Praise for *Colombia E[s Pasión!]*

'Matt Rendell's passion for Colombia is evident in this wonderful sequel to *Kings of the Mountains* – another of his cycling books about that country. Here, he explores a new generation who have beaten poverty, violence and corruption, and can now, via two wheels, tell a story of a more peaceful, happier nation'
Ben East, *Observer*

'Matt Rendell's latest book *Colombia Es Pasión!* takes you into the heart of both a sport and a country. The journey is well worth the effort'
David Walsh, *Sunday Times*

'Enjoyable, authentic and thorough . . . this book will enrich your understanding of many of today's top riders and the long, arduous paths they've taken to reach the top of their sport'
The Inner Ring

'Remarkable, a masterpiece, one of the best books written about cycling . . . The result of decades of knowing and understanding Colombia. Meticulously researched, and written with a lightness of touch. In particular, the dialogue is outstanding. Matt's best book – and he's written some stonking books'
Ned Boulting and David Millar, *Never Strays Far* podcast

'The 'Mr Colombia' of the cycling press [has] an infectious enthusiasm for [his] subject that the army of online encyclopedia devotees could only hope to capture'
Cycling Weekly

'These real-life stories are humbling and inspiring, and if reading them doesn't turn you into a fan of Colombian cycling it can only be because you already were a fan or because your heart is made of stone'
Rolf Rae-Hansen

COLOMBIA! ES PASIÓN!

Matt Rendell survived Hodgkin's Disease and lecturing at British and Latvian universities before entering TV and print journalism. He first visited Colombia in 1998, and his Channel 4 documentary *Kings of the Mountains* (2000) was described in the *Observer* as 'a gem, telling us more about the essence of sport in under an hour than a season's worth of Premiership matches'. His first book, *Kings of the Mountains: How Colombia's Cycling Heroes Changed their Nation's History* (2002), was described in *The Times* as 'meticulous, elegant and sensitive'. He has worked on the British terrestrial coverage of the Tour de France since 1997, he has won three National Sporting Club awards, and his book *The Death of Marco Pantani* was shortlisted for the William Hill Sports Book of the Year Award. *Colombia Es Pasión* is his fifth book about Colombia.

COLOMBIA!
ES PASIÓN!

THE GENERATION OF RACING CYCLISTS WHO CHANGED THEIR NATION AND THE TOUR DE FRANCE

MATT RENDELL

WEIDENFELD & NICOLSON

First published in Great Britain in 2020 by Weidenfeld & Nicolson
This paperback published in 2022 by Weidenfeld & Nicolson
an imprint of The Orion Publishing Group Ltd
Carmelite House, 50 Victoria Embankment
London EC4Y 0DZ

An Hachette UK Company

1 3 5 7 9 10 8 6 4 2

A CIP catalogue record for this book is
available from the British Library.

ISBN (Mass Market Paperback) 978 1 4746 0972 2
ISBN eBook 978 1 4746 0973 9

Typeset by Input Data Services Ltd, Somerset

Printed and bound in Great Britain by Clays Ltd, Elcograf S.p.A.

MIX
Paper from
responsible sources
FSC® C104740

www.weidenfeldandnicolson.co.uk
www.orionbooks.co.uk

For Ana Marín

. . . hasn't the point
Of all this new construction been to provide
A protected medium for the exchanges each felt of such vital
Concern, and wasn't it now giving itself the airs of a palace?
And yet her hair had never been so long.

John Ashbery, 'Clepsydra'

Contents

Introduction:
A Change of Climate

Prodigious hailstones pummelled the hard earth. Lightning flashes turned night to day – 73,700 of them one squally Saturday, according to the national observatory. And, between the storms, the heat was so intense, the very sky seemed made of fire. The day the 2019 Tour de France entered the Alps, eighty of France's ninety-six mainland departments were on severe weather watch. The next, mudslides trapped a hundred travellers between their flows, 35 kilometres beyond the stage finish at Valloire, while, in Paris, shoppers on the Champs-Élysées wilted in 42-degree heat.

It was a summer of extremes.

Yet, at Saint-Jean-de-Maurienne, for the start of stage nineteen, blue skies welcomed the riders and hung over them for 85 kilometres. Only high on the Col de l'Iseran did the shadows lose their sharpness. Dark clouds brewed beyond the pass but, with 44 kilometres still to ride, Egan Bernal had other things on his mind.

The youngest rider in the race, he had won the eight-day Paris–Nice in March and then taken third place at the Volta a Catalunya. Then he had returned home to far-off Colombia, to prepare at altitude for the Giro d'Italia. On Saturday 4 May, in Andorra, now, he suffered a metaphorical thunderbolt of his own when he crashed on the descent from the Port d'Envalira. He knew instantly that he would not be going to Italy.

Driving behind him was his coach Xabier Artetxe.

'When I reached him, he was on the ground. He said, "Xabi, I'm sorry. The collarbone is broken." He didn't even mention the Giro. That evening, even before he went in for surgery, he wanted to talk about a training programme that would get him to the Tour in top form. Our goal was to make it to the final week as strong as possible.'

On the Iseran, his teammate Wout Poels set a searing pace, lining out the group of contenders into a neatly sewn seam while, further back, the stitches were beginning to slip as, rider by rider, the group thinned out. Another teammate, Geraint Thomas – the reigning Tour champion – was tucked into Poels' slipstream. Next came Egan, and, behind him, a knot that had somehow to be disentangled.

Julian Alaphilippe had not spent his season building gradually for the sustained endeavour of the great, three-week tours. He had been winning explosive, hard-fought stages and one-day races all spring. Then he had come to the Tour and taken two swashbuckling stage victories, disdaining the energy efficiency that current wisdom deemed imperative to Grand Tour success. He was so good, he raised the question: could the current wisdom be wrong?

True, he had shown signs of weakness on the Col du Galibier twenty-four hours earlier, crossing the pass a handful of seconds behind his rivals, but on the long descent into Valloire he had regained the group and, going into stage nineteen, he still led Bernal by a minute and thirty seconds in the General Classification, with Thomas five seconds further back. Thomas and Bernal outnumbered him, and had to make it count without allowing others to profit from their work. But how? If Alaphilippe could not be distanced, and decisively, there was every chance he could win the Tour.

With the gradient at 9.3 per cent, and 43.4 kilometres left in the stage, Thomas set off in search of an answer, springing past Poels and away. Egan drifted wide, coaxing Alaphilippe forward, and slipped in behind him. He would watch the next episode of racing unfold from here.

The Austrian Gregor Mühlberger led his teammate Emanuel Buchmann and the other favourites back up to Thomas's wheel. Then the Dutchman Steven Kruijswijk stole away, casting a backwards glance, seeming to invite a response. Thomas accelerated, Mühlberger again gave chase – and then, some way back, a gap appeared.

Out of the saddle, heaving his bike from side to side, Alaphilippe is in trouble.

Egan ducks right, describes a wide loop around the flailing yellow jersey, and crosses in an instant to Buchmann. Mühlberger, Thomas and Kruijswijk look back in succession – and Bernal goes again.

Still seated, he darts past Kruijswijk. To close the gap, the Dutchman rises out of the saddle for twelve laborious turns of the pedals. Then he too sits, a glance down disguising pain – and surrender. The effort has taken him deep into oxygen debt. With little body movement, Egan rides away. There are 42.5 kilometres left in the stage, and five to the top of the Iseran.

Over the next four kilometres, he overtakes the best riders from the earlier breakaway – accomplished champions like Vincenzo Nibali, Simon Yates, Warren Barguil, his compatriot Rigoberto Urán. Some match his pace for a moment. All eventually drop away. He crosses the col alone, picking up an eight-second time deduction. Fifty-eight seconds later, Thomas, Kruijswijk, and Buchmann cross in the slipstream of Kruijswijk's mountain helper Laurens De Plus. Alaphilippe makes the line two minutes and seven seconds after Bernal: 48 seconds off the race lead, although, with fifteen downhill kilometres before the final 7.4-kilometre climb up to the finish line at Tignes, the day could still hold plenty of racing.

While the riders were climbing the southern side of the Iseran, however, the weather had moved in to the north. In fifteen torrential minutes, dark clouds deposited six inches of frozen water on the race route. Quick-response snow ploughs bulldozed floodwater from the road, only for more to close in behind them. Worse, 13.5 kilometres from the finish line, beyond the Brevières tunnel, a landslide had buried the road in half a metre of debris. There could be no final ascent, no stage finish at Tignes. The stage was stopped, the riders informed, and the time gaps at the Col d'Iseran confirmed what everyone knew: Egan Bernal was in the yellow jersey. Two days later, on the Champs Elysées, he celebrated Colombia and Latin America's first Tour de France win.

It had been the strangest of Tours, marked not just by a freak weather front but by long-term climate change. And Egan Bernal, at just 22 years and 195 days – the youngest Tour de France winner for 110 years – was young enough to start an era.

With such talented young riders as Daniel Martínez, Sergio Higuita and Iván Sosa – not to mention Ecuador's Jhonatan Narváez – having also broken through to cycling's elite World-Tour, and an army of young hopefuls behind them, it was an era that could last a decade or more. Except, of course, that it had already begun. After all, Egan's Tour de France win followed hard on victory in the 2019 Giro d'Italia by Richard Carapaz, an Ecuadorean who rode in the Colombian domestic scene before moving to Europe – indeed, who lived so close to the border with Colombia that he crossed it several times a day on his training rides. And, before him, in the six seasons between 2013 and 2018, a quartet of Egan's compatriots – Nairo Quintana, Rigoberto Urán, Esteban Chaves and Miguel Ángel López – accumulated no less than thirteen podium finishes in the great three-week Tours of Italy, France and Spain.

It is sometimes thought easier to see the beginnings of things than the ends. But beginnings we identify only after the fact, and Egan's win can be seen as harvesting what had been sown by any number of predecessors. Certainly, since in 2013, when Nairo Quintana, aged 23, became Colombia's first runner-up in the Tour, a Colombian win could be said to have been imminent. Much the same was felt in 1988, when Fabio Parra became the first to stand on the podium. All three – Fabio, Nairo and Egan – hail from the same high-altitude plateau north of Bogotá. See them side by side, and you could be forgiven for thinking they were related.

But there are other beginnings, for it was a son of Egan's home town, Zipaquirá, some forty kilometres north of the capital, who, in 1949, read about the Tour de France and proposed a national stage race. Efraín Forero Triviño, a pharmacist's son, and a team pursuit gold medallist at the 1950 Central American and Caribbean Games, brought the idea to the attention of the sports correspondent of the national newspaper *El Tiempo*. His persistence was rewarded in October 1950, when he was asked to prove it could be done by climbing the formidable, 50-mile Alto de Letras, accompanied by a Ministry of Public Works truck. The truck got bogged down in the mud. Forero made it to Manizales, the town on the shoulder of the climb. There, apprised of his feat, the townsfolk raised him above their heads and carried him around the square.

El Tiempo's director, Enrique Santos Castillo – whose son Juan Manuel Santos would, as President of the Republic, win the Nobel Peace Prize and welcome Nairo Quintana and Esteban Chaves to the presidential palace – was convinced. But history was against the project, or would have been anywhere else. The country was deeply divided into two opposing factions, the Liberals and the Conservatives. In rural communities where party affiliation was more a matter of collective identity than personal choice, relations between them consisted at best of a simmering stand-off. In 1946, when a Conservative took up the presidency despite Liberal majorities in both houses, fighting broke out. The assassination, in central Bogotá on 9 April 1948, of the Liberal leader Jorge Eliécer Gaitán, led to nationwide conflict.

Historians simply call the years between 1946 and 1958 *La Violencia*. Perhaps 180,000 were killed and two million were displaced – impossible conditions for a national bike race. Yet, in a historical paradox that says much for this country of surprises and cycling's place in it, the first Vuelta a Colombia went ahead as planned in January 1951. By winning it, Efraín Forero became the country's first cycling superstar. Zipaquirá was already well known for its salt mines, which had made it a major economic centre even before the Conquistadors arrived. Indeed, despite their skill as gold, silver and copper workers, the indigenous Muysca people are thought to have used the town's salt as currency. Efraín Forero indelibly associated the town with something else: cycling prowess, manifest in his *nom de guerre* 'El indomable Zipa' – 'The Indomitable Zipa' – a *Zipa* or, more properly, a *Psihipqua*, being, or having been, a Muysca leader of such intense spiritual power that he could only be approached backwards: to behold him face-on could leave the reckless supplicant blind or worse. So, on Wednesday 7 August 2019, it was with a sense of closure, or of completion, that Efraín Forero, aged 89, joined Egan Bernal on stage in the town's central square to celebrate his Tour de France win. Colombian cycling had come full circle.

Forero's Tours of Colombia, the early ones, attracted enormous crowds. More than just capturing the national imagination, they proved there could be such a thing. They allowed a nation to reveal itself to itself, opening new horizons to communities that could see no further than the view from the nearest hilltop. In a country later characterised, for its introversion, conservatism and the sheer difficulty of communications, as 'the Tibet of South America', the racing was brutal, with horrific injuries suffered on boulder-strewn roads. The riders seemed to carry the cross of their deeply Catholic homeland into the mountains, as if paying penance for Colombia's sins fell to them. Cycling started out in Colombia as an intimately national and surprisingly spiritual affair.

At the same time, sport has long offered a gateway into the community of nations, and Colombia's international ambitions have always been interwoven with it. In 1953 Forero led his country's first team at the Route de France (now the Tour de l'Avenir, a sort of miniature Tour de France for under-23s). Ill-prepared and ill-equipped, he and his teammates were out of the race within four stages. Forero then went to the 1953 World Championships in Lugano, Switzerland, and made the decisive breakaway until an untimely puncture ended his hopes.

In December 1957 Tour de France winners Fausto Coppi and Hugo Koblet, semi-retired and thinking of future business opportunities, toured South and Central America. There they met the extraordinary Ramón Hoyos, the winner of five Tours of Colombia, the 1954 Tour of Puerto Rico and the 1955 Pan-American road race. Coppi tried to secure him a start at the 1958 amateur World Championship road race at Rheims. It could have been designed for him, he said. But Hoyos's sponsor, the Swedish bicycle manufacturer Monark, wanted him at the Six Days of Stockholm, and held him to his contract.

Cycling quickly metamorphosed into a means of national projection. In 1966 the country's foremost road and track rider, Martín Emilio Rodríguez, known to all by his childhood nickname of Cochise, won the first Tour of Táchira State in Venezuela. In 1967 his rival Álvaro Pachón won the Tour of Mexico. In 1970 Colombians won another Venezuelan race, the Tour of Barinas, and the Tour of Costa Rica. In 1972 it was the Tour of Guadeloupe. By the mid-1970s they were winning throughout the Americas.

Then another threshold was crossed. Cochise Rodríguez had all but retired from the road in 1970 when he broke the amateur world hour record. A year later he became amateur world individual pursuit champion. While preparing for the Munich Olympics, he was accused of professionalism and barred, so he joined the Bianchi team in Italy, achieved Colombia's first two Giro d'Italia stage wins, then became the first Colombian to ride the Tour de France.

Cochise blazed his trail largely alone. It was not until 1980, when Alfonso Flores won the Tour de l'Avenir at the head of a national team, that the gates of cycling's greatest event finally opened. In 1983, in the hope of attracting Eastern European and Latin American teams, the Tour de France declared itself open to amateurs. Only the Colombians showed. Within a year they had taken their first stage win – on the hallowed ascent of Alpe d'Huez, no less – through the country's first international cycling superstar, Luís Herrera, a figure so slight he seemed a sculpture in steel wire, spliced in a town whose indigenous name, Fusagasugá, tied European tongues in knots. In 1987, two years after his compatriot Francisco Rodríguez had finished third in the Vuelta a España, Herrera snared it to become the developing world's first Grand Tour winner – and did so in the colours of the nation's insignia brand, Café de Colombia. A year later Fabio Parra, from Sogamoso, a pre-Columbian centre of sun-worship, made the top three in the Tour de France. In 1989 he was second in the Vuelta a España, one place ahead of yet another Colombian, Óscar Vargas.

Then the sun seemed to go in. Café de Colombia withdrew from cycling sponsorship at the end of 1991, followed by other long-time national sponsors like the soft drinks brands Glacial, Manzana Postobón and Pony Malta. Regional concerns filled the vacuum: lotteries, public authorities, sports bodies, and the regional licencees for rum and the sugar-cane-derived, anise-flavoured spirit known as *aguardiente*. A handful of private companies – digital service providers, fruit juice producers, couriers – sponsored teams, but there was little in the way of structured sports development or integration. As the use of performance-enhancing drugs reached epidemic proportions, Colombian cycling, once a key vector of international communication, cut itself off from the world.

And that was the least of the country's problems.

☰

In 1960 Colombia's principal causes of death had been intestinal, respiratory and perinatal infections. In the 1970s they were cancer, heart and cerebrovascular disease. A decade on, among males at least, the most common cause was murder. The cocaine billionaire Pablo Escobar, avowing his preference for a tomb in Colombia to a prison in the United States, started by targeting judges, lawyers, policemen – everyday heroes who refused his corruption – and ended up planting bombs in city streets.

In a modern, globalised version of Prohibition, in which one set of countries funded violence in another through their drug purchases, Colombia tore itself apart. No country has suffered more in the war on drugs.

The cyclists described in this book were very young or not yet born when Escobar was hunted down and killed, and still small when it emerged that the Cali Cartel, by then supplying about 80 per cent of US and European cocaine, had funded the successful campaign of Ernesto Samper, President of Colombia from 1994 to 1998. But they and their generation were stigmatised the world over for the crimes of the few, which left Colombia de-certified as an anti-drug partner by the Clinton administration and with its economy in tatters, its institutions infiltrated, its president disgraced, and illegal armed groups controlling vast territories.

Yet the economy remained robust. In the 1980s, as hyper-inflation and negative growth tore through Latin America, 30 per cent inflation and 1.4 per cent growth made Colombia a hemispheric exception. Even so, when the World Bank and International Monetary Fund prescribed a full economic overhaul of the hemisphere, Colombia was not spared. So, in February

1990 – Nairo Quintana was two weeks old at the time – import licences were abolished, duties slashed, employment deregulated and the Colombian economy opened to international investment. What was lost in weakened industry was more than made up for in boosted trade and services. At least in the cities. In the countryside, export crops like African palm, timber, cocoa and fruit trees flourished, inflating fuel, energy and agrochemical prices beyond the reach of the nation's small farmers or *campesinos*, a quarter of a million of whom were left unemployed between 1991 and 1993.

To complicate matters still further, a modernising, inclusive new political Constitution was drawn up to reform the old two-party system. When it came into force in 1991, it handed political power to the regions, funded by transfers from the centre that amounted to 8 per cent of GDP. Guerrilla and paramilitary groups in outlying regions appropriated both the money and the influence. The state ended up as the central financier of its own subversion.

The largest of the rebel groups, the Revolutionary Armed Forces of Colombia (FARC), who aimed to take over the country and do nothing they could articulate in a coherent manifesto, already had rich revenue streams in kidnapping, extortion and drug trafficking, and were soon deploying forces a thousand troops strong, and overwhelming entire military bases. Under-armed, undertrained, repeatedly humiliated, elements of the military forged links with the paramilitary groups who were vying with the FARC for control of the drugs trade. In August 1998 Samper's presidential successor Andrés Pastrana was told by his military commander, 'Mr President, we are losing the war.'

Between 1996 and 2001, a million nationals moved abroad. Many rural Colombians fled to the cities. A tiny minority, trapped by geography or the dream of easy riches, sought a living in illicit crops or the illegal armed groups. By 2000, Colombia was the world's greatest producer of coca leaf. Thirty per cent of its towns and villages were occupied by the FARC or its guerrilla rival, the National Liberation Army (ELN), and another 30 per cent were under the control of paramilitary groups. The FARC were thought to number 18,000, the ELN another 6,000 and the paramilitaries from 10,000 to 14,000, although there could have been far more: in 2010 President Álvaro Uribe claimed that 52,000 subversives of all colours demobilised during his eight years in power.

The decommissioning of illegal armed groups was just part of a remarkable turnaround. These days Colombia is a complex, multicultural, mid-to-high income country with a diverse population, a vibrant public sphere, a combative and independent press, and Free Trade Agreements with the United States, Canada, the European Union and the European Free Trade Association; it supplies the world with avocados and bananas, coffee, cut-flowers and crude oil – even dance, for salsa owes much of its global spread to Colombian out-migration. The world's largest producer of emeralds, Colombia also exports gold, silver, platinum, nickel and coltan. If history had taken a different path, the word Colombia would instantly evoke brightly coloured orchids, hummingbirds and amphibians. The biologist E. O. Wilson has written that Colombia should be counted as 'one of Earth's "megadiversity" countries, with a fauna and flora rivalled in richness only by Brazil'.

Foreign investment and tourists are flooding into its Western-style cities and picture-postcard beaches. The cyclists Peter Sagan and Chris Froome were just two of the 3.1 million overseas visitors who holidayed there in 2018, up from just under two million in 2014. Meanwhile, the newspapers proclaim: '"Goodbye, Weapons!" FARC Disarmament in Colombia Signals New Era' (*New York Times*), 'Colombia – a nation transformed' (*Miami Herald*), 'Colombia: from failed state to Latin American powerhouse' (*Daily Telegraph*). Since December 2015, Colombian travellers, once unwelcome, have been welcomed into the Schengen Area, no visa required.

It is hard to imagine that cycling success has played no role in this dramatic reversal. Since Rigoberto Urán moved to Europe in 2006, and Nairo Quintana won the Tour de l'Avenir in 2010, many talented Colombian riders have featured in cycling's elite WorldTour and on the world's television screens. One of the principal conduits for this stream of talent was the cycling project launched under the aegis of a national rebranding campaign called Colombia Es Pasión.

The campaign chief was Luís Guillermo Plata, chairman of ProExport – the government agency responsible for fuelling Colombian tourism and trade – under President Álvaro Uribe (2002 to 2010). In a restaurant in the chic Bogotá district of Usaquén, he explained its genesis:

When we came into power in 2002, Colombia was on the verge of being a failed state. You can take pretty much any indicator: where up is good, we were down, and where down is good, we were up. Uribe starts changing things. Around 2005, after more or less three years in government, we reach the point where the reality has changed significantly. But international perceptions couldn't keep up. So, we're thinking, how can we close the perception gap? That's why we started Colombia Es Pasión.

The idea was to find something unique, something very Colombian, a brand that we could use in many areas. Like, you make a shirt and say, 'Made in Colombia with passion.' Or you sell coffee or fruit or whatever, and you say, 'Grown with passion in Colombia.' And that became the tagline of the umbrella organisation for tourism, investment and business.

We launched the campaign sometime in 2005, and Coldeportes – the state ministry for sport, more or less – said, 'Why don't we pick a sport and use it to promote Colombia.' So I said, 'Great idea. We're OK at football, but we're not Brazil or Argentina. The only sport that we really excel at is cycling. Let's sponsor a team.'

Nairo Quintana, Esteban Chaves, Darwin Atapuma, Jarlinson Pantano, Sergio Luís Henao, Fabio Duarte and Sergio Higuita all passed through Colombia Es Pasión or its subsequent manifestations, 4-72 Colombia and Manzana Postobón. They helped normalise the presence of Colombian riders in World-Tour teams. From Colombia Es Pasión then sprang two more teams, Team Colombia and Claro-Coldeportes, which nurtured Sebastián Henao and the sprinters Fernando Gaviria and Álvaro Hodeg.

Their achievements represent a form of soft power which has helped fuel their country's integration into the world economy. The irony is that most of the Colombian riders in the international WorldTour – the great majority, if we include their parents and grandparents – derive from a social group whose form of life represents no one's idea of development: that of the *campesinos* or peasant farmers – the inhabitants, typically, of low-tech family farms on poor, marginal land, where religious belief is still profound and individual freedom has traditionally been subordinate to wider community strictures. The story of Colombian cycling is inescapably the story of the Colombian peasantry and their responses to a time of crisis.

In Western Europe and North America, the peasantry has largely disappeared. Indeed, the great three-week Tours around Italy, France and Spain, with their Milan, Paris or Madrid conclusions, can be read as a celebration of their passing – annual re-enactments of the population shift from the rural to the urban world: a declaration, in the language of sport, that the future lies inside the city walls.

Yet, in Latin America the peasantry has survived, and has a fascinating hybrid identity. Of course, under European rule, the prior inhabitants lost their best land, water supplies, social complexity and most of their population. Even so, the Spanish crown sought to limit the Conquistadors' independence: historians even speak of a second conquest that followed the first – that of the conquerors by the crown. The ultimate authority over territorial acquisition and settlement, the Spanish monarch also insisted on retaining control over the protection of its indigenous communities and the salvation of their souls. To do so, it conceded them a degree of autonomy. This equivocal protection allowed them to endure as communities sometimes known by the composite term *campesindio*, from *campesino*, peasant farmer, and *indio*, the erroneous product of Columbus's geographical perplexity.

For centuries the peasantry has been controlled, exploited and kept safely away from political power. Only now, under the pressure of free-trade deals and the numinous attractions of the smart phone and urban connectivity, are the rural economy and, with it, peasant identities, collapsing – not least because, in a nation which would prefer to be thought of as emerging, their way of life is ultimately something of an embarrassment. And this, in turn, is a reflection of the contradictory ways in which Colombians, even urban, educated ones, feel not just about the rural world of their cyclists' childhoods, but about the integration into the wider world represented by their sporting successes, as if Colombia fixes its aim on development and incorporation into the international order, even as it sees its most authentic instincts, its better self, in its rural origins.

Yet, unacknowledged by the global sports industry, the sons of the peasantry have found in cycling a refuge from rural decline, a place where they can apply the traditional peasant virtues of patience and persistence, lucid observation and the stoic forbearance of physical pain. It has allowed them to transition to the heart of global capitalism and earn considerable livelihoods from the marketing arms of companies looking to sell their goods to national and transnational markets. Some have even turned global sport against the forces of uniformalisation and used it to strengthen their own local identities. A few even have the President of the Republic on speed dial. And, in a country that has seen such sudden, disorienting change, their success and status are interwoven with Colombian nation-building. Such is the story explored in this book.

It is of course true that adaptations to altitude could hardly have failed to play their part in the story of Colombian cycling. Writing in the 1950s of a peasant community living in the village of Saucío north of Bogotá, at an altitude of 2,689 metres, the Colombian sociologist Orlando Fals Borda observed:

> The *mestizo* of Saucío has some special characteristics. Living in a rarified atmosphere with oxygen partial pressure only about 120 millimetres (as compared to 153 millimetres at sea level), he is equipped with a remarkable lung capacity. Men are chesty and broad shouldered, have unusual physical endurance and are excellent long-distance runners. The heart-rate tends to be slow (bradycardia); the Saucite has many of the characteristics of an athlete.

It would have been possible – and, perhaps, more in keeping with the times – to weave a popular-science fable (it could have been called *The Muysca Gene*) that mentioned individual drive and desire only in passing, and ignored broader cultural factors altogether, extolling instead genetic inheritance. But *The Muysca Gene* would overlook the high places around the world that do not produce champion cyclists, and omit the current wisdom that if sleeping at altitude is beneficial, training is better done at sea level.

Instead, this book starts with the lives of the riders. To see them in the context of the families and communities that formed them, as trade, development, digital technologies and new forms of identity transformed their country and the wider world, is to see, in each individual, a universe – and one in which the new Colombia can be seen emerging like a rushing spring of the fresh water in which the country is so remarkably abundant. And all this entails other contexts and longer durations: the history of the peasantry, Colombia's relations with Europe and the wider world, and the arrival in the Andean highlands of the first Europeans half a millennium, or a moment, ago.

1

Cold Energy

To a flicker of sheet lightning, the quick tropical night engulfs the mountains of Iguaque, which rise like a great wave over Vereda La Concepción, a *vereda* being a unit of farmland divided among a number of households. The night is cold here in the high-altitude Colombian department of Boyacá and, at ten thousand feet above sea level, you sigh involuntarily after each movement.

The gathering darkness above obscures the lake from which, according to the narrative cycles of the Muysca people, Bachué, the primordial woman, emerged in the time of the ancestors to populate the earth. Lower down lie the hillsides where, in what we can only call March 1537 – the other calendar involved being lost – a bearded wayfarer named Gonzalo Jiménez de Quesada appeared at the head of 170 half-starved Spaniards.

The aspiring Conquistadors had left the Caribbean coast eleven months earlier. Six hundred of their men had succumbed en route to exhaustion and disease, before the peaceable Muysca offered them their wary assistance. But the expedition was just one of eight that would subdue these highlands before 1550. Today, the only remaining traces of their culture apparent to the casual observer are the place names. Vereda La Concepción lies on a hillside about six kilometres from the village of Cómbita, thought to mean either 'Hand of the Tiger' or 'Strength of the Summit'.

I asked Nairo about them: Bachué, the primal mother, Bochica, the lawmaker, Chía, the moon-goddess. What did the old ancestral stories mean today?

He told me, 'That is who we are.'

Yet, as the centuries pass, we seem to understand less and less of the Muysca. The last native speaker of their language is believed to have died in around 1870, and most of what remains of it is contained in two documents dispatched from the New World at the end of the eighteenth century for inclusion in Catherine the Great's *Comparative Dictionaries of All Languages and Dialects*. When he recieved them, Charles III, who had ordered the eradication of the indigenous languages in his dominions, decided not to send them on to Saint Petersburg but to keep them in his Chamber Library – which is to say, the idioms described in those priceless parchments were made extinct by their collector.

It could well be that the colonial rulers simply corralled a dozen distinct groups into camps and pressed together an array of complex dialects into an elementary Muyscaranto. If so, what we thought we knew of their language, we didn't – and the Conquest did not so much destroy the Muysca people as create them.

◈

The front door opens onto an empty conservatory and then the house proper. Emiro López, in his early sixties, stands on the threshold between the kitchen and the room where his wife, Isabel Monroy, known as *Mamá Chavita* (*Chavita* simply means 'small', although she is not especially slight), has for many years run the Pato Lucas Kindergarten. Emiro's eyes glisten as he travels a quarter of a century back in time.

'He was crawling slowly across the floor just here,' he says. 'I picked him up' – he mimes picking up a tiny child and encountering a gaze devoid of all recognition – 'and said to Isabel, "There is no life in him. The boy is going to die."'

Nairito – 'Little Nairo' – eight months old, was emaciated and

18

weak with diarrhoea. His stomach was shockingly swollen, his hair on end. Few believed he would survive infancy.

Standing opposite Emiro, her back to the stove, is Mamá Chavita herself. She tells me, in beautiful peasant Spanish, '*Tentaron de ese tiempo que lo había tentado era antes de defunto*,' which I take to mean something like, 'Around that time, he was tempted by a dead body,' the verb *tentar* having shades of 'to goad', 'to try the mettle of'. In other words, Nairo had been somehow courted or put to the test by a strange force of attraction emanating from the dead woman.

He had come into the world on 4 February 1990, the son of Luís Quintana, a market trader from neighbouring Vereda Salvial, and his wife Eloísa Rojas. Their faces tell the history of these hills: Luís is ruddy, light-skinned, green-eyed; Eloísa has long straight hair and dark Muysca features. As a young man, Luís had rented a shack beside a busy road and started selling groceries. It is easy to find: open any online map and search for Tienda la Villita. The imposing house you find now is proof of Luís's acumen: the store allowed him to buy the land – some of which he turned to agriculture – extend the property and marry Eloísa Rojas, a customer from Vereda San Rafael across the road.

By the time she was twenty, Eloísa was pregnant with Willington Alfredo, named after the footballer Willington Ortiz who played 49 times for Colombia, although everyone calls him Alfredo. Then came Esperanza, meaning 'Hope', and Leidy, a name that became common after Diana married Prince Charles in 1981. Alfredo thinks his parents found the names of siblings four and five, Nairo Alexander and Dayer Uberney, in the newspapers.

Eloísa had been abandoned as a child. She told me, 'I was one of eight children, although I found out only recently. I was brought up by a woman named Sagrario Rojas, who loved me like her own daughter.'

Sagrario died a few months after Nairo's birth. Eloísa went to pay her respects and took the baby with her.

'The illness began three days later,' Eloísa said. 'The man who had dressed the corpse must have touched little Nairo.'

Later, Nairo spoke to me of a belief system going back many years, according to which dead bodies emit a cold energy that, on contact, impregnates unborn children or babes in arms.

'Only natural remedies can be used to treat it. It's not a matter of scientific medicine.'

As an athlete, Nairo has been subjected to scientific method since his teens, and knows exactly what he is saying: that modern science and medicine, for all the good they do in the world, belong to a way of life that has forced the thought-world of his own childhood into retreat, which makes Nairo's illness and survival, more than medical or biographical facts, markers of identity, even forms of resistance.

'*Los antiguos*,' Isabel Monroy told me, meaning the old people of the community, 'told Doña Eloísa to collect the buds of nine medicinal plants, boil them, and bathe Nairito in the water.' It was unclear to me whether the ritual of collecting the buds was not itself part of the cure.

⑪

The Quintana children scarcely saw a television. As a result, the filmic language of gesture and expression, second nature to those socialised before the small screen, was foreign to them. Nor did they have much time for music and dance, although the hills around Cómbita resonated to the sound of *tiples* – three-quarter guitars with twelve strings arranged in groups of three – and even more diminutive *requintos*, and a genre of music known to the outside world as *carranga*, practised by singers like Jorge Velosa and Ildefonzo Barrera, both of whom, many years later, would compose songs about Nairo.

Incorporated into this culture of local music and dance was

a form of improvised speech in four-line verses called *coplas*. Orlando Fals Borda's study of Saucío gives the example of a dance called the *tres*, which sees three revellers trace a figure of eight on the floor: 'When a dancer "cuts", that is, passes between his two partners, he is expected to "sing" a *copla*, or ditty, of four verses rhymed *a-b-c-b*. By the time the dancer twists his way to trace his next "eight", he has finished singing and one of the other partners takes a turn.'

A remarkable local teacher named Elba Rosa Camargo – Colombia's Teacher of the Year in 2015, no less – taught me more about *coplas*. Posted in 2006 to the Environmental Technical Institute in Vereda Sote Panelas, close to the house where Nairo grew up, although higher on the hillside, further from the main road, she told me, 'I had been working in Tunja, at an urban school where the children talked loudly and freely. Suddenly I found myself in a very quiet community, living in dwellings set far apart, uncomfortable with house visits. I was only twenty minutes from Tunja but it felt quite alien. I found the silence terrible.'

Coplas provided a means of breaking her classroom's icy quiet. Before her children, she recited one she had made up:

> *Dame un besito, mi vida,*
> *como siempre me lo dabas,*
> *con un tricito de lengua*
> *con nariz, mocos y babas.*
> (Kiss me, my darling,
> the way we used to kiss,
> With a touch of tongue,
> some nose, dribble, and spit.)

Calibrated expertly to provoke the surprise and disgust of her young pupils, it drew their rapt attention. Did any of them, she wondered, know any *copla*s?

'A boy raised his hand:

> *Y allá arriba, en aquel alto*
> *y allá abajo en aquel otro,*
> *se ríen la gallinas de ver*
> *el gallo en peloto.*
> (On that mountaintop, soaring;
> and that other, elated,
> The hens all laugh to see
> the cockerel stark naked.)

The other children laughed. Then another hand went up, and another. Soon all of them had their hands up.'

Their enthusiasm engaged, they boasted, 'My father knows a thousand *coplas*,' 'My mother knows two thousand,' and the ice was broken.

A format for sometimes bawdy humour, *coplas* are also the library of the Boyacá peasantry. Traditional forms of knowledge like medicinal plant use are preserved not in books but in *coplas*. They were part of Nairo's upbringing and give us some idea of his inner life.

He told me, 'I have liked poems and *coplas* since I was very small. I used to make up little rhyming sayings. Sometimes I still do.'

But when I asked him and his brother Alfredo to recite some for me, they declined. I realised only later that I had been asking them to stage the childhood world that had endowed them with their identities as a kind of performance.

☰

From the medicinal *coplas* collected by her pupils, Elba Rosa Camargo found that much of the vegetation around Sote Panelas is used in traditional treatments. 'They only see the doctor when they have failed to cure the ailment with their own medicine.'

But Luís Quintana had suffered mobility problems since childhood and was compelled to make frequent hospital visits.

Nairo explained: 'When he was seven, my father was hit by a car and fractured his hip and legs. His father was in the army, so they took him to a military hospital. The surgery didn't go well and he was in plaster too long. Since he was still growing, one foot atrophied. Then he had another accident when he was playing at school, and there were more fractures. He has walked on crutches and lived with pain ever since.'

Alfredo recalled, 'They wanted to amputate his bad leg. My mother and uncles went with him to the hospital, and the doctor explained his reasoning, but the family wouldn't allow it.'

After primary school at Vereda San Rafael, Alfredo and Esperanza went to the Colegio Normal in Tunja. However, by the time Leidy, the third of the siblings, was ready to move up, there was no easy way of getting to the school in Tunja. Instead, there was a direct bus service to the Institución Educativa Técnica Alejandro de Humboldt in the village of Arcabuco, 16.5 kilometres downhill from Vereda La Concepción, so Leidy went there and her younger brothers followed.

The family finances fluctuated with the rural economy, and the credit they extended their customers in good years became debt when times turned hard. One of these crises hit soon after Nairo started high school.

He told me, 'We were small producers, but the rural economy was in crisis. Various blights had set in, and the land we had turned to agriculture was repossessed. We gave up farming, and from then on we only grew food for ourselves.'

The Kindergarten teacher Isabel Monroy remembers Nairo's mother knocking on the door early one morning on the day of a school trip: 'She said, "Señora Chavita, you don't have a pair of shoes from one of your boys by any chance? They're taking Nairo, and I don't have any shoes for him."'

The Quintanas responded to the rural crisis with relentless

rounds of the local markets. Nairo's week during his first two years at the Humboldt school in Arcabuco, when he was aged twelve and thirteen, is exhausting just to contemplate:

> We started loading the truck late on Monday nights. We had to be at the wholesale market in Tunja for three in the morning to buy fruit and vegetables. I'd get home from loading up, and I'd have an hour to wash and get ready before setting off to school. I'd finish classes at lunchtime, join my father in the market square and eat at the stall. By 10 p.m. we had to be packed up and leaving, because it was a different type of market at Moniquirá, which meant another 3 a.m. start to pick up supplies.
>
> I would take the bus to Arcabuco, go to school, take the bus back and work until eleven o'clock at night, although there were times we weren't home until four in the morning. I had to be ready to leave for school at six. We didn't work on Thursdays, but we were up in the early hours on Fridays for the market in Tunja, then it was off to school, back again at lunchtime, hard work until eight or nine, and home at ten. If there was no market at Barbosa we had Saturdays off, but on Sundays we were back in the square in Tuta.

To make the market stall as attractive as possible, Nairo would arrange the fruit meticulously, then set off on home deliveries. When the market closed, he would wheel the unsold products along the backstreets, selling them off cheap.

The world of rural silence that Elba Rosa Camargo had described was one to which the Quintanas both belonged and did not belong. They lived in a community in which old ways like medicinal plant use, and culture-bound syndromes like Nairo's childhood illness, were still relatively intact, but, at the same time, they lived on the main road, traded with passing motorists, and travelled to the markets in surrounding towns and villages bringing food, salt, sugar, news and conversation. It gave them a certain status. It could still be impossible to get a word from Nairo as a child, but his family's special position as intermediaries perhaps gave him the conviction he needed to pursue the life project of his choosing.

Meanwhile, Alfredo taught himself to drive and contributed to the family coffers by operating a taxi in the hours of darkness, so the police couldn't see he was underage. Nairo, not much more than ten but observant and streetwise, kept him company and advised him who to pick up and who to leave. Nairo then began finding jobs of his own: at one point he was working with Dayer at a fuel station. At another, they were collecting scrap metal. And they found other ways of economising: at Christmas they made presents by melting plastic waste and pouring it into moulds.

Looking back, he recognises that it was a demanding childhood. 'Dayer and I were lucky in that we were able to go to a good school and take our school certificates. A lot of kids who grow up in difficult, demanding circumstances, and have to work so hard, so young, end up drinking or in a mess.'

But, somehow, the Quintana kids had the mental resources to cope. Nairo, in particular, had a kind of genius: a structured inner life that allowed him, barely in high school, almost to take over his family and infuse them with his inner drive and purpose. Alfredo speaks of him with great admiration. 'He was sensitive, proud, focused, ambitious. A leader at school and at home, very neat and disciplined, with big plans and his own outlook on things.'

It prepared him for his future career as a sportsman.

Then something unforeseen occurred that changed the course of all their lives.

From the tiny daily allowance Nairo and Dayer were given to pay for everyday school expenses, Nairo, aged fourteen, set aside enough to buy an old mountain bike. It offered him something hard to come by in a peasant world of limited possibilities, a means to a kind of self-realisation, and he seems to have come to regard the bike as a close companion, almost human. As Alfredo puts it, 'It was more like his right hand than a means of transport.'

After mastering it himself, Nairo taught his younger brother – 'The old way,' says Dayer. 'By pushing me down a mountain!' Three days after his initiation, Dayer somehow managed to procure a bike of his own and the two boys hatched a plan: to coast down the 16.5 kilometre descent to school and then ride back up again.

Dayer says, 'We had heavy bikes, jeans and school bags. We just about made it.'

Then they did it again. And again.

'From then on,' Nairo says, 'we didn't take the bus.' Anticipating the conclusion I might draw, he adds, 'It wasn't because we couldn't afford it: it was only a thousand pesos [about twenty pence] there and back. I did it because I had a bike and I liked it.'

Weeks passed, and neighbours and school friends joined them, eventually forming a group of ten or twelve, all told.

'We covered our bikes in stickers, reflectors and lights,' Dayer says. 'It was quite a spectacle.'

But Nairo was the most dedicated of them. Alfredo remembers how, when it rained, Nairo would arrive wet and dirty at school. His teachers were indulgent with him, and cleaned him up when he fell. So were the bus drivers, who would take him and his bike home at no charge.

On one of his first outings, Nairo crashed near his house: 'I didn't have a helmet or anything like that. I was unconscious for a time, but I didn't go to hospital.'

That he carried on suggests how much of himself he had invested in his new passion.

A year later, in Tunja, he was hit by a taxi and, this time, hospitalised.

Alfredo says, 'We worried about him, but we supported him too.' His family understood that cycling had a special meaning for Nairo.

The dangers of the Tunja–Arcabuco highway were not lost on the family of another Humboldt pupil, who led Nairo to the next milestone in his cycling career: racing. Cayetano Sarmiento, the son of a *campesino* family who lived close to a fresh-water spring called Agua Varuna, halfway up the climb from Arcabuco to Vereda La Concepción, told me, 'My father grew potatoes and kept cattle, so I helped him with the harvest and the milking, then sold our potatoes from a stall in the square. At the time the Tunja–Arcabuco highway was the main road to [the department of] Santander. It was very dangerous for a child, so my father didn't let me go to school until I was seven, and I didn't take my high school diploma until I was seventeen.'

He, Nairo and Dayer became firm friends, although Nairo was three years younger and Dayer five. That was in 2004, when a young sports-loving mayor named Víctor Hugo Silva was elected in Arcabuco and brought the Departmental Schools Games there. Weeks before the tournament in May, Silva's sports coordinator, Rusbel Achagua, visited the school. Cayetano remembers, 'I put my hand up for cycling.'

Achagua gave Cayetano basic training advice, and Nairo became curious. 'I began to train with him,' Nairo told me, 'and we spurred each other on.'

Despite his late start, Cayetano went on to win the Under-23 Tour of Italy in 2009, then race professionally in Europe for five seasons.

Cayetano also gave Nairo his first pair of padded cycling shorts. Nairo used them until the colour had faded and the padding had collapsed, then handed them on to Dayer, who wore them until they fell apart at the seams.

Arcabuco had another young cyclist, Camilo Moyano, who would win a silver medal in the omnium at the 2007 Panamerican Games and spent 2009 in Europe riding for Colombia Es Pasión. His father ran the first bike shop of any note in Arcabuco, although Cayetano, Nairo and Dayer found support at a more modest establishment.

A local businessman named Héctor Garabito, who bottles natural mineral water from one of the many springs that surface around the village, rented an empty shop near Arcabuco's church to a man named Raúl Malagón, who was both a bike mechanic and a bee keeper.

'When I started,' Nairo told me, 'I went to Raúl's workshop to set up my bike and learn. He used to repair our machines and talk to us about cycling. In exchange, we used to wash bikes and mend punctures.'

Raúl developed training strategies suited to the time and place. He fitted out Nairo with a heavy bike to strengthen his young charge. And, Nairo recalls, 'He fed us pollen and royal jelly, and put water in one bidon and a honey solution in the other.'

Raúl's sister, Maribel Malagón, who still runs a general store in Arcabuco, remembers, 'My brother had thirteen or fourteen young riders,' she says, 'although Nairo was the most promising of them. Raúl held raffles and *matachines* [parties with folk dancing] to raise money. After one, he bought a bike for Nairo.'

Nairo, she says, was 'tiny, shy and noble'.

Raúl introduced Nairo to Mayor Silva, his sports coordinator Rusbel Achagua, and a young and enthusiastic councillor named Jaime Póveda. 'We were lucky to have them,' Nairo remembers. 'When we needed something, they were always there for us, giving us as much support as circumstances allowed.'

On schooldays Nairo would ride down to Arcabuco, go round to the workshop and do a session on a set of rollers that had been repaired so many times they were effectively homemade.

He would go back after school, spend another half hour on the rollers, and then time trial up to Agua Varuna.

Nairo recalls, 'The school bus would set off, stopping from time to time to let the students get off. We would start one at a time, at two- or three-minute intervals, and try to beat the bus. Raúl, Rusbel or the councillor would go up by car or motorbike and take our times – if they made it.'

Pedro Camargo, an agronomist with the mayor's office who still volunteers with the cycling club, remembers the first time Nairo tagged along with his group. 'You could see he was special. He was young and tiny, and he had no training, but it was impossible to drop him.'

The village came together to support its budding cyclists. Héctor Garabito told me, 'We all made small donations. All the shopkeepers and small businesses. The local radio station, Radio Estéreo, organised races and raised funds to cover race expenses and bicycle parts. Cayetano Sarmiento rode the junior Tour of Colombia using bike parts donated by Radio Estéreo, and wheels donated by [national cycling] teams like UNE and Colombia Es Pasión. Afterwards the parts went to Nairo and Dayer.'

Nairo began to take part in village races every few weeks. Maribel Malagón brought out a plastic trophy and placed it on the counter of her shop. It is inscribed *1ra Copa Ciclo Mtañismo MONIQUIRÁ 2/05–06* ('1st MTB Cup MONIQUIRÁ 2 April 2006').

'It was his first win. Nairo gave it to Raúl as a way of saying thank you.'

ᛞ

The eldest sons in rural families had more important things to do than ride bicycles. On 24 November 2003 – a date burned into his consciousness – Alfredo followed in his grandfather's footsteps and took the traditional career path for the sons of the poor: he joined up. It was a propitious moment for Colombia's armed forces.

In the mid-1990s, 60 per cent of Colombia's military personnel were conscripted school-leavers, and military equipment was basic. Reinforcing troops under FARC attack in isolated areas was near-impossible. The military wanted Black Hawk helicopters but, under the disgraced President Samper, access to US military hardware was denied. When Harvard-educated Andrés Pastrana replaced him in 1998, he proposed an ambitious, internationally funded Marshall-type Plan for Colombia. Under President Clinton, US aid doubled to US$280 million. In August 1998, a week into Pastrana's term, the Colombian army purchased the first of fourteen Black Hawks. The armed forces began replacing conscripts with professional soldiers, improving their intelligence services and purging officers with paramilitary contacts.

Pastrana's two headline policies were shared responsibility in the war on drugs between producer and consumer countries, and peace negotiations with the FARC. However, the FARC, with drug money pouring into its coffers, saw no pressing need for peace, and demanded a safe haven larger than Switzerland as a precondition for talks. Pastrana inexplicably complied. Yet, on 7 January 1999, the day of the opening ceremony, the FARC's veteran leader Manuel Marulanda failed to appear, leaving Pastrana beside an empty chair, posing for the photographers. When the negotiations finally started, the FARC continued to kidnap, murder, build air strips and sow coca.

On 20 February 2002, FARC hijackers forced a scheduled flight to land close to the demilitarised zone and kidnapped one of the passengers, the chairman of the Peace Commission of the Colombian Senate. Pastrana terminated negotiations, sent 13,000 troops in to reoccupy the DMZ, and penned an acid open letter to Marulanda, with the words, 'I gave you my word and kept it to the end, but you have abused my good faith and that of all Colombians . . .'

The FARC reacted by kidnapping the presidential candidate Ingrid Betancourt and her campaign chief Clara Rojas. They bombed oil pipelines, electricity pylons and water-treatment plants, assassinated the Archbishop of the city of Cali, kidnapped twelve deputies of the Department of El Valle del Cauca, and, most notoriously, during a shootout in a tiny village near the Pacific coast called Bojayá, fired a gas cylinder bomb at a church, killing 117, including 48 children.

Until that explosion of violence, the hardliner Álvaro Uribe, whose father had been murdered by the FARC, had been little fancied as a future head of state. Oxford-educated, a former mayor of the city of Medellín and governor of the surrounding department, Antioquia, and suspected of proximity to certain paramilitary groups and leaders, Uribe had left the Liberal party to campaign for the presidency. The last two major candidates to do the same, Jorge Eliécer Gaitán in the 1940s and Luis Carlos Galán in the 1980s, had both been assassinated.

But, in the May 2002 elections, a wave of public outrage swept Uribe into power. On the day of his investiture that August, the FARC fired mortar shells at the Presidential Guard and detonated a cylinder bomb near the presidential palace, killing seventeen.

Uribe set about strengthening the armed forces and police, dismantling the paramilitaries, and waging war on the guerrillas. Alfredo Quintana was soon operating in the special forces in the worst of the fighting. Through the money he sent home, the boosting of Colombia's military budget made a small contribution to Nairo's early cycling career.

The many relationships Nairo formed as he passed from local to national to international competition are as strong today as ever.

During one of our interviews, I commented, 'Nairo, you are like America. So many people say they discovered you.'

He said, straightforwardly, 'There were a lot of people involved.'

Rusbel Achagua was a case in point. Achagua is another aboriginal name: tiny Achagua communities survive on reservations in the department of Casanare. But Rusbel was Arcabuco-born, and, as Mayor Silva's sports coordinator, became part of Nairo's relentless schedule of work, school and competition.

'We supported him in every way we could,' Rusbel told me. 'We took him to the swimming pool and the gym. Some days, when darkness fell and caught him unawares, he stayed in Arcabuco with us. On the bike he was instantly recognisable. There was no body movement, and you couldn't tell from his face if he was going well or badly.'

Nairo was well known for his reticence, yet, by the time he started racing at the age of fifteen, he had perfected a sponsorship appeal which he recited on race-day mornings in local shops, bakeries and cafés.

'*Señores y señoras, buenos días.* We are here for the bicycle races in the village. We have a good chance of winning. We have taken the bus from Arcabuco, the entry fee is ten thousand pesos and we need to eat, so you can sponsor us for twenty thousand pesos and, if we win, we'll mention you in the radio interview on the podium. *Muchas gracias!*'

The response was either 'No, thanks,' or 'Take this, *chinito*' – a term of affection Colombians use with children (something like 'My little Chinaman') – 'Now go and win your race, you hear?' and, signing in, it would be 'Nairo Quintana, such-and-such Bakery.'

Yet, he insists, even at this stage in his life, he did not know that professional cycling or the Tour de France existed. His home department, Boyacá, had produced dozens of professional cyclists. Two of them – Fabio Parra, from Sogamoso, 75 kilometres away from Nairo's home at Tienda La Villita, and Francisco Rodríguez, from Duitama, 60 kilometres away – had stood on Grand Tour podiums. Nairo had never heard of any of them, nor of the Grand Tours themselves. He was still living in the tiny, close-knit world of his childhood. A vast cultural gulf separated him from the world where he would one day make his fortune.

'We were never sports fans,' Nairo simply says. 'We didn't have time. The thought of becoming a professional cyclist never crossed my mind. It was only later I saw that people were earning a living doing what we were doing.'

All that was soon to change.

In 2005, Mayor Silva supported the creation of Arcabuco's own cycling team, Alcaldía de Arcabuco ('Mayoralty of Arcabuco'). Nairo quickly established himself as its star rider. In October that year Nairo's father Don Luís spent the considerable sum of 360,000 pesos (about £86 at today's rates) on a light-blue, steel-framed machine for Nairo, with a Giant sticker indicating the prestigious brand with whom it plainly had no connection.

Rusbel Achagua tells me, 'It was so heavy, people were amazed he could win on it.'

Soon afterwards, over a beer at Agua Varuna with an Arcabuco carpenter colourfully named Belarmino Rojas, Don Luís fell into conversation with the father of another budding cyclist. Juan Guzmán cherished high hopes for his son Jhon, also known as *Pistolas*. Jhon had made occasional appearances for the Alcaldía de Arcabuco team but he was not a regular member, much less its leader. Even so, Guzmán challenged Luís: 200,000 pesos that Jhon would beat Nairo in a race from Arcabuco to the Alto del Sote, back to Arcabuco, and then back to Agua Varuna, half-way up the mountain. Having recently paid for Nairo's bike, Don Luís was short of cash, but Belarmino Rojas covered the bet and the race was on.

Rusbel drove the car behind the riders, with Luís and Juan Guzmán. 'Both were proud fathers. Pistolas had a better bike and proper kit, but Nairo dropped him from the start.'

Afterwards, Luís met up with Belarmino Rojas to pay back the loan. Belarmino told him to give the money to Nairo.

'The boy deserves it.'

The famous wager exists in local folklore as Nairo's first great test, although Nairo plays it down. 'It was just a bet between a couple of fifteen-year-olds, or their fathers. And I won.'

'And so,' Rusbel Achagua told me, 'we went from village races to departmental races, and Nairo began to make a name for himself.'

Nairo's father went to as many of these races as possible. Another parent, Rodrigo Anacona, whose son Winner was a year and a half older than Nairo, remembers, 'The races were usually circuits, so we would see them come past, then run two or three blocks to see them again and encourage them. Despite his crutches, Don Luís ran with the rest of us. I remember the emotion he showed when Nairo won. I found him admirable.'

Nairo was soon winning races against riders in higher categories. 'They paid more than in my age group. I was third in a mountain time trial for elite riders at Cómbita, which was followed by a circuit race. One of the directors complained because I was only seventeen and they threw me out.'

His winnings he divided into three: one part for his family, one part for bicycle equipment, and one part for himself. Without a doubt it was in these village races, against young riders inspired by dreams of winning the Giro, Tour and Vuelta, that the horizons of Nairo's life began vertiginously to recede.

◈

In November 2007 the fragility of life was brought home to him when Raúl Malagón was found dead on the road between Arcabuco and his bee hives at La Palma. He used a heavy baker's bike with a rack that allowed him to carry trays of honey pots, small gears and mudguards. No one was ever entirely sure what had happened, although it was possible that one of the mudguards had crumpled into the front wheel, sending him headfirst into the road.

Pedro Camargo remembers, 'Everyone in the village said, "Those poor Quintana boys. What are they going to do now?"'

Raúl was the first person Nairo had lost in his young life. 'It hit us hard,' he remembered, searching for words. 'We were friends. We had . . . an affinity. He indulged us and taught us things we remembered for the rest of our sporting careers.'

In her store in Arcabuco, Raúl's sister Maribel told me that 'When Nairo came back to Arcabuco after winning the Tour de l'Avenir [in 2010], he said in his speech, "I owe this victory to someone who is no longer here." I started crying, and I looked around and saw that everyone was crying with me. They all knew who he was talking about.'

Raúl Malagón's imprint may be felt not only on Nairo's brilliant career, but also on the pronunciation of his name. In Arcabuco, Nairo is invariably pronounced 'Nairon'. All my interviewees pronounced his name that way. Indeed, one of the nicknames sometimes foisted on him, 'Nairoman', only really makes sense in the village diction, the 'n' allowing the rhyme with the Spanish pronunciation of 'Ironman'. No one seemed able to explain this anomaly. I came to suspect that it originated with Raúl, whose nephew, his sister Maribel's son, was named Byron. Perhaps, talking animatedly around the village about his remarkable protégé, he inadvertently added the final 'n' – as if Nairo were a variation on Byron – and, enthused by his emotion, the entire village followed suit.

Hernán Darío Casas was the assistant coach to the Boyacá track cycling team when he first met Nairo:

It was on a windy day early in 2008. I was on my motorbike driving from Duitama and there he was. I said, 'Hey, *mijo* [a term of familiarity, literally 'My son']. Sit on out of the wind and I'll accompany you to Tunja.' I set a very good rhythm, but he had no trouble following. He told me where he was from, and I invited him to the track in Duitama.

When I got home I said to my father, '*Papá*, I met a kid, *negrito, negrito, negrito* [meaning 'small and very dark-skinned'] and he's going to be something.' He was serious, poised, very much his own man. You could see the ambition.

Guided by Hernán, Nairo began to train and compete on the track. At Duitama's Colombian Track Cup in March 2008, Nairo rode the points race.

'He had a skinsuit and a lenticular wheel,' Hernán Casas told me, 'and he was very happy with both. But when I set up his bike with a 51×14 gear, he protested. "No, *Profe* [the Colombian athlete's standard form of address for his coach, from *Profesor*], give me a 52, I'll be fine."'

'No, *mijo*, on the track it's about cadence and agility. Don't worry.'

During the early sprints, Nairo crossed far back in the pack. Then, using hand signals and whistles, Hernán Casas sent him on the attack, but held him short of gaining a lap. For sprint after sprint, Nairo gained full points and took the race lead even before riding into the group and lapping the field.

It was a rare closing of the distance Nairo preferred to keep from the established teams and departmental structures. He had reluctantly joined the Tunja Cycling School, sponsored by a local printer called Ediciones Mar, to obtain his racing licence. But he regarded the licence regime as a racket.

'To get your licence from the Federation, you had to belong to the League, and to belong to the League, you needed a club, so the clubs had high membership fees, and gave you nothing for them but a uniform with a sponsor's name all over it. If you weren't of a certain economic level' – meaning, if you couldn't make under-the-counter payments – 'it was hard to find a place, unless you were a big signing. I was neither, so I preferred not to get involved.'

Instead, he rode for the highest bidder. As a result, there are photographs of him in many different team jerseys. If, in later life, he would become a seasoned campaigner on rural issues affecting the peasantry, and would even take on the Cycling Federation itself, this refusal to conform was an early sign.

In particular, he did not join the biggest team in Tunja, Chocolate Sol, for whom Mauricio Soler, who would win a stage and the mountains classification at the 2007 Tour de France, had triumphed at the 2001 Vuelta del Porvenir.

Dayer Quintana recalls, 'Chocolate Sol brought in riders from all over Boyacá and waged war in the races. Nairo often rode alone, and won, against an entire Chocolate Sol team of eight or nine riders, including talents like Michael Rodríguez, Edward Beltrán and Darwin Pantoja.'

But Nairo did not get on with the team manager, Serafín Bernal. 'I didn't like his character or the way he treated other people, so I didn't want to be in his team. And he didn't like me either.'

Yet Nairo's first journey beyond Colombia's borders was to ride for Chocolate Sol. In June 2008, aged 18, he left home with his faithful, heavy bicycle on his back, boarded a bus for Cúcuta, on the border, to meet a team car heading for the nearby Venezuelan town of San Cristóbal and take part in the five-day Junior Tour of Venezuela.

For one race only, Serafín Bernal had found extra sponsorship from a Cúcuta sports goods outlet called Zapatillas Ulloa. Nairo's father's brother José, a bus driver in Cúcuta, saw to it that Nairo was part of the deal. It was an odd arrangement, and epitomised Nairo's sense of independence: in the race documentation, his teammates were listed as *Zapatillas Ulloa – Chocolate Sol* riders. Nairo's name appeared next to *Ulloa Deportes*.

He was given a more modern, lighter bike to race on. It reduced him to tears to forego his own machine. Even so, he helped his team leader, Heiner Parra, win the race, while finishing comfortably in the top ten overall and second in the time trial.

But he had not asked his school for permission to go. His social science teacher, Leonardo Cárdenas, showed me the classroom where Nairo had his desk, by the far wall, two or three places back.

'Don Luís came to speak to the headmaster, who said he could not authorise the trip. Luís told him, "Too late, he's already gone."'

Afterwards, his PE teacher failed him and the principal ordered him to ask his classmates' forgiveness in a public speech. Instead, Nairo held them in thrall with tales of his adventure, including how he won a fight against a group of Venezuelan riders who had attacked him during the race.

'He was no fool,' says his old teacher Leonardo Cárdenas. 'He never let anyone get one over on him. He was never bullied. He was well-mannered, but he was no coward. And he was noble.'

In spite of the disagreement, he appreciated his old school and returns there regularly to speak to the children, although he never passed PE.

At around this time, Nairo stopped going to the Friday and Sunday markets at Tuta and Tunja and launched a new initiative: 'We installed ovens in the shop at home, and I started baking bread when I came home from school. I served at the counter until ten or eleven at night, then went back to the ovens and baked for the following day.'

It did nothing to improve his sleep patterns: 'When I started cycling, I would be up until four making bread, and at six in the morning we would set off for the village where I was racing.'

Hernán Casas tells me, 'My father was a baker, so Nairo asked him how to make things, and my father showed him.'

Since that time, Nairo has been an enthusiastic and skilful cook in the family kitchen.

A month after his Venezuelan trip, on 20 July 2008, Nairo went to the town of Sogamoso, 70 kilometres north-east of Tunja, for the annual Independence Day race. There, he approached Jenaro Leguízamo. A Sogamoso native, Jenaro had been a domestique with the amateur Café de Colombia team until 1991, when the sponsorship dried up and Colombian cycling went into a ten-year decline. He had started coaching, before taking a degree in physical education and pioneering sports science in Boyacá. In 2008 Leguízamo had joined Colombia Es Pasión as team coach.

Ten years on, at his studio in the house where he grew up, Jenaro remembered the moment that shy, determined peasant child approached him.

'Professor Jenaro, I want to ask you a favour. I'm racing today, and again in two weeks' time. I want you to watch me and tell me if you think I'm any good.'

Jenaro was curious. 'With other riders, it was, "Coach, I need a contract." With Nairo, it was, "Tell me if I'm any good." He was always different.'

Nairo's result in the 20 July event is forgotten. Not so his performance a week later in the Clásico Club Deportivo Boyacá, a three-day race with a time trial and two mountain stages. It was Chocolate Sol's home race and Nairo faced their leader Darwin Ferney Pantoja, seven months his junior but already the winner of the 2007 Vuelta del Futuro, the national stage race for fifteen-and sixteen-year-olds.

In the windy opening time trial Nairo was only sixth. In stage two he finished second to Pantoja, who took the leader's jersey by 37 seconds. The final stage, from Moniquirá to Tunja, included the climb Nairo rode every day after school. He attacked on the lower slopes and rode Pantoja off his wheel. At

Vereda La Concepción, his mother Eloísa threw rose petals into the road before him. Rusbel Achagua filmed events for posterity from the driver's seat of a red Chevrolet Jimny belonging to the mayor's office, as the sentimental Don Luís, in floods of tears, shouted, 'Come on, *mi chinito*. That's it, *mi negrito*,' from the open window.

Nairo rode alone into Tunja's Plaza Bolívar to win the stage, the general classification and the mountain and sprints jerseys. The video, and the race winner's jersey, now framed on his wall, are among Rusbel Achagua's most prized possessions.

After singlehandedly dismantling the strongest team in the department, including the nationally feted Darwin Pantoja, Nairo saw new pathways open before him.

2

Colombia Es Pasión!

In February 2004 President Álvaro Uribe had visited Brussels and Strasbourg, where MEPs staged walk-outs and waved white flags as if to say, 'Don't shoot.' In October that year a Danish group named Oprør held a fund-raiser for the FARC and sent them US$8,500. Uribe concluded that Europe was getting its information from guerrilla sympathisers and decided it was time to do something.

At the time, the director of ProExport, the government agency responsible for fuelling Colombian tourism and trade, was Luis Guillermo Plata Páez. A Business Administration graduate from the University of Arizona with an MBA from Harvard Business School, Plata was typical of the young, English-speaking, foreign-educated technocrats Uribe had brought in to help transform the country. Selected by the World Economic Forum as one of the Young Global Leaders of 2006, he would go on to become Colombia's Minister of Commerce, Industry and Tourism. But at the time of Uribe's resolution, the transformation of Colombia's image abroad fell within Plata's purview.

His mellifluous American English is replete with business jargon and statistics.

'Did you know that over 90 per cent of the coffee Colombia exports is unroasted? Great coffee but, in the value-added chain, at the very bottom. It is as if France was exporting grapes instead of wine. I mean, which business do you want to be in? Exporting grapes, or making fine wines and charging a hundred bucks a bottle?'

We met in Usaquén, one of Bogotá's most upmarket *barrios* – a *barrio* is a small urban area, something like a ward or precinct, bundled up into a larger district called a *comuna* or *localidad*, depending on the city. Surrounded by colonial architecture, restaurants, boutiques and market stalls laden with curiosities, he explained how, in 2005, he earmarked some funding, Coldeportes did the same, and the Colombia Es Pasión team was born.

'Then I called a friend, someone I've known a long time, and asked him to run it.'

The friend was another US-educated technocrat: a financial consultant from Medellín named Ignacio Vélez, who had studied mathematical modelling at Stanford University. Passionate about cycling, Vélez started devouring coaching and sports science manuals, although at the outset his role was purely external. The new team's first year was a fiasco.

Blood tests conducted the day before the 2006 Vuelta a Colombia showed more than fifty cyclists with suspect results, suggesting massive use of the hormone erythropoietin – in sports parlance, EPO – then undetectable. The transgressors included Colombia Es Pasión riders. Vélez was livid.

He told me, 'We were representing a country beset by its association with violence and the cocaine trade. The words "drugs" and "Colombia" could not be allowed to appear in the same sentence. Promoting Colombia with a team using illegal methods was totally contradictory.'

He need not have worried: the corrupt anti-doping authorities ensured that the blood samples were disposed of, the results deleted and a second round of tests was held on the morning of stage one. There were still suspensions, but, by the previous day's standards, the outcome was deemed acceptable.

On every mountain stage, a group of riders aged 35 and over

seemed to ride away from the twenty-somethings. The race leaders included three riders – José Castelblanco, aged 36, Libardo Niño, 38, and Hernán Buenahora, 39 – who had ridden for the Spanish team Kelme and been treated by its notorious doctor, Eufemiano Fuentes, the figure at the centre of the scandalous Operación Puerto doping investigation in Spain. On the eve of the final stage, news broke that Buenahora, the race leader, had been disqualified, although no full explanation was given. The race was won by Castelblanco, who had won in 1997, 1998 and 2002, and also in 2004, although that result had been annulled when he tested positive for testosterone.

This was the world in which Vélez and Colombia Es Pasión were seeking to find a place. In the first three years of the team's existence, as Vélez attempted to inculcate the values of clean sport in his staff and riders, the team lurched from crisis to crisis.

In 2007 he approached cycling's world governing body, the Union Cycliste Internationale (UCI), about joining its biological passport screening scheme, but the infrastructure did not exist in South America. Instead, he promoted his staunchly anti-doping assistant coach Luis Fernando Saldarriaga, who took over as principal coach in 2007, and brought in a new general manager.

Saldarriaga had been a good but not outstanding junior rider who had studied Physical Education at the University of Antioquia, and Sports Science at the Grancolombiano Polytechnic. He had been a track coach in Medellín, Bogotá and Tunja, before moving to Colombia Es Pasión part-time in 2006. He went on to become Colombia's greatest ever cycling technician.

Luisa Fernanda Ríos, a former adventure sport competitor turned event organiser, was brought in as general manager in 2008, soon after yet another Colombia Es Pasión rider, Rafael Anibal Montiel, had tested positive.

'I was brought in for a period of six months to put the team's accounts and inventories in order, and to help change its internal culture,' Ríos told me. 'If I failed, Ignacio Vélez was going to wind up the team. I didn't know anything about pro cycling. I didn't even know what a peloton was, or a breakaway. Ignacio said, "That's what I need: someone new to it, with a clear mind." I didn't want to get too involved and lose the freedom to work on my own projects, but I fell in love with the project of clean cycling, and spent the next ten years there.'

Vélez, Saldarriaga and Ríos pioneered much that was new in Colombian cycling: the latest in sports science and psychology, training based on power meters, a no-needles policy. Ríos brought in a private health firm, Colsanitas, as sponsors. As part of their involvement, Colsanitas subjected the riders to twice-monthly testing using the UCI biological passport protocols, but went beyond them by monitoring hormones like thyroxine and testosterone as well. Each rider was provided with a booklet – the team's own bio-passport – that provided potential employers with a detailed physiological profile.

Vélez, Saldarriaga and Ríos bombarded their riders with anti-doping education, and, even as the team fought a constant, low-intensity war with the sporting institutions, including those that provided its funding, it created an oasis of clean sport in Colombian domestic cycling.

3

Darwin's Parrot

Late in 2006 Colombia Es Pasión held what Luís Fernando Saldarriaga called his 'Reality Show'. 'Team selections in Colombia always come down to politics, family connections, someone putting a word in, that sort of thing,' Saldarriaga told me. 'I've always been against it, so our working group devised a process to test strength and stamina, technical skills, the ability to interpret team orders based on a race profile, and psychological aptitude. We awarded points for each test: two points if they produced 5.0 to 5.2 watts per kilo, three points for 5.3 to 5.4, two points for 60 metres in 8 or 9 seconds, but four for 7.5 or 8 seconds, and so on.'

A group of riders who had shown ability during the 2006 Vuelta del Porvenir were invited to take part. When the points were added up, the riders selected were Camilo Torres, Óscar Sánchez and Jarlinson Pantano. In May 2007 Pantano went to the prestigious Ronde de L'Isard in France and won the best young rider title. Saldarriaga remembers it as a turning point in the Colombia Es Pasión project: 'It marked the moment we really began to concentrate on the long-term development of Under-23 riders.'

Pantano's story today is overshadowed by a positive for EPO at an anti-doping control on 26 February 2019. Four months later, in mid-June, he told the journalist Jairo Rodríguez: 'I cannot explain it, and I feel cheated. I have decided not to fight to the bitter end because I do not want to squander my family's assets just to get an explanation two years from now.'

Pantano's coach at Trek-Segafredo, Josu Larrazabal, informed me, 'We were very surprised. Jarlinson had been ill for long periods of his time at the team, so he had a lot of tests and we have a very full physiological picture of him. There was never a question mark or red flag, never the slightest suspicion of untoward practices.'

Indeed, Jarlinson Pantano spent six years with Colombia Es Pasión, and then seven years as a professional, during which his integrity was never at issue.

◈

It is a curious name – and it could have been worse: Jarlinson's father, José Gabriel Pantano, was going to call him Fafier. 'What's funny about that?' he asks me. 'I have a friend called Fafier who runs a barber's. But I liked Harley Davidsons, so I thought, Harley, Harlin, Jarlinson. The day we baptised him the priest grumbled, "What? Jarlinson? Unpronounceable. Makes no sense. What's wrong with normal names?"'

His mother, Olga Sofía, tells me, laughing, 'José gave him the name. I just went along with it.'

Be that as it may, everyone called him *País* – meaning something like 'countryman' – because that is what Jarlinson called everyone else.

His home town, Cali, sprawls across a plain between two mountain chains, 450 kilometres south-west of the capital. It is surrounded by climbs with names like *Dapa* and *La Cumbre* ('The Summit') and towering *Tenerife* – a thirty-kilometre ride up to the altitude of Bogotá – or with barely any name at all, like 'Kilometre Eighteen' because that is how long it is. Situated at only 1,000 metres, Cali is famed for its music and salsa dancers, its football, and its sweltering heat.

'And one more thing,' Jarlinson says, laughing. 'Laziness.'
Anything but cycling.

It does, however, have a history of producing excellent sprinters. Cali-born Leonardo Duque finished second in a stage of the 2008 Tour de France, sandwiched between Oscar Freire and Erik Zabel, while locals Luís H. Díaz and Jaime Galeano were both excellent sprinters in the 1960s and 1970s and rode alongside Cochise Rodríguez on his Caribú team.

Jarlinson Pantano's father, José Gabriel, had grown up with two keen cyclists. One, Ricardo Gallego, known to all as Richard, got as far as the Vuelta de la Juventud then became a jeweller: his sponsorship was crucial to Jarlinson's progress into the top flight of world cycling. The other, Camilo Sepúlveda, became a track rider at national level.

'Camilo invited me to the velodrome to use the gym,' José Gabriel recalls. 'When I got there, he said, "Have a go on a bike."' He adds, wistfully, 'We dreamed the dream handed down to our generation by Lucho Herrera and Fabio Parra, of being in a cycling team.'

He was fifteen, and the group of friends with whom he started racing included William Palacios, later sixteenth in the 1990 Tour de France and a stage winner in the 1992 Dauphiné Libéré.

Around that time, José Gabriel's family moved to Barrio Floralia, a poor area in the north-east of the city, prone to flooding and populated mainly by displaced people. There he met Olga Sofía, who had spent her first two years in San Antonio del Prado, Medellín, until her mother brought her to Cali. By 3 March 1984, the day Olga Sofía turned sixteen, she was pregnant. Their son Carlos Andrés was born eight days later, on the eleventh. José Gabriel had to give up his dream and get a job.

Jarlinson came along four and a half years later. They were a cycling family from the start. Olga Sofía's sister Carolina married Dubán Ramírez, Cochise Rodríguez's nephew, fourth in the World Championship time trial in 1995. Meanwhile, José Gabriel kept an open house. If you were in town for a race or a training camp, there was always a bed at the Pantanos'. The future UnitedHealthcare rider Carlos Eduardo Alzate regularly travelled the 90 kilometres from Tuluá and stayed with the Pantanos. Franklin López came to stay and never left, becoming Andrés and Jarlinson's unofficial, adoptive brother.

'My mother and Olga were at home,' José Gabriel says, 'and I had a good job with the council, so I never charged anyone a penny.' There was just one condition: 'I started work at seven a.m., so we all went out training at three.'

José Gabriel had been brought up on early starts. Not a city boy at all, he was born in rural Sopó, north of Bogotá, where his grandparents were farm superintendents, managing a team of labourers and a hundred head of cattle whose milk went to a dairy called Alpina, created by Swiss immigrants in the 1940s to churn out Colombian versions of Emmental and Gruyère cheese.

When José Gabriel's grandfather fell from a ladder and suffered a life-changing disability, his son – José Gabriel's father, Ángel Gabriel Pantano – became responsible for keeping the family: 'My mother was up with the cows and goats at three or four a.m., when it is bitterly cold. My father drove the milk truck to the factory.'

Colombia's priority in the 1960s was industrialisation: the substitution of imports with home-produced goods. Manufacturing industry, which accounted for only 8.9 per cent of GDP in 1929, had expanded to 16.5 by 1945 and to 20.6 per cent by the early 1960s. A family visit to an uncle in Cali tempted Ángel Gabriel to join the wave of progress.

Taken on to paint a village school near Cali, he learned that Sidelpa – *Siderúrgica del Pacífico*, or Pacific Iron and Steel – was hiring. After a spell there, he moved to a new hydroelectric plant. It was only then that he brought the family to Cali. His son José Gabriel was seven.

Eight years later, with Olga Sofía expecting, José Gabriel

started work, in construction, then loading and unloading trucks, then security. He ballooned to 17 stone. Finally he found steady work with the city council as a works inspector and started riding again. He competed in masters events and in the national games for public sector employees. But the only time he had for training was in the early hours.

Olga Sofía tells me, 'Jarlinson was only three, but he would get up and beg to be allowed to go out riding with them. He would take the pump and put air in José's tyres.'

José adds, 'I would say, "You're too small. Go back to bed." When he was ten and started riding seriously, people used to say to me, "Be careful, you'll burn him out." They didn't know I had been holding him back all those years.'

When he was eight, Olga found a folder under his bed containing a school essay that laid his desires bare.

It read, 'My name is Jarlinson Pantano and I want to be the departmental cycling champion, then the national champion, and my ambition is to enter the Tour de France and win a stage.'

José says, 'He had the secret of a happy life: passion. He used to ride his kid's bike all day, from the patio to the front door and back.'

Whenever there was a race in Cali, Jarlinson went to watch. If his uncle Dubán was there, he would come away with a water bottle or a pair of gloves as a souvenir.

By then, the family was living in Barrio La Independencia, in Cali's Comuna or District 11, built to receive the survivors of a colossal explosion that rocked the city in August 1956, when ten military trucks transporting dynamite blew up in front of the old Pacific Railroad station. The blast razed the station and forty city blocks, killing four thousand.

Jarlinson's elder brother Carlos Andrés was talent-spotted while playing football for the Comuna and invited to join América de Cali's Under-15s. By the time he was 16 he was training with the first team. A great future seemed to beckon. 'There were two other players in the same situation. One of them was the son of an ex-América player. He was always picked ahead of me.

'One week América were playing Millonarios. I had had a good week in training and I was hoping to make my debut. Instead, the ex-player's son was in the team and I was left out. I decided, "That's it."'

Used to seeing his father and brother out riding their bikes, Andrés took up cycling. Within a month he had finished second in the time trial and third on the road at the departmental championships.

Jarlinson loved football too but lacked his brother's ability, so he cultivated other ambitions. He began to train and compete in children's races. As his proud father puts it, 'He could win with one leg, either sprinting or alone.'

José Gabriel coached him – 'There were no heart rate monitors, so it was "Ride at 60 per cent," "Ride at 70 per cent," and so on.' – and Ricardo Gallego created a team to support him, Joyería Richard, and paid Jarlinson small cash prizes for winning.

Jarlinson's daily schedule started with training at 3 a.m. By 7.30 he had to be at school: 'Sometimes I got there at eight, but I couldn't be any later. If I wasn't too tired, I would spend time with my friends at break time. Otherwise I would get my head down.'

José Gabriel recalls a headline in the local newspaper, *El Caleño*: '*Triunfan los Pantano en Palmira*' – 'The Pantanos win in Palmira'. Andrés and Jarlinson had both won their races, and José Gabriel had finished second in his. The following year Andrés made the national team for the Pan-American Championships.

In 2001 Jarlinson, twelve now, started riding at Cali's celebrated track under Hernán Herrón, who had ridden at the 1960 Olympics and then become national track coach. At the 2004 departmental championships in Yumbo, Jarlinson took gold medals in the individual and team pursuit on the track, then won the road race. Then, in July 2005, the national selector, Luís

Fernando Saldarriaga, paired him up with another of the young stars of Colombian cycling, Rigoberto Urán Urán, for the madison at the Pan-American Cycling Championships at Barquisimeto, Venezuela. Rigoberto was 18, Jarlinson two years younger.

In Venezuela, the evening before the final, Urán fell ill. But he reassured Jarlinson: 'Don't worry, País, tomorrow we're going to win.'

Saldarriaga remembers, 'Rigo had come down with flu, but it didn't make any difference. They put on an exhibition and took the gold medal.'

Jarlinson also rode the team pursuit and the points race, and then he rode in support of Urán in the road race, where Rigoberto, who had already won the time trial, duly triumphed. In August, Jarlinson travelled to Austria to compete in the World Junior Track Championships. He won his scratch race qualifying heat but finished only seventeenth in the final.

In 2006 Dalivier Ospina, a rider from Palmira, just north of Cali, was invited to Aigle, Switzerland, to train at the World Cycling Centre, the headquarters of cycling's world governing body, the UCI. Three years Jarlinson's senior, Ospina was asked to recommend a junior to attend the centre, and suggested Pantano. The Colombian Cycling Federation and Cauca Valley Cycling League contributed to his expenses, and Ricardo Gallego and other family friends provided the rest.

Jarlinson recalls, 'I spent three months there, but I was young and it was hard because I didn't speak the language. Because of the schedule, I had breakfast but missed the other meals, so I ended up eating bread washed down with Coca-Cola and putting on weight.'

Even so, in 2007 Jarlinson and Dalivier were invited back to the World Cycling Centre to ride the Tour de l'Avenir in their colours. Between April and September 2007, Jarlinson rode several north European races with another World Cycling Centre trainee, Chris Froome. The Tour de l'Avenir, however, was a hard one for the Colombians: 'It was very flat. I wasn't used to riding in the wind, so I suffered.' Jarlinson was 37th.

He rode his second Avenir in 2008, again for the World Cycling Centre team: 'Andrey Amador won the Prologue, and in the end I worked for him. He finished fifth and I was seventh.'

During these European adventures, Jarlinson wrote home regularly, signing off with one or other of the pseudonyms he adopted from his favourite riders: 'Thanks. I love you. Attentively, Ullrich.' Or, if he'd been in a sprint, 'Cipollini.'

His father still has the letters.

In 2008 and 2009 Saldarriaga calculated that he could get more from his team if he increased his contact hours with the riders. This meant asking them to move to Medellín. Jarlinson Pantano left his family in urban Cali and moved into the peasant *finca* – a rustic smallholding – of one of the other riders: Sergio Luís Henao. Henao was a formidable racer: in 2005 he had taken two stage wins and finished second in the Vuelta del Porvenir, won by his teammate Rigoberto Urán. The following year, as an eighteen-year-old competing against elite athletes, he had won his first stage race, the 2006 Clásica Norte de Santander. Third at the Vuelta a Antioquia, he was then fifth overall and the best Under-23 rider at the Clásico RCN. It was this result that had earned him the call-up from Colombia Es Pasión.

He told me, 'I grew up doing agricultural work: hoeing potatoes, picking beans, helping with the harvests and doing various jobs for other small farmers.' When I ask which side of the peasant–urban divide he falls, he tells me, 'Somewhere in between: country with some town, although,' he says, smiling, 'not much.'

His cousin Sebastián joked to me that they were 'backwoodsmen made good!' – 'backwoodsmen' being a rather kind English rendering of *auténticos montañeros*, a pejorative Colombian expression for those most remote from urban influences. 'It used to be applied to people in isolated regions with no water or electricity. Sure, we come from the countryside, but life there today is much more comfortable than it once was.'

The boys' grandfather Eduardo came unambiguously from the land. His first wife died giving birth to their fifteenth child. Eduardo remarried and had four more. Sergio Luís's father Omar was the seventh of the nineteen. He worked as the caretaker on a private finca before inheriting his own patch of land and sowing it with beans, maize and potatoes.

Sergio Luís says, 'We set aside a small amount to eat at home and sold the rest. That was how my father supported a wife and five children.'

As a young man, Omar had had his own ambitions as a cyclist, Sergio Luís tells me. 'He would go out to ride at five or six in the morning after a breakfast of bread and *aguapanela*' – concentrated sugar-cane juice dissolved in water, the Colombian cyclist's traditional on-road refreshment. 'It was train, then down to work, which meant hoeing in the sun until sundown. Dinner was not much more than potato broth with a pinch of salt. They didn't know what it was to eat meat.'

Omar's brother Alcides had the same dream, and his son Sebastián paints much the same picture. 'He didn't have enough to eat, let alone a good bike, so, yes, he raced, but on an empty stomach. He never made it to the national level.'

Omar and Alcides had seen one of their childhood friends, a man named Reynel Montoya, later turn professional and win consecutive national championships in 1987, 1988 and 1989. Both men wanted their sons to have the opportunity that they had never had.

Sergio Luís says, 'I saw my father's bikes and photographs and the idea of cycling began to sink in. He gave me my first bike, a green Torres with an aluminium frame, and my first uniform.'

Growing up, Sergio Luís saw Colombia's violence close up.

The family farm, Vereda Río Abajo, was vulnerable to guerrilla and paramilitary incursions.

'The main road was only a hundred metres from the house, and when you heard cars and trucks racing past at high speed, at two in the morning, you knew it was either the guerrillas or the paramilitaries. At times I thought they were coming for me and my family. I went through periods of fear and anxiety.

'In those days, if the paramilitaries knocked on your door wanting food or land to camp on, you cooperated or they put a bullet in you,' he went on. 'But that made you a collaborator in the guerrillas' eyes, and that was a death sentence too.'

From the age of eleven, Sergio Luís, the oldest of the five children, rode the eleven kilometres of dirt track from the family finca to school in Rionegro. In 2001, the year he turned fourteen and started training, the territorial conflict between the illegal armed groups had been at its height.

'I used to go out on my mountain bike at six in the morning, along a dirt track,' he recalled. 'One day I came across the bodies of two people who had been dragged outside in their underwear and executed. You could see the bullet holes. The image is still burned into my mind.'

Vereda Río Abajo – *río abajo* means 'downriver' – belonged administratively to the town of San Vicente, an hour due east of Medellín, although it was closer to Rionegro, an important industrial centre that provides a home to a number of Colombia's best-known enterprises: the paint brand Pintuco, the paper manufacturer Sancela, confectionary producer Nutresa, textiles firm Riotex, as well as the country's second largest airport, José María Córdova International. The countryside around Rionegro is covered by the vast greenhouses of Colombia's cut-flower industry, second globally only to Holland.

The collapse in agricultural prices hit Antioquia hard, and Omar took a job as a night watchman at a cut-flower producer ten kilometres from home: 'He worked from 6 p.m. to 6 a.m., came home to sleep, then went back to work. Life was hard.'

A cousin named Jhonatan Marín was already racing. Sergio Luís tells me, 'I was competitive, and I thought I could beat him, so we raced up the climb from La Ceja to La Unión and I lost. I demanded a rematch, and, later the same week, my father bet Jhonatan's father lunch that I would beat him second time around. I did. As a result, he gave up cycling, and I took it up.'

When the Uribe government came into power in August 2002, operations against the FARC intensified in the region: 'From inside the house I could sometimes hear bombs exploding and salvoes from the helicopters attacking the guerrillas in the mountains. I remember thinking, "This is what war must sound like."'

After three years with the local cycling club, Club de Ciclismo CICO Rionegro, Sergio Luís was selected for the cycling programme of the Indeportes Antioquia (Antioquian Institute of Sport). Known as *Orgullo Paisa*, 'Pride of Antioquia', the project had been established in 1993 and had the rare virtue of longevity. Based at the Atanasio Girardot Sports Complex in western Medellín, it brought together riders from throughout Antioquia with some of the nation's top sports scientists.

In an open-plan office at Indeportes Antioquia, beside a desk covered with neat paper files, Dr Luís Eduardo Contreras, who joined the Institute in 1993 and became one of the architects of the cycling programme, sketches its history:

We were very advanced in physiological and biochemical evaluation. We were already doing ergospirometry with direct measurement of maximum oxygen uptake, and working out thresholds and lactate curves, in the 1990s, and measuring urea and CPK [creatine phosphokinase, an indicator of fatigue] in-race to monitor recovery.

Our juniors used to finish first, second and third in the Vuelta del Porvenir, and the Under-23s did the same in the Vuelta de la Juventud. In 1997 the newspaper *El Espectador* named Orgullo Paisa 'Colombian Sports Phenomenon of the Year'. I still have the cuttings.

A rider complained recently that he had never received any support. I told him, 'You lived and ate at the Villa Deportiva for six years. We provided coaching, paid for your studies and high school certificate, and offered you a place at university, although you turned it down. That's 500 million pesos [£120,000]. Then there are all the appointments with the doctor, the physio, the psychologist, the nutritionist, the orthopaedist, and the testing: ergospirometry, ECGs, blood tests. All paid by Indeportes Antioquia.'

His archives include physiological data on virtually every rider who ever passed through the programme. He scrolls down a screen on his desktop: 'I have' – there is a pause – '327 maximum oxygen uptake tests taken on the cycle ergometer.' He jumps from file to file. 'Here is Sergio Luís Henao in 2004. Ah, here we have dynamometry and ergospirometry for Rigoberto Urán, Rigoberto again, Sergio Luís, José Nicolas Castro, Julián David Arredondo, Carlos Julián Quintero . . .'

It is a contemporary history of Antioquian cycling.

At the centre of all this expertise, Sergio Luís Henao developed into one of the best young riders in the country. Then, in 2007, he joined Colombia Es Pasión and stayed for three years. In 2008 he won the Under-23 Vuelta a Colombia ahead of his teammate Fabio Duarte, with Cayetano Sarmiento third. Darwin Atapuma, riding for Orgullo Paisa (officially Indeportes Antioquia-Idea), was fifth, and Jarlinson Pantano, in his second year with Colombia Es Pasión, was ninth.

Like Jarlinson's place in Cali, the Henaos' finca became, in Sebastián's phrase, a high-performance home. 'Friends or teammates often used to come for dinner, sleep over and then come out training with me. We didn't have much money but there was always a plate of rice or lentils.'

In 2008 the Henaos opened their door to Jarlinson Pantano. Sergio says, 'He stayed a year and became part of the family.'

Sergio's cousin, Sebastián, then only thirteen, joined Sergio and Jarlinson on some days. He told me, 'We kept our road bikes in a cousin's flat in Rionegro, so I would arrive at Sergio's at six in the morning, in a track suit, with my kit in a backpack. We would ride there on mountain bikes in half an hour. Sergio always started really fast, with me and Jarlinson behind, our breakfast coming back up our throats. We used to get changed in Rionegro, and head out on the road.'

Sebastián adds, 'There were days when Sergio did five hours and Pantano only did an hour and a half to recover. I remember Pantano saying, "You train too hard, Sergio!"'

Sergio tells me, 'When Chaves joined Colombia Es Pasión, he wanted to train with me too. Saldarriaga had given him the opportunity to join the team, but he was very skinny, with no muscle mass, and he had knee problems. But he came and lived at my house in 2009, and then Carlos Betancur came in 2010 to prepare for the Vuelta de la Juventud.'

To the many cyclists who stayed at the Henaos' finca, Cecilia Marín, Sergio's mother, became a legend as the generous supplier of traditional Antioquian sweetcorn, beans and *aguapanela* to the future champions who visited the family farm.

◈

In 2008 Colombia Es Pasión was reinforced by another of the riders who had been dominating Colombia's junior ranks.

Darwin Atapuma and Jarlinson Pantano had first met at the 2001 Vuelta al Cauca, a circuit race around the charming colonial town of Popayán in south-west Colombia, won, as far as either can remember, by Darwin.

'He was always a nightmare for me!' Jarlinson tells me, recasting adversity as laughter.

Five years later – ten days before the 2006 Vuelta del Porvenir – the six riders of the Valle del Cauca team moved into a Túquerres hotel to prepare for the race. The contrast could hardly have been greater.

Darwin recalls, 'Jarlinson had come from thirty degrees in Cali to five degrees and pouring rain here [in Túquerres]. He was shivering with cold, and I remember us looking at each other and laughing, and Jarlinson saying, "It's a different sport here . . . !"'

卌

Darwin Atapuma is seventeen. He has long left the family finca and is living with his brother Remigio at an altitude of 3,100 metres in the town of Túquerres, beneath the sulphurous, semi-active Azufral volcano in the rural, high-altitude department of Nariño, close to the Ecuadorean border, where the Andes diverge northwards across Colombia.

Darwin has a cow and weaning calf at the finca. His mother milks the cow, sells the milk and sends the proceeds to Darwin, who uses them to pay his rent, food and schooling in Túquerres. But Darwin faces a dilemma. He needs a light, modern racing bike. Without it, his chances of winning the 2004 Vuelta del Porvenir, the national stage race for seventeen- and eighteen-year-olds, will be slim. But if he sells his cow, he disposes of his only source of income.

Darwin's dilemma is one that faces many Colombian riders from peasant farming families. He weighed up the pros and cons and took the plunge. But how many young talents decide the risks are too high, costing Colombia in soft power and depriving it of more sporting ambassadors?

Darwin prepared for the Porvenir, in another volcanic department, El Huila, on a Giant TCR carbon frame. The favourite was the previous year's winner, Rigoberto Urán, now, like his teammate

Sergio Luís Henao, in his final year at under-19 level. On his new bike, Darwin took the lead in the mountains competition, fought his way into third place overall – then crashed. He finished the race on a spare bike, keeping the mountains jersey but dropping to nineteenth overall. Worse, his carbon frame was broken.

'That's it,' he decided. 'I need a job. I'm giving up cycling.'

Another rider's career would have finished then and there. But, in one of those large peasant families with many siblings born years apart, Darwin had his brother Remigio, eighteen years his senior, to support him as his coach and companion.

There were nine Atapuma siblings: Alirio, Carmen, Remigio, Doris, Pablo, Damaris, Elsa, Alex and Darwin, with twenty-two years between first and last. They had all worked in the fields. Remigio tells me, 'In the countryside, when you are five or six you have to go and bring down the cows or the horses, or run errands, or bring the water. Whatever your father tells you to do, you do, pronto.'

The father in question, Ignacio Sigifredo Atapuma, had grown up on Vereda Chambú, 23 kilometres from Túquerres. When Sigifredo and María Bersabeth Hurtado, from a neighbouring vereda called Guaisés, decided to build a life together, Sigifredo had been no more than an agricultural labourer, working wherever there was money to be earned. But the land was fertile and Sigifredo was tenacious, and, by the time Darwin, the last of the children, came along in 1988, Sigifredo was employing twenty labourers on two fincas, growing his own crops and buying those of his neighbours and taking them all to the surrounding markets on his own pack horses.

It was a remarkable success story for a small peasant farmer, although it belonged to its time: it would have been inconceivable after the opening up of the national economy. Sigifredo and his men farmed maize, beans, potatoes, carrots and cabbage, but earned most of their income from wheat and barley, which they sold to a malthouse in Ipiales, near the border with Ecuador. But in 2000 the malthouse closed – a catastrophe, even for successful families like the Atapumas. By 2006, 75 per cent of Colombia's commercially traded maize, 95 per cent of its wheat and 100 per cent of its barley were imported.

In the 1980s, Sigifredo and María's eldest, Alirio – born in 1966 – started listening to cycling. During the Vuelta a España and the Tour de France the radio would come on at two in the morning and, until the day's stage had finished, Alirio would not appear for work. Remigio, four years his junior, soon caught the bug.

Remigio told me, 'My father used to get angry with us. "Listening to the radio. What good does it do you?" But when we told him, "Lucho Herrera won today," or "Fabio Parra won today," he brightened up.'

Three kilometres from the house, along the main road to Túquerres, there is a testing climb. In those days it was all thick stones and sand. Alirio would mount his bike, challenge the other young men who made up his father's work force, and beat them to the top, Lucho Herrera-style. That was until Remigio took his savings, added some money from his father and bought a Standard steel racing bike with gears. Then *he* took over as the best cyclist in the family.

Aged twelve or thirteen, Remigio met a group of cyclists who invited him to join the Túquerres club. Within a month, he was competing at national level. He won races as a junior and made the top thirty in the Vuelta de la Juventud, then, for lack of support, he retired, although not before discerning, in the bicycle, a means of escape. Aged nineteen, Remigio sold his horses and took on a team of temporary workers to plant, harvest and market what turned out to be a bumper crop. Converted to cash, it allowed him to leave the family vereda, open a bike shop and marry his sweetheart Aida.

Then he set about turning his youngest brother into a professional cyclist.

The wall of windows gazes up at another volcano. Pasto, the capital of the department of Nariño, sits beneath Galeras, whose daily threat as Colombia's most active volcano overshadows the lives of the city's half a million inhabitants.

Darwin Atapuma fell in love with cycling as an eight-year-old, he says, watching Remigio race: 'I dreamed of copying him and travelling to far-off places like Bogotá, which I had never seen. Remigio gave me my first bike when I was eight or nine. I rode it all the time, even after dark. My father sometimes got angry because I was still riding at ten o'clock at night.'

A peasant child enamoured of his bicycle and the country-side, he found urban life, even in a garden town of 17,000 like Túquerres, unbearable. Darwin's brother Alex recalls, 'When he was eleven or twelve, he was sent to Túquerres to start secondary school. Remigio even paid his school fees, but Darwin refused to go.'

Remigio's wife Aida tried to convince him to study, but Darwin, who missed his mother terribly, ran away, first to Vereda Chambú, and then Vereda Guaisés, where he hid with his maternal grandmother.

Around this time, Don Sigifredo went down to the market in the nearby village of Piedrancha and came home with a small parrot. He tried to domesticate the creature and teach it to speak but, unable to adapt to life indoors, the parrot died. Alex recalls, with an affectionate smile, 'Darwin said that he felt so sad in Túquerres that he was afraid of going the same way as the parrot. He hated school and lost a year of his studies.'

The family decided it would be best to let him live in Chambú. Darwin spent another year there, travelling to town only to take part in the children's races that Remigio organised. For Alex, Darwin's obduracy was normal: 'In the countryside, you are responsible for yourself from the age of ten or eleven. Darwin would string a bag over his back and ride into town to race, or he would say, "I'm riding out to visit my mother. No need to come with me," and he wouldn't come back.'

At Vereda Chambú, Darwin and his brothers spent hours with their sister Carmen and her son Jesús, who entertained them with elaborate summaries of the week's news. Jesús was Darwin's nephew but only nine months his junior.

'They were more like brothers,' Alex remembers. 'Darwin made things out of wood: stools, chairs, toy cars. Jesús helped him. At one point they were stealing bed slats to work with. They were found out when someone fell through the gap. They knew they would get into trouble, but they knew they would be forgiven too.'

After Darwin had moved to Túquerres, Jesús and his friends would ride their bikes into town to meet him. One Friday, dusk caught them unawares. Alex, on his motorbike, told them, 'Go ahead and I'll light the way for you from behind.'

'When we reached the descent, they sprinted ahead. A car was coming towards them on the wrong side of the road. It only had one headlamp, so they assumed it was a motorbike. My nephew [Jesús] was the most badly hurt. I placed my hands lightly on his shoulders. The sensation has never left me. He felt like a bag of broken glass.'

Darwin told me, 'He was in intensive care for three days but never woke up. It was the first time I had lost a loved one. The vereda was never the same without him. Our visits became fewer and further between. Remigio became like a father to me, and Aida, like a mother. Their children, Jennifer, Johana and Duván, were like brothers and sisters.'

Darwin agreed to go to evening school, intended not for twelve-year-olds but for working people who had not had the opportunity to study as children and wanted to take their school certificate: 'I got up at half past six to train. I would arrive home at about midday, eat, then go to my brother's bike shop to help him until five. Then I studied from six in the evening to a quarter past ten.'

Alex says, 'Finally he adapted to life in the village.'

Darwin's passion for cycling eventually infected Alex too. Coached, like Darwin, by Remigio, he finished seventh in the 1999 Vuelta del Futuro in Fusagasugá, Lucho Herrera's home town, and third in the 2000 Vuelta del Futuro at Yarumal, Antioquia, where his Nariño teammate Robinson Chalapud, from Ipiales, was the champion.

Despite their potential, Nariño wasn't Boyacá. You didn't see small businesses contributing to help young cyclists. What Nariño did have in its favour was Ecuador. As Alex explains, 'Ecuador's cycling scene is mostly near the border, from Quito northwards. It is harder for us to get to central Colombia than it is to get to the country next door, so we went to race in Ecuador and they came to race in Nariño.'

Until 2004, the Vuelta al Ecuador was open to elite riders, under-23s and juniors. The juniors waited at their own stage start, and when the peloton reached them, they joined in and contested the mountains, intermediate sprints and stage finishes.

'It was against international regulations,' Alex continues, 'so the older riders complained when we won. We felt sorry for them too, because we were riding shorter distances, but it was a good apprenticeship. There are things you can learn only by racing. Afterwards, the age group categories in Colombia were easy.'

Chalapud and Alex Atapuma became fixtures in the departmental team, which was feared throughout Colombia.

'If the team from Nariño was coming, they knew they had a hard race in store.'

Alex won the Vuelta Juvenil al Ecuador in 2000. Chalapud then won the Colombian Vuelta al Futuro for fifteen- and sixteen-year-olds in 2000. At the 2001 Vuelta del Porvenir for seventeen- and eighteen-year-olds, won by Mauricio Soler, Alex finished both of the big mountain stages in the top ten, and his teammate Robinson Chalapud was seventh overall. Their performances earned invitations from Serafín Bernal, the Chocolate Sol manager, to go and ride in Boyacá.

Alex tells me, 'Soler was moving up into the Under-23 ranks, so Don Serafín was scouring the nation for juniors to replace him. I spent my second year as a junior with them, including three months living in Tunja.'

With Chocolate Sol Alex finished fifteenth in the 2002 Vuelta del Porvenir.

'I couldn't move up to Under-23 with Chocolate Sol because I had to go home to Túquerres and finish my school certificate. When I'd finished, I called Don Serafín but by then the team was full.'

Alex moved on to a small team in the Valle del Cauca called Gripofen, where he became a teammate of Carlos Andrés Pantano, Jarlinson's elder brother, but it was a distinct step down.

He won the Vuelta al Ecuador in November 2007, rode December's Vuelta a Costa Rica for the money, finishing sixteenth, started the 2008 season tired and never recovered. In 2009 he returned home and rode for Nariño, making ends meet over the next three years by racing for appearance money alone.

'Then they offered me a position as a coach for the department. I took it, no regrets, and I'm still here.'

◈

Until a sudden, brief growth spurt during his twentieth year, Darwin was boyish and very slight. When he was thirteen, Remigio had to take a hacksaw to a normal frame and weld the pieces back together to make a bike that would fit him. He gave him a helmet, uniform and shoes, and, thus attired, Darwin started a new phase in his cycling career.

In 2004 he won the Tour of Carchi, the Ecuadorean province closest to the border, then triumphed in his own country's Vuelta del Futuro for fifteen- and sixteen-year-olds. He followed in his brother Alex's footsteps by winning the Vuelta Juvenil al Ecuador in 2005, and did so again in 2006. Then, he won the mountains jersey in the 2005 Vuelta del Porvenir, after facing his dilemma: peasant or cyclist?

It cannot have been an easy decision: after the race, in financial and temperamental meltdown, he was ready to walk away from the sport: 'I had won the mountains competition representing Nariño, but the department didn't want to pay for the repairs. And I no longer had the cow. I took my school certificate at seventeen, so, with no more studying to do, it was time to make a decision.'

But Remigio would have none of it. He botched a repair and packed his brother off to the Junior Tour of Venezuela. His Venezuelan host promised Remigio he would call when the race had started. The phone did not ring until the evening after stage three.

'How is he?'

'He crashed in stage one, he lost two minutes in stage two, but today he won the hardest stage.'

It was the story of Darwin Atapuma's young career.

Meanwhile, Remigio spoke to Serafín Bernal, who had directed Alex at Chocolate Sol. Bernal invited Darwin to Tunja. The day Remigio took him to the bus station in Pasto is etched in the family memory.

Remigio says, 'I was happy because he finally had his opportunity, but the moment he was on the bus, I wanted him to stay. He was so small. What was going to happen to him?'

Darwin remembers, 'From the bus I saw he had tears on his face, and I began to cry too.'

The journey to his new life took a day and a night. Serafín Bernal was waiting for him at Tunja bus station. Darwin moved in with his coach and helped him run the car park that he owned.

'My life consisted of training and racing. I went from asking my brother or father for help, to being paid – only a little, but even so – and having somewhere to sleep, nice uniforms and a car to the races. I was very happy, and Serafín Bernal helped me develop.'

At the 2006 national time trial championships in Popayán, Darwin won the silver medal. Then he began to prepare for his season's goal, the Vuelta del Porvenir. Remigio, an experienced organiser of local and departmental events, had won the contract to organise the race in Nariño, so, in November that year, the leading junior teams made a rare trip south.

Darwin dominated from the start. He won three stages, the mountains title and the team competition with Chocolate Sol. He won the race overall by five full minutes, with a teammate, Gabriel Álvarez, second, and the Antioquia rider Carlos Betancur third, 6 minutes 27 seconds behind.

In 2007, recommended by Serafín Bernal, Darwin moved to Medellín and joined Orgullo Paisa. Darwin acknowledged his good fortune: 'For a rider like me who was just coming through, it was an incredible opportunity. I earned enough to buy a better bike, help my family, even make a few savings. I lived in the Villa Deportiva, and I often rode in the same team as Betancur and Arredondo.'

There, Darwin succeeded Sergio Luís Henao as Under-23 champion at the Clásico RCN. The result led to the call-up to Colombia Es Pasión, which, with its formidable young squad, was almost ready to challenge the world.

4

Carpenters and Their Sons

Before the call from Colombia Es Pasión, Luís Fernando Saldarriaga had been training juniors on the track for the Bogotá Cycling League. One day in 2005 a local team, the Monserrat Club, was training at the velodrome. One of the fathers asked Saldarriaga if he would draw up a long-term programme to turn his son, still fifteen, into a champion.

Saldarriaga asked: 'Does he have a heart rate monitor?'

'Yes, sir.'

'Is he disciplined?'

'Yes, sir.'

Saldarriaga mulled it over, and cut a deal. The boy's name was Jhoan Esteban Chaves.

Every week, Saldarriaga sent him his training plan. Esteban's father, Jairo Chaves, still has a pile of exercise books from those years, containing detailed written notes.

I wondered what long-term meant: 'Three years? Four?'

Saldarriaga told me, 'Much longer. Many years. His father was a visionary.'

♯

'I was born with a gift.'

At a table in Tenjo, north of the capital, Jairo Chaves is telling me his story.

'I was forced into learning a trade. I learned it properly, mind. I made every item of furniture in this room.'

I give the table a closer look. 'This is a work of art,' I say.

'My father was a carpenter. He decided I would be one too, and that was the end of it. I was unhappy for many years because I didn't enjoy my work. I have always told my sons, "Whatever you want to be in life, be good at it. But the day you stop enjoying it, go and do something else."'

His father worked at home and the radio was always on:

There was a silver-tongued cycling commentator from Argentina called Julio Arrastía Bricca who described the racing and the landscapes. I'm sure he made a lot of it up, but to me it was magical, and I fell in love with cycling when I was five, riding my tricycle around in circles, listening to the Vuelta a Colombia and dreaming I was one of the cyclists.

My father promised to buy me a bicycle: he even made me work to pay for it, then made up excuse after excuse. When I raised the subject, he told me sport was for idlers. So when I was eighteen, I took my first wage packet and bought my first bike.

It was only then I understood that the world was more than the ten blocks around my home. We were poor, so I had never been anywhere, and my mother wouldn't let me go far.

A remembrance of real danger may have underlain his mother's injunction.

In 1953 the Chief of Staff of the Colombian Armed Forces, General Gustavo Rojas Pinilla, overthrew the government and, through talks and amnesties, quelled much of the violence. Military rule ended in 1957, when a plebiscite supported by four million voters and opposed by only 300,000 led to an arrangement called the National Front, according to which Liberal and Conservative governments would alternate for the next four terms. It was an imperfect proposal, leaving the victims of atrocities with no redress, but no other solution would stick.

Gangs of brigands known as *bandoleros* were left roaming the mountains. Some were army or police deserters. Others were members of proxy militias abandoned to their fate now that the political elites had decided that armed groups had outlasted their usefulness. They killed, stole harvests and took over smallholdings for themselves or paying clients.

Jairo's mother was born in 1943 in the town of Purificación, in the coffee-growing department of Tolima, 200 kilometres south-west of Bogotá. In 1957 she joined millions of small farmers displaced by the bloodshed.

'They had to leave that night,' Jairo told me. 'They would have been killed the following day.'

They settled in Barrio Simón Bolívar, in north-west Bogotá. It was there that Jairo's mother met and fell in love with his father – there that Jairo grew up and began to explore the world by bike. All traces of the few blocks where Jairo grew up were destroyed in 1983 when bulldozers cleared the area and a shopping mall called Metropolis opened its doors. They were an urban family now.

When Jairo was eighteen, he decided he wanted to be a professional cyclist.

'Imagine!' he exclaims, recognising the extravagance. 'I've always wondered what my life would have been like if I had succeeded. But my mother had other ideas for me. Over many years she had saved enough to pay for my first semester at university. She said that I would have to pay the rest myself.'

His brief stint of higher education had a life-changing outcome.

'I was heading to university, Carolina was on her way to school. She seemed very pretty, so I said hello.'

Carolina recalls, 'Jairo's room was covered in posters of cyclists. Those were the Lucho Herrera years. My father used to take me to the Vuelta a Colombia. You'd stand there for four hours, then they would race past in ten seconds, but I liked it. So when I met Jairo, I thought, "Great, he likes cycling."'

Many years later, when their sons, Esteban and Brayan, began to show ability, Jairo told them, 'I'll go to the end of the world and back to help you, but you have until you are 23. If you haven't made lives for yourselves in cycling, then you will have to go and study.'

They never went back to their books.

Jairo tried at least to correct the errors of judgement that blighted his own childhood: 'My father took us to live in parts of the city where the conditions were not the best. I grew up with that, but my mother always told me, "Try to live better."'

'I decided never to make my family live the way I had. I lived on my wits: a down-payment here, the rent there, but I wanted the family to live well, so, when I had money, I spent it: we went somewhere special, or bought some clothes, or moved to a better area.'

Colombian barrios are categorised by levels or 'strata' which determine the costs of social services. The wealthiest areas are classified six; their residents pay higher rates for water, electricity and other public services. The poorest are classified one: services are cheap, but living conditions basic. When Jairo and Carolina's first child, Jhoan Esteban, was born, they were living in a single room in Barrio Minuto de Dios, a 'lower middle' neighbourhood rated three. Due on 18 December 1989, he emerged on 17 January 1990 requiring oxygen and incubation. As soon as Carolina had recovered from the birth, the family moved down to a two: Barrio París Gaitán, between Calle 83 and Calle 89, east of the Avenida Ciudad de Cali. Dropping a level meant they could afford two bedrooms, a dining room, kitchen, bathroom and terrace, with a small supermarket nearby and a shopping street at Carrera 92, in Barrio Quirigua, eight blocks away.

Saturday 12 May 1990 was the day before Mother's Day, and

Carrera 92 was crowded with families buying gifts. Carolina tells me, 'We didn't have money for presents.'

It may have saved their lives. At 4.15 that afternoon there was a colossal explosion. Then came the baby's cries. Carolina collected little Esteban from his bed. He was just sixteen weeks old, and it took a moment to calm him.

Mother and child joined Jairo on the veranda. A plume of smoke rose from the place where seventeen lay dead, seven of them minors, and 150 injured. A Fiat 147 crammed with a hundred kilos of dynamite had been abandoned outside a household goods store called Bombazo. The word means two things: 'cut-price' and 'bomb blast'.

Another device had exploded outside a supermarket three kilometres away, killing four more. A third went off at 8.50 that evening in Cali, outside another supermarket, killing nine and injuring fifty. And there were twelve assassinations in Medellín that day.

They were all part of the Medellín cocaine cartel's campaign of terror to force the government into abandoning the extradition of drug traffickers to the US. Between August 1989 and May 1990 eighteen car bombs exploded in Colombia. Between 21 and 25 May three more devices exploded in Bogotá and Medellín. The so-called Extraditables had threatened what they termed the Bogotá oligarchy, but Barrio Quirigua was a working-class area.

Carolina told me, 'We'd never had one so close.'

Pablo Escobar's death on 2 December 1993 did not end the nightmare of inner-city drug violence, but it did draw a chapter of Colombian history to a close.

☷

Jairo told me, 'The city sucks the dreams out of you.'

But Jairo never lost his.

Wherever there was sport, Jairo steered his sons towards it, whether it was the Olympics or Pan-American Games on the television, or the events at El Salitre park in central Bogotá, the heart of their childhood activities. There were cyclo-cross meetings there each Sunday: Esteban took part in his first one when he was six. He went back four or five times until, one day, he fell flat on his face.

'Instead of coming to help me, my father said, "Get up. You can do it. Be brave!" I said, "If you want a champion in the family, you get on the bike!" And I never went back.'

A few hundred metres from the cyclo-cross track was the Red Cross pool where, aged eight, Esteban learned to swim. At the same time, he started competing in athletics. When he was twelve, his father took him to a triathlon in the Tominé Reservoir, north of Bogotá. By then, he was going to the 1st May Velodrome every Saturday for his first serious training sessions.

At the time, Jairo still had ambitions to be among the best senior riders in the country. 'I wasn't improving, so I found a coach, who told me to buy a heart rate monitor. I started seeing results immediately. But, when Esteban started, I said, "Let's do this right," and I gave him my heart rate monitor, my cycling shoes – everything he needed.'

At the time, the department of Cundinamarca had a vast cycling project whose architect was a former rider named Oliverio Cárdenas, five times the points champion at the Vuelta a Colombia in the 1980s.

Cárdenas told me, 'Of the 166 municipalities in the department, sixty had cycling schools. Lucho Herrera fronted the project. Condorito' – the former rider Edgar Corredor, fifth in the 1984 Vuelta a España – 'was the mountain bike coach, and I was head of road.'

The Bogotá District Recreation and Sports Institute (IDRD) had opened a school called the Centre for Elite Sport with a Cuban coach named Jorge Pérez. Cárdenas asked Pérez to work with Esteban.

But, in 2004, a new governor, Pablo Ardila Sierra, disbanded the cycling project, and the IDRD terminated the Cuban's contract.

Jairo Chaves thought to himself, 'What am I going to do now?'

Then Luís Fernando Saldarriaga appeared.

Jairo reflects, 'I always say that life follows a path, and that destiny brings you everything you need . . .'

'We had to pay him fifty thousand pesos per month' – about £12 – 'and there were times I simply didn't have the money, but Saldarriaga never made it a problem. My son was growing stronger, but Saldarriaga was honest with us. He said, "Don't expect any results for two years. We have to build him slowly."'

However, the first results came sooner than expected. Saldarriaga selected Esteban for the 2006 national time trial championships at Popayán and the points race at the national track championships in Duitama. His protégé came away with two silver medals. Saldarriaga wanted Esteban to ride the 2007 Vuelta del Porvenir for seventeen- and eighteen-year-olds, but before he could, he had to find a team.

In mid-2007 Bike House, a chain of bicycle and triathlon stores, announced a new team, Bike House-Trek. The team director was an old friend of Saldarriaga's father, Gonzalo Agudelo, also known as Parlante, 'Loudspeaker', for his incessant articulacy.

To select his future riders, Agudelo was holding a three-part event, with a hill climb, time trial and circuit race, around Medellín, starting on 31 August 2007.

That morning, Esteban stood in the pouring rain on the start line of an 18-kilometre race finishing on the Alto del Chuscal, 14 kilometres above the village of San Antonio de Prado, close to Medellín. Saldarriaga followed him in a Colombia Es Pasión team car driven by one of the soigneurs, Nicolás Restrepo, who lived in San Antonio de Prado and knew the road perfectly. He told Esteban, 'I'll sound the horn when you need to attack.'

With Restrepo's help, Esteban finished second in the climb,

third in the time trial, and fifth in the circuit race. He won the tournament overall, a Trek bike frame, and a place on Parlante's team.

Jairo told Agudelo, 'But we want Luís Fernando Saldarriaga to keep training him.'

Esteban travelled to Medellín for training camps and races, staying with Saldarriaga's parents Fernando and Amparo. He finished twentieth in the 2007 Vuelta del Porvenir, won by his future teammate Darwin Pantoja.

By 2008, his second year with Bike House-Trek, Esteban had become the team leader. Saldarriaga, building a strong Under-23 team for the coming season, told Esteban, 'If you make the top five in the Vuelta del Porvenir, you're in Colombia Es Pasión.' He finished sixth, which meant that his place in Colombia Es Pasión depended on factors that were out of his hands.

5

Against the Grain

Under Jenaro Leguízamo's watchful eye, Nairo had won the 2008 Clásico Club Deportivo Boyacá in style. Days later, Leguízamo gave the Colombia Es Pasión management meeting an animated account of his victory.

When he said, 'He lives on the Alto del Sote at 3,100 metres above sea level,' the team doctors exclaimed, 'Bring him in!'

After the test, the team doctors raised their eyebrows. Jenaro remembers, 'The maximal oxygen uptake seemed excessively high, so they turned to me. "Why don't you do a field test and see what you find?"'

Jenaro described what happened when he and Nairo rendez-voused a few days later in Paipa, between Tunja and Sogamoso.

Only nine kilometres of the climb up to Palermo were tar-macked. We had times for Sergio Luís Henao, Atapuma, Pantano and Fabio Duarte, but Nairo was riding a bike that probably weighed twelve or thirteen kilos. The first three kilo-metres were really hard, with gradients at around 15 per cent. Halfway up, Nairo stopped. 'Coach, I messed it up. I started off too hard and died. Let me try again tomorrow.'

The next day, he was calm, upright, with no head movement and that face that gives nothing away: the same Nairo we see today. The time was very good. The power was very good. I called Ignacio Vélez and said, 'Coach, he's the one.'

Ignacio said, 'OK. I'll call Luísa and tell her to get him a contract. Tell the boy he has a team.'

Days later, Nairo travelled to Antioquia for the 2008 Vuelta del Porvenir. His main rival was Darwin Pantoja. While they watched each other, two other riders broke away and built an insuperable lead. Nairo won the time trial and finished the race third overall.

At the start of November, Jenaro gave him a call.

'Are you ready to sign the contract?'

'No, coach, I'm really sorry.'

◈

On 24 February 2009, under the title 'My name has never been connected with Operación Puerto,' the Colombian daily newspaper *El Tiempo* published comments by Vicente Belda, a well-known former rider. 'I had nothing to do with it,' he stated. 'I don't know where the rumours come from.'

An accomplished climber who had taken stage wins at the Vuelta and Giro d'Italia, and finished on the podium of the 1981 Vuelta a España, Belda was the former manager of the cycling team sponsored by the sports clothing brand Kelme. In March 2004 an ex-Kelme rider named Jesús Manzano had given the Spanish sports daily *AS* a detailed account of his doping practices as a member. In May 2006, after Madrid police raided a series of apartments, finding 153 bags of blood in cold storage – blood extracted from athletes and evidently intended for reinfusion – Spanish police made a series of arrests, including Kelme coach and sports director Ignacio Labarta, team doctors Yolanda and Eufemiano Fuentes – sister and brother – and the team director Vicente Belda.

Doping in Spain did not contravene any specific national law. It was a matter purely for the sporting authorities. Yet the sheer magnitude of the operation persuaded investigators to try a prosecution under public health law. In April 2013, after years of legal wrangling, Fuentes was sentenced to a year in prison and four years of disqualification as a sports doctor, and Labarta was jailed for four months. But both sentences were then quashed on appeal. The doping was proven but not the contravention of any national law.

Belda was acquitted first time round. But when he flew to Colombia in June 2008, Operación Puerto still hung heavily on him. It was not his first visit: in 1985 he had won two stages of the Vuelta a Colombia. This time, he had been contacted by Spanish ex-pro Pepe Del Ramos, the owner of the cycling helmet brand Catlike, about a job offer in Boyacá.

The rivalry between the departments of Antioquia and Boyacá had stirred the Boyacá leadership into action. In May 2008 a Boyacá native, Giovanni Báez, had won the Vuelta a Colombia riding for a Medellín-based team. Belda's former pupil Hernán Buenahora, now 41, had finished second in Boyacá colours, but, as everyone knew, he hailed from the neighbouring department of Santander.

With wounded regional pride, José Rozo Millán, Governor of Boyacá from 2008 to 2011, and Fernando Flores, director of *Indeportes Boyacá* (Boyacá Institute of Sport), approached the distributor of Orbea bikes and Catlike helmets in Bogotá, Luís Gabriel Roa, and asked him if he knew any good young coaches. Roa contacted Del Ramos in Spain.

Vicente Belda told me, 'Pepe said, "Well, I know one. He's not young, but he's good."'

Belda's appointment as director of the Boyacá Institute of Sport cycling team was announced on 10 July 2008.

It was the start of an influx of Operación Puerto refugees. Óscar Sevilla had been the Best Young Rider at the 2001 Tour de France and the runner-up at the Vuelta a España later that year, but his career had stalled in 2006 when documents, tapped telephone conversations, blood bags and surveillance evidence proved his involvement in Operación Puerto. Sevilla was sacked by his team, T-Mobile, and in 2007 joined four other Operación Puerto riders at a small Spanish team called Relax-Gam. When the Vuelta a España announced that Relax-Gam had failed to adhere to its moral charter and would not be invited, Sevilla's career in European cycling was effectively over. The same range of evidence also implicated Sevilla's former Kelme teammate Santiago Botero, Colombia's 2002 world time trial champion. In 2008 Sevilla, Botero and fellow outcasts Tyler Hamilton and Francisco Mancebo joined an American team named Rock Racing, with whom Sevilla became the first non-Colombian to win the Clásico RCN.

Vicente Belda was already in Colombia. He installed Ignacio Labarta as head coach. To those contracting them, it may have felt like globalisation, although it was the very absence of integration into the world system that allowed them to find employment in Colombia, to the detriment of local athletes and coaches.

Without a hint of irony, Belda told me, 'Colombia has a reputation for doping and taking the easy route.'

Labarta modifed their riders' diet, training and post-race practices, and, says Belda, 'In 2008 we began to win races again. We improved the technical side, the physical side, training, everything.'

Belda continues: 'There were hardly any youth and junior races, so we started creating school events and went talent hunting.'

In December 2008 and January 2009, Belda and colleagues began testing athletes. 'We conducted forty-six effort tests, with physiological analyses.'

Nairo was tested twice.

Belda says, 'The second test confirmed the first.'

Belda called the sports institute: 'We have discovered a jewel, an 18-year-old with the same values that Santiago Botero had when he was 29.'

Seen from Tunja, Nairo's imminent move to Colombia Es Pasión, with its Medellín-based management, looked like an Antioquian takeover. Keeping Nairo in Boyacá became a priority. Nairo's father Luís later recalled, 'A lot of people called to persuade me not to put Nairo in that *Paisa* team' – the term *Paisa* indicating the people of the Department of Antioquia.

'Even [Governor of Boyacá] José Rozo Millán sent an emissary, asking me to convince Nairo to sign a contract with them. The contract was for 18 million pesos a year' – not much more than £4,000 – 'to be paid in three instalments: April, June and November. It seemed a lot of money to me,' he remembers.

Vicente Belda told me, 'The maximum contract was 60 million pesos' – about £14,000 – 'the minimum I think was 12 or 18 million, I do not remember which.'

Luisa Ríos remembers the telephone conversation with Nairo: 'He said, "I'm sorry, but this weekend I signed with Belda. I had no choice. But do something for me: promise me you will have a place for me next year."'

At that moment, the door opened for Esteban Chaves, who joined his coach at Colombia Es Pasión.

6

Touring the Future

The Tour de l'Avenir was a race of great historical meaning in Colombian cycling: by winning the 1980 edition, Alfonso Flóres had opened the doors of European racing to his country. Martín Ramírez triumphed again in 1985, and Henry Cárdenas took the mountains competition in 1987, but since then no Colombian had made the final podium. The last Colombian stage winner had been Mauricio Ardila in 2002. Colombian domestic cycling had become so cut off from the outside world that by 2009 the race no longer figured in the Colombian Cycling Federation's ambitions. That year, Vélez, Ríos and Saldarriaga made winning it their season's goal, partly as a vindication of their methods and philosophy, and partly because they thought they could. But it was also a first step in reconnecting Colombian cycling with the wider world, and, as such, would have lasting significance – provided they managed to qualify.

Thanks to Sergio Luís Henao, there was never any doubt. He won the Grand Prix Portugal at the end of March (with Pantano twelfth) and the Cinturón Ciclista Internacional a Mallorca in April (with Pantano eighth); in June he finished third in the Coupe des Nations Ville Saguenay (with Atapuma sixth) and second in the Tour de Beauce (where Atapuma was third).

With qualification assured, Henao started the Avenir on 5

September 2009 as one of the favourites. His bid for victory ended on stage one, ten 13-kilometre circuits around the town of Dreux, just west of Paris. The short Côte de la Grande Falaise stood just before the finish line. Two French riders, Julien Berard and Romain Sicard, broke away early, in the rain. Behind them, the Colombia Es Pasión riders started aggressively: Sergio Luís was third in the first climb after 27.5 kilometres, and third again in the first intermediate sprint after 39 kilometres, while Jarlinson Pantano was second in the second intermediate sprint, after 65 kilometres. Then, adversity struck.

'I punctured on a short descent and stopped, then one of the Spanish riders rode into me from behind,' Sergio Luís remembers. 'I remember waking up and hearing Saldarriaga saying, "Henao, Henao." I could feel bruising on the top of my head but I couldn't remember what had happened. Parts of it came back to me over the following days.'

The race was largely decided that day: Berard and Sicard stayed away, gaining a minute and a half on the main peloton. With Darwin Atapuma still in contention, Saldarriaga drove on, leaving orders that not everyone should wait with Sergio Luís. But there was a misunderstanding. The rest of the team waited for Sergio Luís, and finished together, 83rd to 87th in the stage, 7 minutes 15 seconds behind the stage winner.

Sicard went into the final day with a lead of 2 minutes 1 second over the American Teejay Van Garderen. During the stage, Sicard, on team France A, suffered a puncture and swapped bikes with another Frenchman, Aurélien Duval, who was with France B, and the commissaires imposed a two-minute penalty on Sicard for irregular assistance. It meant he still won the race by a second.

Meanwhile, for Colombia Es Pasión, the Tour had been a debacle, their best result being fourth place in stage six and fourteenth overall, both thanks to Darwin Atapuma.

It had been a difficult year, as Luisa Fernanda Ríos told me:

'At the start of the 2009 Vuelta a Colombia, nearly the entire peloton had a red blood cell count above the legal limit. Our riders were clean, but we were bombarded with insults. We felt totally alone against the world.'

Meanwhile, Nairo Quintana was continuing his apprenticeship, in cycling as in life. Vicente Belda had brought two Spanish riders with him to Boyacá's departmental team: his son David, and Antonio Olmo, from Extremadura in south-west Spain.

'Some of my companions did not want to learn from them as a matter of pride,' Nairo recalls. 'I took in as much as I could: dietary habits, timing, training. I didn't know anything, because I had gone from school to a team that was practically professional.'

At the Under-23 Vuelta a Colombia in April, Nairo went into stage three in sixth, 11 seconds off the lead. As a nineteen-year-old in his first year at Under-23 level, he caused a stir by attacking in the early, hilly part of the stage. The move gave him the race lead on the road, but the peloton chased him down.

The following day, the Antioquian rider Carlos Betancur joined a five-man breakaway that included one of Nairo's teammates. The quintet gained two and a half minutes, and Nairo, barred by team strategy from chasing, dropped to ninth overall, 2 minutes 51 seconds behind. He took some consolation on stage five, a 20.8-kilometre time trial, when he came within two seconds of the stage win behind his future Colombia Es Pasión teammate Juan Pablo Villegas. It was Nairo's breakthrough ride on the national stage.

A week later, on 1 May, in the oppressive heat of Barranquilla on the Caribbean coast, he won the national Under-23 time trial title. A fortnight after that, he won another time trial in the departmental Under-23 stage race around El Huila, over a 32-kilometre course. It earned him a place on the elite Boyacá Es Para Vivirla team's European tour, starting in June.

At the Vuelta a la Comunidad De Madrid in mid-July, Nairo won the best young rider category. Then, at the Subida a Urkiola on 2 August, he took the most significant result of his career so far by finishing seventh and conceding just 36 seconds to the winner, Igor Antón, one of Spain's best climbers. The top five included three more top Spanish mountain specialists: Xavier Tondo, David Arroyo and Beñat Intxausti. Intxausti, the youngest of them, was three and a half years older than Nairo.

'It was a hard race, and I was inexperienced,' Nairo remembers, 'but the result told me that this' – professional cycling – 'could go well for me.'

However, while the team was away in Europe, a change of political alliances led Governor Rozo to terminate his backing for the cycling project. The team simply stopped paying its riders.

'The politicians and the people running cycling were brazen,' Nairo told me. 'They paid out what they wanted to pay, and kept the rest.'

Ríos recalls seeing Nairo at the Vuelta a Madrid: 'He came over to the car and repeated what he had said the previous year: "Make sure you have a place for me next season."'

In mid-October, as the Colombian domestic peloton rode into Tunja during the Clásico RCN, Nairo met Luisa Fernanda Ríos in a coffee shop several blocks from the finish line and signed a three-year contract worth 56 million pesos annually – about £13,000 – negotiated by Vicente Belda. When he left the Boyacá structure at the end of the season, Nairo was still owed two million pesos.

Already one of the most talented young riders in Colombian national cycling, it was in 2010, as part of a new-look structure, now styled Colombia Es Pasión-472-Cafe de Colombia, that he began to attract attention from the world's top cycling teams.

They went back to Europe in March that year. At the three-day GP Portugal, Sebastián Salazar, a time trial specialist from San Rafael, 100 kilometres east of Medellín, was fifth. At the four-day Cinturón a Mallorca, Jarlinson Pantano was fourth. Then the team decamped to the altitude of the Sierra Nevada in Spain to prepare for one of Italy's top Under-23 stage races, the Giro delle Regioni.

For the first few days the team worked well in the mountains above Granada. Then the temperature plummeted and training became excruciating. When snow began to fall, it became impossible. As soon as arrangements could be made, they moved to Guadarrama, 50 kilometres north-west of Madrid, but the riders still lost days of crucial preparation.

On stage one of the Giro delle Regioni, Nairo and Darwin Atapuma attacked together. Their director at that race, Oliverio Cárdenas, recalls, 'They gained three or four minutes but they were caught, and finished the stage dead on their feet. It was inexperience. I had told them, "Eat and drink," but they just said, "I'm fine, I'm fine." The peloton brought them back on the final circuit. They lost a minute that day, and two the next.'

On the evening of stage one, Saldarriaga called Cárdenas, who said, 'We won the mountains jersey, but we lost a minute on the leaders. They're only kids.'

'Put Atapuma on.'

Atapuma ended the call in tears.

Cárdenas asked, 'What happened?'

'He says we're stealing our wages.'

For a moment, relations between the riders and Saldarriaga were fraught. Darwin took his director's anger so badly that he considered walking out.

Nairo's reaction was rather different from Darwin Atapuma's. He shed no tears and told his boss, 'Don't fuck with me. I'll go and find another team if you want.'

Looking back, Luís Fernando Saldarriaga says that the weather and the limited training were just two of the issues: 'They were eating too much and sleeping too little, because they were calling home late at night. So, at ten each evening, we started going from room to room collecting their laptops. We weren't going to lose races because they were using Skype instead of going to sleep.'

The measure created even more ill-will, although, all these years later, Nairo observes, 'It's true that Saldarriaga was hard on us, but he was right, and I could see that.'

The 2010 Tour de l'Avenir started on 5 September. The start list included the cream of a generation of riders born in 1990: the outstanding French climber Romain Bardet; Poland's 2008 junior world time trial champion Michał Kwiatkowski; a remarkable young Dutchman named Tom Dumoulin who had won the 2010 GP Portugal, and his even younger compatriot Wilko Kelderman, born in 1991. A little older were the Dutch Under-23 champion Tom-Jelte Slagter, born July 1989, and the Eritrean, Daniel Teklehaimanot, already sixth in the 2009 Tour de l'Avenir.

The 7.8km prologue, around the town of Vierzon, 200km south of Paris, started with an early climb, shallow but, at 1.7km, requiring sustained power and stamina.

Saldarriaga says, 'I followed all of my riders. Nairo rode well. Pantano too. But Puma was distracted. We'd ridden the route and identified a curve that they were not to take on the bar extensions, but he stayed down and crashed.'

A second separated Nairo, seventeenth, from Jarlinson Pantano, nineteenth, 33 and 34 seconds behind the stage winner, Taylor Phinney, already in his second year as world individual pursuit champion. Darwin Atapuma lost 1 minute 41 seconds.

Atapuma told me, 'We were up against riders on WorldTour teams like AG2R, Rabobank and Lotto, so it was intimidating – until we started climbing. Then we could see the suffering on their faces. That calmed our nerves. By the final two or three days, they were pleading with us: "No, Colombia, not today."'

Stage three took them into the Massif Central. In the French department of Puy-de-Dôme, the riders crossed the category-two Col du Chansert, then negotiated the exacting descent to the foot of the Col de Béal. Saldarriaga had taken his riders to reconnoitre the stage the previous week. They had familiarised themselves with the descent as well as the final climb, and Saldarriaga had a plan: 'The last two stages suited us perfectly. I calculated that we could lose 2 minutes 45 seconds before stage six and still win, so I told them: no risks on the descent. We didn't want the race lead so early anyway.'

Esteban Chaves rode at the front to bring back the break-aways. Atapuma finished second in the stage, 21 seconds after the stage winner and new yellow jersey, the Dutchman Yannick Eijssen. Overall, Pantano was the best placed of the team, 21 seconds off the race lead, with Nairo 56 seconds behind him and Atapuma 8 seconds further back.

On stages three and four, the Colombians received racist insults and blows. Jarlinson Pantano remembers one incident clearly: 'There were sidewinds, and a French rider grabbed Puma and pushed him out of the group. It made me angry, so I moved alongside him and punched him. He squared up to me and we hooked handlebars. I went down. Nairo saw it all, so he went over and put the Frenchman in the ditch.'

On the morning of stage five, Saldarriaga went to speak to the French team directors and asked them to tone it down.

On stage five, Esteban Chaves broke away, taking the lead in the mountains competition while his teammates saved energy. Then, sixty kilometres from the end of the stage, descending from Lachamp-Raphaël, the highest village in the Ardèche, a gust of wind caught him. His teammate Camilo Suárez glimpsed him among the rocks, bloodied and broken, and they finished the stage together.

The standings then remained largely unchanged until stage six, a 204-kilometre odyssey from the old Huguenot stronghold of Saillans, where the Drôme and Rieussec rivers meet, to the ski resort of Risoul.

Saldarriaga still remembers the race situation clearly. 'We had three riders with a chance of overall victory: Pantano was the best placed of them. The first climb of the day was the Col de Pennes, rated category two. It split the peloton. Pantano, Nairo and Atapuma were all in the front group until the start of the descent. Pantano is a brilliant descender and, by following wheels, he ended up in a breakaway group of four or five.'

For much of the stage Pantano was the virtual race leader. His presence caused concern in the peloton. Darwin Atapuma recalls, 'We were stretched out in single file. It was like riding behind a car. Then we realised Taylor Phinney was at the front, setting a blistering pace.' Phinney was working for his teammate, the recently crowned American Under-23 time trial champion Andrew Talansky.

Saldarriaga drove alongside Pantano and told him the chase was coming very fast behind him. Pantano quietly dropped out of the lead group, took a natural break away from the road where he couldn't be seen, and waited. 'The Belgians, French and Americans didn't know he'd stopped and continued the very high pace. Pantano eased back into the peloton behind them.'

The chase continued until the foot of the final climb. Atapuma says, 'I think Phinney did more or less ten kilometres at full speed. I saw him when he pulled off the front, and he had come to a complete standstill.'

By the foot of the final ascent to Risoul, the peloton had been reduced to a group of about thirty that included the Belgian race leader Yannick Eijssen, and second-placed Bardet. Thirteen and a half kilometres of climbing remained.

Russia's Dmitriy Ignatyev was the first to attack. The peloton thinned. A group emerged of Nairo, Atapuma, Andrew Talansky, Mikel Landa and Tom-Jelte Slagter. They caught and dropped Ignatyev, who was joined by Pantano in a second, chasing group.

With four kilometres to go, Atapuma turned to Nairo and said, 'You or me?'

'Me first. When they catch me, you go. Today we win this.'

But Nairo was never caught.

Darwin recalls, 'He wasn't so far ahead, but I could see the suffering in the chasers' faces and I knew he was going to win. I waited with them as Nairo took the stage and the race lead. I was fourth in the stage.'

Between Nairo and overall victory lay a second climb up to Risoul, a mountain time trial this time. Slagter lay 20 seconds behind him, with Landa 41 seconds back and Talansky, a time trial specialist as well as a formidable climber, at 57 seconds.

Atapuma remembers speaking to a member of the Spanish team in the start ramp area before the time trial: 'We were warming up and he said, "Today is Colombia Day. You could be first, second and third on the podium by evening."'

He was failing to take Atapuma's bad luck into account: 'The route descended for a kilometre and a half, and then there was a dangerous curve. I don't know what happened, but the bike slid away beneath me, and I went down hard. I rode the rest of the stage in pain.'

Nairo started two minutes behind Slagter. Ignacio Vélez was in the car behind him: 'At the first split we were already beginning to close in on Slagter, who was second overall but didn't ride a good time trial. I was being interviewed live on my mobile phone by a Colombian radio station. The signal was very weak, but I managed to describe the moment when Nairo gained the first five seconds. In the end, he was so close to Slagter that he nearly caught him.'

Slagter was relegated to fourth place, 1 minute 45 seconds behind Nairo. Pantano was third. Nairo's closest rival, Andrew Talansky, could only come within 47 seconds of him. Nairo had won the Tour de l'Avenir by 1 minute 44 seconds. He was certainly the darkest-skinned winner in the race's history, as he would one day be at the Tours of Italy and Spain, and on the final podium of the Tour de France.

Jarlinson Pantano, third overall, won the mountains category. Atapuma finished the final time trial only 26th, conceding 3 minutes 25 seconds to Nairo: not the clean sweep of the podium the team had hoped for, although his ninth place overall ensured that Colombia Es Pasión added the team classification to its achievements.

On the final podium, Saldarriaga hugged all of the riders except Atapuma, who turned away, still simmering with resentment.

Before their return to Colombia, the team stopped over in Barcelona. Luisa Ríos asked Nairo if there was anything special he would like to do.

'Go to the beach," he said.

So, to celebrate his victory, Nairo had his first ever day at the seaside.

On Tuesday 14 September, well-wishers greeted the team at Bogotá's El Dorado International Airport. The following day, they went to the Palacio de Nariño, the official home of the President of Colombia, for a reception with the new president, Juan Manuel Santos.

In July 2010 Santos had announced a change from Uribe-style 'Democratic Security' into what he called 'Democratic Prosperity'. To power growth he identified five 'locomotives': infrastructure, housing, energy (meaning minerals and petrochemicals), innovation and agriculture. Now, standing beside Nairo, he announced, 'We want sport to be a locomotive driving all the children and young people in Colombia. What better activity to develop in Colombia, apart from studying, as a complement, because it is part of the education of any human being.'

Away from the cameras, Nairo seized the moment and asked Santos to recall his brother Alfredo from the conflict in the jungle. On 18 September 2010, just four days after the reception with the president, Alfredo Quintana left the thick forest of the Meta, and returned to Tunja.

Despite enormous public support, Uribe's re-election in 2006 had required a change to the 1991 Constitution. Any further change being politically impossible, Uribe had put his party, the Social Party of National Unity (or, put simply, 'La U') at the disposal of Santos, his former Minister of Defence, who took over the presidency on 7 August 2010. Uribe had put the FARC on the back foot. The country expected his former Defence Minister to follow the same line. However, in his inaugural speech, Santos announced to the FARC and the country, 'The door to dialogue is not locked.'

Days later, Santos met Uribe's nemesis, the Venezuelan Premier Hugo Chávez, in Santa Marta. When political adversaries of Uribe were appointed to his new cabinet, including advocates of a negotiated peace with the FARC, many perceived a U-turn in state policy towards the guerrillas.

Four days after Alfredo Quintana's surprise recall, laser-guided bombs rained down on a forest clearing where one of the FARC's most bloodthirsty leaders, known as *El Mono* Jojuy – *El Mono* is a nickname meaning 'blondie' or 'whitey' – had been identified days before. When the bombing was done, special forces moved in. In vicious jungle fighting, at least twenty guerrillas, two soldiers, and an explosive-detection dog named Sasha were killed. When the fighting subsided, an immense military complex was unearthed, complete with accommodation, a network of tunnels, and a concrete bunker where Jojuy's corpse was found, fifteen laptops and seventy USB flashdrives. The war on the FARC had taken another decisive turn in favour of the state.

Meanwhile, Nairo's new-found status had another positive spin-off. The parents of his girlfriend Paula, like his mother from Vereda San Rafael opposite Tienda La Villita, disapproved of her relationship with the hopeful young cyclist.

While he prepared to be escorted home in triumph by the fire brigade, as tradition dictated, Luisa Ríos told him, 'Wait till they see you arrive in a fire engine.'

And so it proved: from the day of his triumphant return, Paula's parents finally accepted Nairo into their family. Their daughter, Mariana, would be born on 4 February, Nairo's birthday, in 2013.

Later in 2010, Nairo backed a team, Boyacá Es Para Vivirla-Nairo Quintana, at November's Vuelta del Porvenir, where his brother Dayer finished eighth overall. Future professionals Richard Carapaz and Sebastián Henao were fourth and fifth, respectively. In 2011 Nairo financed a National Police team, for whom Dayer, by then a commissioned police officer, also rode. The team's best rider, Juan Ernesto Chamorro, finished 43rd in the Under-23 Vuelta de la Juventud that May.

From that time on, Nairo was constantly involved in financing and supporting cycling in his home region. But the real legacy of his first major win on the international stage resonated far beyond Colombia's shores. Of his Tour de l'Avenir win, the team president, Ignacio Vélez, says, 'I think of it as the most decisive victory in the history of Colombian road cycling, the beginning of our return to Europe, although if Sergio Luis Henao had not crashed on the first day of the 2009 Tour de l'Avenir, the story might have begun a year earlier.'

7

Chance

Perhaps one day in the new Colombia, the village of Urrao, set in a storybook valley between green lines of fertile hills, will be celebrated as the gateway to some of the most biodiverse square miles on Earth, many still unexplored. The cloud forest of the Orchids National Park, north of the town, teems with life: not just orchids but butterflies, hummingbirds, monkeys – Capuchin, howler, spider, squirrel – snakes, dwarf squirrel and tapir. There are rivers, streams, waterfalls and abundant rain.

Everything seems to flourish here in preposterous abundance – not surprisingly, Colombia is said to lead the world in flowers and bird life, lie second in the rankings of butterflies, fresh-water fish, tropical amphibians and plant life, third in palm trees and reptiles, fourth in mammals, and on and on and on.

But most visitors approach Urrao from the south, where avo-cado and coffee plantations form perfect symmetries in the hills, and, about 17 kilometres from the town, the clear Penderisco River flows down into the valley from the hills to your right. A little further on comes the turning for Vereda San Carlos: in 2018 beans from one of its divisions, Finca La Soledad, were judged to make the best coffee in Antioquia, making it one of the finest coffees in the world. When the south-western coffee belt extended into these veredas in the 1980s, it heralded a decade of high living standards among the peasant farmers of south-west Antioquia, until the coffee crisis of the 1990s.

The valley broadens, the river twists and turns playfully, and there, eight or nine kilometres south of Urrao is the turning for Vereda Pabón, where Rigoberto Urán Urán's family have their origins. As is common among peasant farming families, his parents were cousins – his father's mother and his mother's father were brother and sister, hence Rigoberto's twin surnames. In fact, Vereda Pabón has spawned not one but two great stage racing specialists, for Óscar de Jesús Vargas, third overall at the 1989 Vuelta a España, also has his origins there.

An isolated stretch of hillside lost in the Andean vastness, Vereda Pabón is familiar to historians of civil unrest in Colombia as one of the epicentres of the violence of the 1940s and 1950s. As the historian Mary Roldán describes it, 'young Liberals who were persecuted in their towns of origin flocked to Pabón, the village where the guerrillas established their main headquarters.'

Then, Urrao appears before you, the white spire of the Iglesia de San José glistening over the central park. Every appearance suggests traditional Antioquian industry and gentility. But Urrao is a frontier town in every sense. You can drive another hour north, but to continue, it must be by horse or on foot, and it will take three days to reach the end of Urrao's territories.

Dense forest separates the town from the Pacific lowlands of the Chocó to the west. To the north-east, the Páramo de Frontino, touching 3,850 metres above sea level, separates Urrao from the Caribbean coast. Contraband has flowed freely here since colonial times, from the Gulf of Darien, up the Atrato River and into the dense network of hidden pathways that traverse the landscape: mule-train highways, cattle herders' paths, hunters' tracks, smugglers' trails, shallow streams that wash away all trace of people's passing.

I asked Óscar Vargas about Vereda Pabón. He told me, 'My father, José Ángel, lived *la Violencia* first hand. The way he told it, the Conservatives had the government, the police and the army, and they wanted to wipe out the Liberals, who, in turn, created the Liberal Guerrilla.'

It was not about seizing power or starting revolutions, he says. 'It was just defending themselves against people who wanted to kill them.'

Even so, armed struggle remained part of the repertoire of political behaviour in this distant corner of Colombia, and would return with a vengeance in the 1990s, even if the mid-century bloodshed differed qualitatively from the sadistic butchery of the millennium; even if, countrywide, the death of Pablo Escobar, the disbanding of five of the smaller guerilla armies, and the reforms enshrined in the 1991 Constitution, had led to a reduction in violence between 1991 and 1995. But the two largest rebel forces, the FARC and the ELN, remained at large, and many powerful interests preferred to finance paramilitary groups than to trust a weak army to defeat them.

In the mid-1990s, the organisation of so-called Peasant Self-Defense Forces of Córdoba and Urabá (ACCU), formed an alliance with paramilitary groups in western Antioquia and seized control of all the main towns and villages with one exception: Urrao.

As the FARC and the paramilitaries grew in strength, the national army fell into decline and the violence intensified. Individual and mass killings spread terror through the civilian population, bringing poverty and population flight. By then, Óscar de J. Vargas had become one of the world's leading cyclists.

In October 1995 cycling's World Championships were held in Duitama, Boyacá, and Óscar was there, helping his team leader, Oliverio Rincón, finish eighth, then returned home to Urrao.

He told me, 'I owned a finca in Vereda La Magdalena. It wasn't extravagant or beautiful, but I like being in the countryside with the farm animals, surrounded by nature and birdsong. I had some new cattle and I wanted to go and see them.

'I arrived at my father's place in the evening – I think it was 25 October – and we decided we would head up the next day. But that same evening, a bus came into town carrying people from the surrounding veredas, and someone told me, "Óscar, don't go up to the finca. There are people up there." *People* meant guerrillas, or some armed group or other.

'I said to my father, "I'm not going up there."'

He tried to convince his parents to go with him back to Medellín, or to go and visit relations in Cali: 'But my father wasn't afraid of anyone or anything. He said, "We have worked too hard all our lives to give up what we have because we are afraid. Let's go and see the cows." There was no talking him down.'

Óscar decided to head into the village to see friends.

'It was six in the evening. I was sure he would be asleep when I got back. Before I left, I turned to look at him. I will never forget the image of my father on the balcony.'

He left for Medellín early the next morning, without seeing his father again.

Two or three days later, the telephone went. It was a brother-in-law in Urrao: 'Óscar, I think your father had a problem with the guerrillas.'

'Then my sister called to tell me my father was dead.'

The story circulated that Óscar's father had shot two of the guerrillas before they brought him down, although no witness ever came forward.

Soon after the funeral, the telephone rang: 'A voice said, "We have companions requiring medical treatment and we need five million pesos from you. We know where you live, we know where your children go to school—" I hung up the phone. The world came down on top of me. My career as a cyclist ended then and there.'

He called his team director. 'I said, "I know I have a contract,

Colombia Es Pasión!

but I'm not riding any more. I can't train on the public roads. I'm going to have to go with my children to school. I have to disappear from public life."'

According to the official account, a small boy out fishing in the Antioquian forest chanced on a guerrilla encampment. Moving closer, he distinguished a group of prisoners, ten, twelve, perhaps more. The boy happened to have a brother in the armed forces, and news of his discovery reached the intelligence services, who became convinced that they had found the Governor of Antioquia, Guillermo Gaviria Correa, and former Minister of Defence, Guillermo Echeverri, kidnapped by the FARC 383 days before.

Guillermo Gaviria Correa danced, wrote poetry, studied civil engineering and bubbled with charisma. In 2000 he became Governor of Antioquia. In office, he befriended the Reverend Doctor Bernard LaFayette, Jr, who had marched alongside Martin Luther King. In August 2001 Gaviria and his wife Yolanda attended LaFayette's Center for Nonviolence and Peace Studies, part of the University of Rhode Island, to study King and Gandhi. Later that year, LaFayette repaid the trip: in Medellín he spoke to Gaviria's cabinet and held workshops with gangs and prisoners. Gaviria believed the non-violent philosophy could light the path to peace. He even appointed a graduate of LaFayette's programme as his Nonviolence Advisor.

They were violent times. In the town of Caicedo in south-west Antioquia, 35 kilometres from Urrao, FARC gunmen had been killing, kidnapping, and hijacking farm trucks, making it impossible for the coffee growers to get their beans to the Coffee Federation warehouses. When the town priest defied the insurgents by accompanying the farmers, the FARC bombed his church.

Pursuing the governor's non-violence agenda, Caicedo declared itself neutral in the conflict. To show his support, Gaviria set out on a five-day March of Reconciliation and Solidarity from

Medellín to Caicedo on 17 April 2002. His companions included his wife, LaFayette, former Defence Minister Echeverri, a Medellín priest named Carlos Yepes, three bishops and 1,200 followers. According to press reports, the governor ordered the armed forces not to protect him, and not to retaliate if he was kidnapped or killed: 'The cowardice of not going frightens me more,' he said.

On Sunday 21 April 2002, as the march approached the town, FARC militiamen brought them to a halt. They ordered Gaviria, Echeverri, LaFayette and Father Yepes to proceed. Five hours later Yepes returned with news that the governor, the Peace Commissioner and LaFayette had been kidnapped. The marchers prayed, then boarded buses and returned to Medellín.

LaFayette was released the following day. Gaviria and Echeverri, like 2,800 other kidnap victims in Colombia that year, disappeared.

On 5 June, after forty-nine days in captivity, Gaviria noted in his diary: 'Today we changed location to a camp that, it seems, will be our home for a long time. The big surprise was that we found ourselves with eleven kidnapped soldiers. Some have been held for five years, others three and a half, others two and a half.'

The guerrilla bivouac lay between the Murrí and Mandé rivers, fifty kilometres north of the town of Urrao. According to the official account, the little boy who had discovered it was dispatched with his brother in a military aircraft to find it and photograph it.

At ten o'clock on 5 May 2003, five Sikorsky UH-60 Black Hawk helicopters left Urrao airport with seventy-five Rapid Deployment troops and headed for the forest.

Sergeant Heriberto Aranguren had been taken prisoner in June 1999. Eighteen minutes after the Black Hawks had left Urrao airport that fateful morning, he looked up to see one of them hovering over the encampment. A fast rope, which twenty-five heavily armed commandos can rappel down in thirty seconds, hung limply, five metres from the ground. The uneven terrain and high canopy made landfall impossible. The aerial photography on which the operation depended, and the reality of the land, were at ruinous odds. The guerrilla commander, Ricardo de Jesús Agudelo, alias '*El Paisa*', gave the order to execute the hostages. Nine of the thirteen, including Gaviria and Echeverri, were shot point blank. Three of the four survivors were seriously injured.

When President Uribe was informed of the mission's failure, he flew directly to Urrao. 'It is a deeply sad moment for the nation,' he said in an impromptu broadcast. 'Today the FARC terrorist group has committed yet another heinous massacre.'

Until that day, most Colombians had never heard of Urrao.

Álvaro Salazar Herrera, a social sciences teacher at the Institución Educativa Monseñor Cadavid, formerly the Simón Bolívar Lyceum, in Urrao, told me about life in Urrao either side of the botched rescue attempt of Guillermo Gaviria – the very years Rigoberto Urán went to school there.

Between 1999 and 2004, Álvaro Salazar limited his movements to the five blocks between his home, close to Urrao's central park, and the school:

> If I had to go to Medellín, I flew. To go by road was to take your life in your hands. If they stopped you at a road block and saw from your identity card that you were from Urrao, it was, "You belong to the FARC." If you had the same surname as someone known to be part of one or other armed group, it could be a death sentence.
>
> We taught from early morning until ten o'clock at night. The *campesinos* could only study in the evening, and they travelled to school from their veredas. We lost teachers, students, fathers, brothers, sons.

The conflict was a kind of subterranean war. You didn't know when and where the next act of violence would occur. You were always on edge: a killing meant a bereaved family, but soon afterwards it was another one. There was a state of permanent grieving or social mourning.

There were situations almost daily. We often had to close the school or keep the students inside because there was a gunfight outside.

Urrao's cycling club had been relaunched in the year 2000 as the Óscar de J. Vargas Cycling Club and School, with a local cheesemaker, Jorge Flores Guzmán, also known as Jorge *Queso* (*Queso* being Spanish for cheese), as club president.

Sometime in 2000 or 2001, Jorge's son Jorge David rode his first race for the club at the village of Peñalisa, 95 kilometres away. The difficulties of managing a cycling club amid the violence emerge starkly from Jorge's account of that race:

We needed transport, but that weekend most of the local buses had returned to their veredas. The only thing we could find was an *escalera* [a brightly painted, customised truck, known elsewhere in Colombia as a *chiva*] which had survived a massacre in Corregimiento La Encarnación [north of Urrao]. Normally, they killed the driver and torched the truck. In this case, the driver had survived, and the *escalera* had escaped incineration.

To go from Urrao to the next village, Concordia, you had to pass a guerrilla roadblock and then a paramilitary roadblock. There were two more paramilitary roadblocks on the way to Peñalisa. We were worried someone would recognise the vehicle.

When we went through Concordia, we had bikes on the roof, and forty-five kids. The paramilitaries stopped us.

'What have you got there?'

'Just cyclists.'

He said, 'Are you saying that that *pirringa* [tiny child] is a cyclist?'

I said, 'Yes, that *pirringa* is a cyclist. Here's his licence, and that's his bike.'

'They'll join the guerrillas when they grow up.'

I said, 'Let's hope they have more options in life.'

When we came back, the same man was there. He asked me, 'How did the *pirringa* do?'

The boy held up a medal, and I said, 'You see?'

And with that, he let us pass.

Urrao had become a by-word for guerrilla activity and violence. Elsewhere in Colombia, Urrao natives with the name of the village printed on their identity cards found themselves subjected to abuse and prejudice.

Yet Jorge Queso told me of a security meeting he attended with the departmental chief of police, at around the same time. Jorge raised his hand and asked, 'Major, do the people who fight for the guerrillas come from Urrao?'

'No, the majority come from the Urabá, the Chocó, or they are drafted in from the 5th and 34th Fronts.'

'OK. What about the men in the paramilitaries?'

'They are mostly from the Urabá and Córdoba, and some of them come from the eastern plains.'

'OK, so we know where the guerrillas come from and we know where the paramilitaries come from. What about the dead?'

And he said, 'Ah yes, the dead are from Urrao.'

◈

Against this tragic background, in April 2001 a local *chancero* or lottery-ticket seller enrolled his son in Urrao's cycling club. Rigoberto Urán, known to all as Rigo – his son, the future cyclist, was known as Riguito – had started selling *chances* or lottery tickets for Urrao's local lottery company, Apuestas Penderisco, in 1981. Effusive and gregarious, he was known and loved in and around Urrao and among the town's community of seventy *chanceros* and their families, who met regularly for days out and social events.

He took his lottery tickets into the surrounding veredas on his BMX bike, returning with stubs and cash to the lottery offices in Urrao's central square.

The *chanceros* were salesmen, showmen, entertainers. The office manager at Apuestas Penderisco, Olga Lucía Uribe, told me, 'Rigo was the best. He was a hard worker and very organised. He made a hundred thousand pesos a day' – about £21 – 'and kept a quarter of it. It was good money in those days. He had a small shop in the doorway of his house. He fattened pigs and chickens.'

In 2001 Rigo's marriage was going through a bad patch. Riguito's sister lived with their mother, while Rigo and Riguito had moved into rooms in an Urrao barrio called Buenos Aires. Riguito found work washing cars at the gas station, a place of drug use and bad company, with the added risk of what was known as social cleansing, when one or other illegal armed group swept the area and the latest generation of derelicts, prostitutes and drug addicts disappeared. Rigo Urán looked around for something to keep his son away from the gas station's blandishments, and found it at Bicicletas El Ring, a small bicycle workshop just off Urrao's Parque de los Pies Descalzos, or Barefoot Park, run by an ex-cyclist named Juan David Laverde, known to all as JL, pronounced *Jota Ele*. There, JL's assistant Diana Herrera enrolled little Riguito in the cycling club.

The following Saturday, Riguito met his clubmates for the first time. One of them was Jorge Queso's son David, who told me, 'During the week, some of us trained in the morning and others trained in the evening. On Saturdays we all trained together, either a time trial as a test of form, or an easy ride to put a few kilometres in our legs.'

Rigoberto told me, 'It all happened very quickly. One day my father said he was taking me to a cycling school. A week later, there was a time trial. I didn't know what the word meant. They just said, "Start here, finish there, go as quickly as possible." And I won.'

Riguito's first race for the club was around the village of La Pintada, four hours from Urrao. The club had held a bingo night in a local bar and raffled a leg of pork to pay for the trip. The cyclists and their parents completed the journey in an *escalera*, although some of them felt travel sick. They took food and tents and spent the night after the race at a campsite. Riguito, accompanied by his father, enjoyed the adventure and the evening feast with his teammate and school companion Juan David, JL's son.

Diana Herrera remembers that Riguito didn't win but did well, and his father was immensely proud: 'Rigo said things like, "My boy is going to be someone. He's going to be a very important person, not here, out there in the world. One day he'll ride the Tour de France."'

On Saturday 4 August 2001 a group of about thirty went out riding. There had been a teachers' strike during the week, and the pupils had to make up their classes, so Riguito and Juan David Laverde missed training.

Juan David's elder brother César Augusto was one of Antioquia's leading cyclists. He had ridden back from Medellín the previous day, so he wanted a gentle recovery ride with his father JL and Jorge Queso's son Jorge David Flores. The eleven- and twelve-year-olds turned back early. Those left ranged from young teenagers, like Jorge David Flores, up to the two adults, JL and Riguito's father Rigo, who was heading out to sell lottery tickets in Vereda Arenales, on the road to Medellín. He was riding his BMX bike so he left at 6 a.m. and the group overtook him on the way.

Beside a statue of the Holy Infant, at a place known as Quebradona, 17 kilometres from the village, the riders met a line of stationary cars, and then gunmen with black bandanas over their mouths and noses, and armbands with the letters AUC: Auto-defensas Unidas de Colombia, the United Self-Defense Forces of Colombia, the country's biggest paramilitary grouping.

'Leave your bikes there.'

The gunmen were rustling cattle from the fincas. It was a common activity for groups living in the margins of the law, securing food while, at the same time, punishing and terrorising local civilians.

Jorge David, who was thirteen at the time, recalls, 'We knew the routine. We were used to it. Sometimes we went out training and came back to a gunfight in the village.'

The riders were told to wait in a Chevrolet truck, and then to leave the truck and walk up to a farmhouse just uphill from the statue of the Holy Infant. Jorge David's main concern was that they would steal his bike.

César Augusto told me, 'They took various people to help them bring the cattle down to the road. From our group they took my father [JL] and Riguito's father.'

The gunmen went from finca to finca taking all the cattle from the hillside known as the Alto del Pio Nono. Meanwhile, word of the roadblock somehow reached Urrao. JL's assistant Diana Herrera was behind the counter at Bicicletas El Ring. The father of one of the boys came in and told her, 'Don't expect them back any time soon. They've been stopped by the paramilitaries.'

She told me, 'I remember vividly that Rigoberto arrived from school. He used to spend his time with us in the workshop.'

One of the cyclists out at Quebradona was Davíd Ramírez. A contemporary of Rigoberto's at the Simón Bolívar Lyceum, Davíd had already lost his father: armed men had burst into their home and gunned him down in front of his children. The terror that must have been gripping his schoolmate in that isolated farmhouse cannot have left Riguito unmoved.

He said, 'Diana, I'm worried about my father.'

She tried to reassure him: 'Don't worry, my love, he's with the cyclists. Nothing is going to happen.'

She told me, later, 'Riguito stayed with us a while. You could see the anxiety in his face. Then he left.'

On the hillside, the gunmen told JL to go on ahead and not look back. Behind him, Rigoberto Urán was taken to the bank of the Penderisco River, which flows into the valley from the hills behind Quebradona. A gun was put to his head and, moments later, his body lifeless folded into the water.

The murderers then disappeared into the landscape with the cattle.

Understandably, Rigoberto had few words for me about the death of his father. 'He died when I was fifteen, and it was hard because I had to study, work and train – all three. But when you put your mind to it, you can do anything.'

卌

I went to Urrao hoping to solve the mystery of Rigoberto Urán's murder. I initially reasoned that it should not be too hard to work out who was responsible: in July 2003 the Uribe government and the AUC started negotiations. Between 2003 and 2006, 38 paramilitary structures numbering 31,651 militiamen and women disbanded. A Justice and Peace Law offered reduced prison sentences in exchange for cooperation with the provision of justice, truth and reparations, including, of course, a full confession.

On 30 January 2005, 132 members of the Southwest Antioquia Battalion had demobilised, and it seemed to me at least possible that some information about the murder might have surfaced. But I was wrong: not even the most basic steps had been taken to establish the identities of the demobbed. Most received pardons for paramilitary membership, but few were investigated for other crimes, and the opportunity to question demobilising individuals about the AUC's criminal networks and assets had been allowed to pass.

In January 2010 a Medellín court official told the website verdadabierta.com that only seven former members of the Southwest Battalion of the AUC had applied to be judged under the Justice and Peace Law. But, he said, 'The ex-paramilitary gunmen have not told the whole truth. They have not provided information about the people killed or offered goods to make reparations.'

The former leader of the Southwest Antioquia battalion of the paramilitary Self-Defence Forces, Jesús Alcides Durango, better known as 'René', is said to have been under orders from the Self-Defence Forces leader Vicente Castaño to expel the guerrillas from the coffee-growing zone of Antioquia and impose AUC rule. Alias René demobilised with another paramilitary battalion, the Héroes de Tolová, on 15 June 2005, then disappeared. He was arrested in Urabá, northern Antioquia, on 19 June 2007, and sentenced to life without parole for ordering nineteen murders in Urrao during January, May and June 2000, of peasants, housewives, students and traders said to be FARC collaborators. Many of the bodies were thrown into the Cauca River. In March 2011 he was sentenced to a further 24 years for 31 murders between June 1999 and May 2007. In October 2016 he was handed a further sentence of 19 years and 9 months for the murder of four farmworkers on veredas in Urrao and nearby Betulia.

The National Unit of Justice and Peace Prosecutors had records of at least 5,000 victims in Antioquia. Against the background of collective massacres, mutilations, burnings, killings of schoolchildren, a single murder was lost in the statistics.

In any case, as Jorge Queso says, 'We think they were self-defence forces, but they could have been guerrillas in disguise, or common criminals. What difference does it make? The cattle owners were compensated by the government three or four years later, but no one brings back the dead.'

The paramilitaries sought to identify and destroy the

clandestine networks that provided the FARC with intelligence, stashed their weapons and hostages, and served as their legal front men. Suspicion alone was enough to trigger indiscriminate violence, although local people also used disinformation to rid themselves of political or economic competitors, even rivals in love. Rigo, who seemed to know everyone, might have been taken as some kind of informant, although, Jorge Queso concludes, 'In reality he had nothing to do with it. He was just in the wrong place at the wrong time.'

At around the same time, the paramilitaries had given another lottery ticket seller, Jaime Roldán, twenty-four hours to leave Urrao. That Rigo received no such warning suggests he was not previously in their sights.

The illegal armed groups mostly fought their wars by proxy. In their eyes, the group most feared by the civilian population was the winner, and few things engender more terror than random, incomprehensible slaughter. On encountering Rigo Urán at Quebradona that morning, the paramilitaries would have recognised a man whose murder would fill Urrao and its vast territories with dread. One bullet could be made to terrorise an entire community.

I asked Óscar Vargas if he had ever tried to find out who murdered his father.

'No, no. I am fairly certain it was the FARC. They say it was people who are in the peace process now, but it doesn't matter any more. This is my life now: there is no solving anything.'

He continued, 'Imagine you are a peasant farmer, earning your living on a piece of land, without stealing from anyone, without bothering anyone or harming anyone, and the guerrillas arrive and tell you that you have to collaborate, to give them food or pick something up in the village, and you have to do what they say because they will take your money, and either kill you or force you out. And then the paramilitaries arrive, and they tell you the same thing, and you become a target for both sides. Without doing anything. Where is the logic? It is killing for the sake of killing. Whose head can fit this all in?'

Going back to the peace process, he wondered aloud, 'You take an adolescent boy, teach him to use a gun and make him commit fifty atrocities. How do you ever re-socialise him?'

Of the orphaned Rigoberto, Álvaro Salazar Herrera told me, 'There was no time for mourning. There was no time for anything except accepting his family responsibilities. He was away from school for a short time. A week, perhaps.'

Rigoberto took up his father's lottery ticket round and put his mind to cycling.

JL's brother Benjamín, known to all as Mincho, told me, 'JL started going round there at five or five-thirty for him, getting him up every morning, until he became a rider again. He said he was going to become a cyclist in his father's name. He was going to ride because his father wanted him to. He started winning in the villages. My brother trained him, and he got stronger and stronger.'

As Jorge Queso remembers it, Rigoberto had joined the cycling team more at his father's behest than of his own choice. Now he may have discovered in it a means of survival. He began to compartmentalise his life with obsessive rigour.

Álvaro Salazar Herrera watched the transformation: 'I live a few metres from the lottery office. After his father's death I used to see Riguito arrive at nine or nine-thirty in the evening, delivering the lottery stubs and cash, and then, early the following morning, he would get up to train. He was incredible.'

Like Nairo, in very different circumstances, Rigoberto was able to structure his life and mind, and cope.

Another witness to Rigoberto's transformation was Diana Herrera: 'There was a place the kids called the volcano, where they used to go and swim. Riguito would come into the workshop and say, "Where is everyone?" "At the volcano. Are you going?"

'I've got to sell these tickets.' He was incredibly diligent. And his bike was always immaculate.'

Olga Lucía Uribe tells me, 'Riguito took over his father's work. In the lottery office, we did everything we could to help so that he could study, because he needed to do his school work too.'

Olga Lucía's assistance was short-lived: during a gunfight in the main square, a stray bullet flew across the park and tore the hand off one of the office girls. Olga Lucía witnessed the incident. It left her traumatised and unable to return to work. Such illnesses of the spirit were common in Urrao. In her absence, another of the lottery workers, a young man named Jairo Herrera, assisted Rigoberto with the clerical work.

Diana remembers how the community helped Rigoberto sustain his cycling ambitions: 'There was Ramiro Gustavo, Señor Gustavo. There was Darío, who ran a funeral service. There was León Cañas and León Gómez, Eli Samar . . .'

The new mayor, Fidel Marino Figueroa Montoya, elected in 2001, contributed food baskets for the Urán household which he left at Bicicletas El Ring. José David, Diana or Jorge Flores Guzmán would then deliver them. Seeing the enthusiasm generated among the town's children by the revived cycling club, with Jorge Queso and the local ice-cream manufacturer Helados Tonny lending their support, the mayor decided to give the club his backing, and to organise, in October that year, the Clásica de Urrao.

Hundreds of cyclists flooded into the town. The mayor invited the Laverdes, Marlon Pérez, the president of the Cycling League of Antioquia, Javier Ríos, Cochise Rodríguez and his great friend and rival from the 1960s, *El Ñato* (Pugnose) Suárez. Helados Tonny had the bikes of all the local riders painted blue, white and green, the colours of the Urrao flag, and marked up with Helados Tonny stickers. They wore uniforms with Helados Tonny blazoned across their chests.

Local riders either won or stood on the podium of nearly all the categories. The race for thirteen- and fourteen-year-olds attracted particular attention from the Orgullo Paisa talent spotters. In a consummate display of teamwork, the Urrao riders worked hard to close down the breakaways, then, in the final kilometres, Riguito attacked and reached the finish line alone. It was the first official race win of his life.

Diana Herrera remembers Rigoberto raising his hands in the park and saying, 'That's for my *papá*.'

'Everyone cried. Javier Ríos saw Riguito's potential when he was just beginning, and invited him to join Orgullo Paisa. And Riguito, still just fourteen, met Cochise.'

After the races, there was yet another bingo night to raise funds for the team. Cochise Rodríguez was the special guest. Jorge Queso remembers the drink flowing and Cochise being the first to shout 'Bingo!'

He took his card to the announcer who checked the numbers and found that Cochise had not been telling the whole truth: 'He came back to the table and said, like a true cyclist, "We didn't win, but we gave them one hell of a fright!"'

Always more than just a cyclist, Cochise's humour and personality have resonated with ordinary Colombians for more than half a century. He has become a national institution capable of voicing a sort of popular wisdom, expressed most memorably when, after being denied the opportunity to stand for public office by professional politicians, he commented, '*En Colombia se muere más gente de envidia que de cáncer*' ('In Colombia more people die of jealousy than of cancer'). The remark struck home so deeply that it could usefully have been added to the national coat of arms.

In a celebrated comic article published in the magazine *Cromos* in May 1968, the poet and journalist Gonzalo Arango described his encounter with Cochise:

A dog came and lay down in the middle of the room. It was big and gentle. The champion stroked it tenderly.

– What's he called?

– 'Blek.'

I thought of William Blake.

– Blake, like the English poet?

– No. 'Blek.'

Even if it wasn't black, more coffee with milk, I asked:

– Black.

– No, *hombre*, 'Blek.' How many more times do I have to tell you?

[. . .] He peppered his Paisa phrases with popular expressions that I didn't fully understand, like '*Ni piper*' ['Don't even think it'] or '*Ya voy Toño*' [something like 'No way, José'].

Rigoberto Urán seems to have adopted Cochise Rodríguez as a model. At the 2017 Tour, the Radio Caracol reporter Fernando Calle, known as *Piolín* – Spanish for Tweety, the yellow canary in the Looney Tunes cartoons – asked him to explain why he had decided to cut his hair.

'Why did I cut it? My wife always says she does not like my hair like that because it's very *nea*. She says it's *nea*.'

Piolín looked blank.

'You don't know what *nea* is, or what?'

'No.'

'Very left to its own devices. Street urchin, that sort of thing.'

When Rigoberto talks – at least, when he talks without swearing – it is impossible not to hear Cochise. But it is not mere imitation.

In *Blood and Fire*, a remarkable history of *La Violencia* in Antioquia, Mary Roldán writes of Urrao:

Many of the town's residents lived in free union rather than legally sanctioned marriage, and the rate of illegitimate births was considerably higher than the regional norm. The town abounded in taverns and brothels. All this contributed to Urrao's reputation as a place of loose morals and radical politics. Coffee farmers from nearby towns, where their behaviour was closely scrutinised by parish priests and the Legion of Mary, found festive release in Urrao's prostitutes and drink, perpetuating its fame as a place free of morals.

Economic survival and social life in Urrao have always involved activities at the margins of the law. Urrao had a long tradition of moonshine distilleries. Already in the 1950s, customs officers were complaining that the local *tapetusa* – illegally produced cane liquor – was so popular, it forced the legal liquor monopoly to lower its prices in order to compete.

In short, Urrao was a national centre of unruly defiance – which may be how Rigoberto Urán gets away with saying things no one else could.

When Piolín approached him after stage nine of the 2017 Tour de France, Urán probably expected to be asked about the frustration of finishing second in the final sprint. But it was also true that Richie Porte's crash on the high-speed descent from the Mont du Chat was one of the most dramatic, and decisive, talking points of the race. When Porte went off the road, Dan Martin was on Porte's wheel and Rigoberto on Dan Martin's.

Piolín secured the rider's attention while piling question on question.

'Rigoberto, here, for Colombia. I'm live. What happened in the crash? Hello, Rigo? How are you?'

Urán replied, 'What's up? What have you got to say for yourself? All good?'

It raised a smile. His answer to the follow-up – 'What happened in the crash?' – provoked a national guffaw.

'*Yo qué voy a saber, güevón?*' was soon appearing on walls and T-shirts. The audio clip went viral.

By the standards of live, post-stage interviews, the question was not unreasonable. *Güevón*, however, is not a frequent term of address in the Colombian media. From *huevo* meaning egg, or testicle, it is rendered on an ingenious online site as 'Someone so lazy that their testicles drag along the ground'. Inverting its potential for insult, Antioquian males use *güevón* as a term of address – muppet, perhaps – if not a humorous synonym for dude or buddy, although generally not on television.

Admittedly, it had been one of the more bizarre stage finishes in Tour de France history. After crossing the line, the French rider Warren Barguil had raised a fist to celebrate victory. French TV had given him the full stage winner's interview before the finish-line photograph could be carefully analysed and the outcome communicated to the protocal area: Urán, not Barguil, had won the stage, despite being unable to change gear. Pictures seemed to show Dan Martin's heel hitting the rear triangle of Urán's bike in the Porte crash, disabling his rear mechanism. The neutral service mechanic had come alongside Urán and pulled the derailleur away from the spokes, fixing the chain on the smallest cog, the eleven, for the flat run into the finish.

Urán resumed his interviews when the stage result had been confirmed: 'Amazing. It's a surprise because I lost a stage to Barguil in a Vuelta a España, the same *güevonada.*'

How to translate that? *Huevo, güevón, güevonada* – 'The same old bollocks'?

'I only had two gears, 53×11 or 38×11. I did the sprint with the 53×11, to save the day, and obviously when I finished second, I thought, "Oh well, this *güevón* has beaten me again." Fine. Then I was already going to antidoping and all that when someone says, "Listen, you won." This guy's *güevoniando la vida . . .*' – 'ballsing up my life'?

He ends with, '*Una alegría muy grande. No, una puta alegría . . .*'

'Great happiness. Great fucking happiness.'

◈

Sergio Luís Henao was sixteen when he first met Rigoberto, now no longer Riguito but Rigo, like his father: 'It was 2004 and we both took part in the *Regional del Futuro*, a qualification race for the national Vuelta al Futuro, in San Rafael. Rigo won.'

In Rigo and Sergio Luís, and another rider, Carlos Julián Quintero, Orgullo Paisa had an irresistible trio. But they ran into an immovable object in Fabio Andrés Duarte Arevalo.

Dr Luís Eduardo Contreras told me, 'In 2004 Duarte was close to unbeatable. In the peloton they joked, "Don't provoke him or he'll get angry and we'll all finish outside the limit."'

One year older than Rigoberto, Duarte was a formidable opponent. Quintero recalls the 2004 national championships, held on ten circuits of Sogamoso, each including a steep, two-kilometre climb: 'In the middle of the race Sergio Luís said, "Let's make it a bit harder. I'll break up the group and then you two finish it off."

'Sergio Luís increased the pace, leaving three riders out front: Fabio Duarte, Rigoberto Urán and me. I looked at Rigo and said, "We've won the nationals."

'Duarte worked with us until, with two laps to go, at the bottom of the climb, Rigo said, "Let's see how strong he is," and attacked. Fabio followed him at a distance, then chased him down on the flat.

'On the final circuit, Rigo said, "I'm dying here. This guy is strong." On the final climb, Rigo attacked again but Fabio chased him down. Then I attacked and Fabio came after me. He caught me, went straight past and rode off alone.

'I waited for Rigo and we rode together to the finish line,

second and third. The group rolled in five or six minutes later. Duarte was a heck of a rider.'

But in the 2004 Vuelta del Porvenir for seventeen- and eighteeen-year-olds, the Urán, Henao, Quintero trident found a way to make their numerical advantage count. Carlos Julián Quintero won stage one in Tunja. Duarte was second, Urán third, Henao fourth.

Quintero told me, 'The next day ended on another climb in the village of Monguí. I stayed with Fabio while Sergio Luís attacked and took the stage and race lead. I was second, Duarte third, Rigo fourth.'

At Monguí, famous for manufacturing footballs, the riders on the podium were given one each. At Rigo's insistence, they played football for twenty minutes. The coach was angry, but, Quintero says, 'Being with Rigo meant breaking all the rules.'

Duarte won the last stage, a 22-kilometre time trial, but ended the race runner-up, 21 seconds behind Urán, who took the race lead on the final day to secure victory in the country's top stage race at his first attempt. It earned him an invitation to live and train at the new Centre for Sports Development, or CEDEP, which opened in 2005 in the pretty Antioquian village of Jardín, 130 kilometres south-east of Medellín.

Jorge Queso recalls, 'Riguito's mother saw that the family needed assistance, and that Riguito had an opportunity, and she gave them the authorisation they needed to take him.'

CEDEP was a big house, one block from one of Colombia's most beautiful parks.

Three other boys from Urrao were selected: Nicolás Castro Laverde, son of JL's sister Margarita Laverde; Diego Andrés Navarro, and one of Riguito's best friends, Edward Alexander Urrego, also known as *Cholo*.

Carlos Julián Quintero was there, and future stars Julián David Arredondo and Carlos Alberto Betancur. Also there was a local athlete named Daniel Jaramillo, who joined the centre as a distance runner, but changed to cycling and went on to become the only Colombian to win the Vuelta del Futuro, the Vuelta del Porvenir and the Vuelta de la Juventud, the three leading stage races for younger-age group riders.

Quintero had cousins who lived in Jardín. He told me, 'I would go out to train with Rigo, and he would say, "I'm tired," and we would go to my cousins' place and use their PlayStation for three or four hours.

'We didn't have any money,' he remembers, 'but we had fun.'

In June, Urán and Henao travelled to Venezuela for the five-day Vuelta de la Juventud, the national stage race for juniors. Jorge Queso recalls, 'We held a bingo night in Urrao to buy him a mobile phone so that he could communicate with his mother. It was a Nokia 1100. And there was enough left over to buy him a pair of training shoes.'

When Riguito went to compete, his mother, still terribly fragile, took over and sold the lottery tickets.

In Venezuela Rigoberto and Sergio Luís Henao won two stages each. On 24 June, Rigoberto won the race overall, 44 seconds ahead of Henao. Back in Colombia, he headed straight to Pereira for the National Junior Track Championship, under the tutelage of another of Urrao's great cycling figures.

▦

JL's brother Benjamín Laverde, known to all as Mincho, played a key role in Rigoberto Urán's development. One of ten children from a peasant farming family in the chill of Vereda Chuscal, some 17 kilometres north of Urrao, he grew up with no electricity or modern amenities, and a five-kilometre walk to school.

'From the age of eight or nine, you got a bang on the door at five in the morning and it was get up and work, barefoot, in the cold. Clean the finca, milk the cows.'

The family produced cheese and grew potatoes, with smaller crops of sweetcorn, beans, cabbage, carrots and sugar beet.

The children took the first two years of primary education at the vereda school, an hour and twenty minutes away by foot. To continue their studies, Mincho and his elder brother Nicolás went into Urrao, and lived in rented accommodation. While they were there, they raised a pig each. When they sold the two pigs, Nicolás bought a bike. A week later, inspired by his brother, Mincho bought one. Each Saturday, their father needed them to help pick blackberries at the finca, so they rode up by bike, although it was so steep, Mincho recalls, they had to get off and walk part of the way.

Mincho entered the 1977 Clásica del Suroeste for *turismeras*, bikes with no gears, and won. In 1978 he left his home town for Medellín, dreaming of making it as a cyclist. His training partner Óscar de J. Vargas stayed behind to study for his school leaver's certificate.

At the 1984 Clásica de Antioquia, Mincho climbed alongside Lucho Herrera. A crash at the Clásica del Carmen de Viboral left him in a coma, but he came back stronger than ever. In 1985 Mincho found sponsorship with the Conasfaltos team. Training for the two big races in the calendar, the Clásico RCN and the Vuelta a Colombia, he went on long, mountainous rides to Santafé de Antioquia or La Pintada with Alfonso Flores.

But then, seventeen days before the Clásico RCN, Mincho crashed. He could not ride for a year. He was never the same rider again. He married, had his first child, and, as his friend Óscar Vargas pursued his international cycling career, took on a new role in cycling: 'In 1991 I began to bring kids from Urrao to Medellín and made cyclists of them. I lived in Medellín and went back to Urrao to organise races.'

As time went by, a long line of Laverdes passed from José David in Urrao to Mincho in Medellín. Together, they helped forge one of Colombia's most enduring cycling dynasties.

Luís Felipe Laverde, the son of the eldest of the Laverde siblings, Luís Aníbal, would go on to win stages of the 2006 and

2007 Giros d'Italia. José David's own sons César Augusto and Juan David would both show enormous promise. César Augusto won the 1996 Under-23 Vuelta a Colombia, while Juan David, a contemporary and close friend of Rigoberto Urán, showed great potential and rode for Orgullo Paisa until a serious road traffic accident ended his career in 2003. Arles Antonio Castro, one of Colombia's most decorated track riders, is the son of the third Laverde sibling, Margarita. His brothers José Nicolás Castro and Jonny Castro have both had road careers in Colombian domestic cycling. José David's grandson Sebastián Zuñiga Laverde, Margarita's grandson Wilmar Andrés Castro and Andrés Octavio Urrego, the son of one of José David and Mincho's younger sisters, are also promising cyclists. Nicolás Laverde, the sixth of the Laverde siblings, has long been a mechanic with the EPM team.

In the early 1990s, when the forested areas north of the town became a safe haven for the FARC, and the gunmen seized control of the strategic corridors that converged there, Mincho's presence in Medellín offered young cyclists a way out of Urrao.

When Rigoberto arrived at Pereira for the National Junior Track Championships in May 2005, he didn't even have cycling shoes.

'I had a pair of my daughter's cycling shoes with me,' Mincho told me. 'I said, "See if they fit." They were small but he used them anyway. With those shoes, and a bike borrowed from the League, he won five gold medals on the track and two on the road. It's still a national record. He was some track rider! If he was up against a quicker sprinter, you could rely on him to find a winning strategy.'

A year older than Urán, his friend Carlos Julián Quintero also rode the Nationals in Pereira: 'I moved up into elites and won the individual pursuit at my first attempt. I was invited to join the national track team. Rigoberto was still a junior, but he was called up too. He made us all suffer at the training camp, then went to the Junior Pan-American Championships in Venezuela and won everything.'

At Barquisimeto, Venezuela, Rigoberto won the individual pursuit on day two, the points race on day three and the madison, with sixteen-year-old Jarlinson Pantano, on day four. Then he switched to the road and won the time trial by 1 minute 16 seconds and the road race by 40 seconds.

In Venezuela, Jarlinson remembers, 'Rigo gave me a pair of cycling shoes. I said, "Hey, great shoes!" and he said, "They're yours. I'm getting new ones so have them."'

Which is how Mincho's daughter's shoes ended up on Jarlinson Pantano's feet.

The Junior World Track Championships took place in Austria between 7 and 10 August. A visa was hastily arranged via the Colombian Embassy in Vienna, where one of the masterminds behind the dismantling of the Cali and Medellín cartels, General Rosso José Serrano, was now serving as a diplomat, and Rigoberto flew to Europe for the first time. In the points race, he finished second in heat one of qualifying, but faded to ninth in the final. In the individual pursuit qualifying ride, he was a second slower than in Venezuela, but it was only the twentieth best time and his championships ended.

On 12 August he was twelfth in the individual time trial around Vienna, 1 minute 17 seconds behind the winner, Marcel Kittel. He did not finish the road race two days later.

His golden year only got better when he went to the Department of El Huila in November and became the first rider ever to win a second Vuelta del Porvenir: Sergio Luis Henao was second, 1 minute 17 seconds back.

Riguito's results in 2005 earned him a national award as Colombia's best junior. In March 2006 he signed a professional contract with the Italian team Tenax Salmilano, negotiated by fellow Antioquian and Tenax rider Marlon Pérez, and travelled to Europe.

Rigoberto's first three days of racing were in some of Belgium's toughest events: the E3 Prijs Vlaanderen, Brabantse Pijl and Driedaagse van De Panne-Koksijde. On the third day, he went down and broke his collarbone. With his arm in a sling, he moved into an apartment in the north Italian town of Brescia, owned by a landlord named Beppe Chiodi.

His new living arrangements came as a relief to those who cared about him. César Augusto Laverde told me, 'Rigo had been living with Marlon Pérez. I'd ridden with him at Orgullo Paisa for nearly ten years, and I knew Marlon had a very disorderly personal life.'

In Brescia, Rigoberto formed a close bond with Chiodi, his wife Melania and their family. He soon became fluent in Italian, and spoke of Beppe and Melania as his second family. Adopting a foreign language and another family was, perhaps, an instinctive kind of self-healing after the appalling trauma of his childhood.

His thirteen days of racing in 2006 included his first monument, the Tour of Lombardy, but no outstanding results. In April 2007, riding for Unibet.com with his compatriot Víctor Hugo Peña, Rigoberto took ninth place in the Prologue of the Tour de Romandie. He took his first professional victory at June's Euskal Bizikleta, when a storm moved in and the time trial around Abadiño was suspended with six riders still to start: 'I had the best time so they gave me the win.'

At the Tour of Switzerland on 25 June, he attacked with 800 metres to go and crossed the line two seconds ahead of the sprinters. It was his first victory at the sport's highest level – and he was still only twenty.

Two months later, descending the Riedbergpass in the Deutschland Tour, he lost control, careered across a mountain stream and smashed into a wall. Protecting his face and head, he sustained complex fractures of both elbows and the right wrist. The helicopter footage shows him writhing in agony as help arrives.

On the team's website, he said, 'Too bad, because I think I might have had a chance to win the stage in the sprint.'

He underwent surgery on 13 August, then entered a long period of rehabilitation. 'I spent almost three months with both arms in plaster,' he tells me. 'One hand was immobile for almost a month, the other for much longer. I was sidelined for seven months, and the rehabilitation was very hard. When something like that happens, you ask yourself whether to carry on. I couldn't feed myself, but my Italian friends are like a second family and they helped me. Even so, I didn't know how I would be after the fall.'

Yet, despite his injuries, Diana recalls that Rigoberto had offers from four or five teams. 'He chose Caisse d'Epargne and took Marlon Pérez with him.'

He signed a three-year contract in November and rented a house in the Pamplona neighbourhood of Gorraiz. It became a first port of call for Colombians riding in Europe: Mauricio Soler, Fabio Duarte, Mauricio Ardila, Nairo and Dayer Quintana, and Sergio Luís Henao all stayed there at various times.

By 2011, when Rigoberto moved to Team Sky on a three-year contract, most of his career – and his greatest successes – lay ahead of him. Even so, he had already been a professional cyclist for six years, and his achievements so far formed a sort of stepping stone for the Colombians who came after him.

For Jorge Queso, 'Riguito marked a critical moment, a before and an after. He built a bridge to Europe and became a kind of godfather for many who went there after him.'

8

The Bike Exchange

Nairo started his first WorldTour race, the Volta a Catalunya, in March 2011. There, he won the mountains competition, five points ahead of the overall winner, Alberto Contador, and, during an altercation, landed a punch on the Russian rider Vladimir Karpets, despite being 23 centimetres shorter and 20 kilograms lighter. After the stage he explained himself to Saldarriaga: 'He disrespected me.'

It is an illustration of the degree of self-belief needed to become a champion. Saldarriaga still smiles about it.

On a descent during stage six of the Vuelta a Colombia on 18 June, Nairo was caught in a crash and sustained a deep cut to a hand and wrist. The team doctor inserted twelve stitches and sent him home. The slightest pull on the bars tore at the stitches, and the injury cost him two weeks of training. As a result, he approached the 2011 Tour de l'Avenir searching for form.

The injury handed team leadership to Esteban Chaves, who had been the only Colombian rider not to finish in 2010. Saldarriaga had consoled him by saying, 'Next year, you'll come back and win.'

In the meantime, the outstanding French rider Romain Bardet had finished second in the Under-23 Liège–Bastogne–Liège, then sixth, fourth and second in the big Under-23 tours of Friuli Venezia Giulia, Isard and the Savoie.

Saldarriaga says, 'We knew we had to come up with a plan for Bardet.'

In stage one, Chaves joined an early breakaway and took the mountains jersey, while Bardet joined a late, seven-man attack and finished second, gaining 26 seconds on Chaves and Nairo. In stage two, an uncomplicated sprint stage, Nairo, Bardet and Chaves finished together, eighth, ninth and tenth across the line.

Stage three finished at Porrentruy, in the Swiss canton of Jura, after crossing the Grand Ballon, the highest mountain in the Vosges range, and then two steep, testing climbs in the Swiss Jura, the Col des Rangiers and the Col de la Croix. The Colombians knew what lay ahead of them: Saldarriaga had ridden it, then taken his riders to train on it.

During the race, he saw Nairo and Bardet at the back of the group. Bardet was following Nairo's every move.

Three Colombians, Chaves, Sebastián Salazar and Michael Rodríguez, had made the breakaway. A level crossing closed behind them. When it opened, Nairo and Bardet were minutes behind. At that moment, Saldarriaga decided, 'We're not waiting for Nairo.'

Chaves finished the stage seventh. Bardet and Nairo came in 2 minutes 55 seconds later.

Two days later, on the stage to La Salève, sometimes called the 'Balcony of Geneva' for its views of Lac Léman, a series of mishaps and mechanicals threatened Chaves' bid for victory. On a descent midway through the stage he and Nairo crashed. Nairo gave Chaves his bike and pushed him off, then waited at the roadside with Chaves' bike. When the team car arrived, the mechanic, Jimmy Martínez, took Nairo's 'B' bike from the roof of the car and gave it to Nairo, then took Esteban's bike into the car. Saldarriaga accelerated away to find Chaves, who stopped and took his own machine back – as the race radio announced that Nairo had crashed again.

Meanwhile, Esteban's chain jammed between the chain rings and the frame. He stopped again and took Nairo's 'A' bike back. Jimmy fixed the problem in the car, but it meant that Chaves had already had to chase back three times. Saldarriaga was concerned that one more pursuit could cost him the race.

Michael Rodríguez was in the leading group. Saldarriaga asked the race director's car for permission to go ahead. At the end of a long straight, he pulled over. Jimmy positioned Esteban's bike out of sight of the road. Chaves saw them and understood. He peeled away from the peloton, stopped at the car, dismounted Nairo's 'A' bike and took his own, then rejoined the race. It was an illegal move – but it allowed him to finish third in the stage and stay in contention. And the commissaires didn't see a thing.

The final stage was a draining, hilly loop, starting and finishing in the Italian town of Alba. Chaves lay seven seconds behind the race leader, Canada's David Boily.

Saldarriaga reached the team hotel and went out to drive the course. The following day, he told Nairo, 'Leave the race leader nice and tired at the top of the climb.'

Nairo performed his task to perfection. Late in the stage, Saldarriaga drove alongside Chaves: 'Boily is finished. Keep attacking.'

'I have nothing left.'

'It doesn't matter. Keep trying.'

Chaves accelerated on a small climb, taking the Frenchman Warren Barguil, the Italian Mattia Cattaneo and his teammate Michael Rodríguez with him. Barguil bided his time, then rode away to the stage win. Cattaneo, Chaves and Rodríguez finished in that order, two seconds behind him.

Boily finished near the back of a group of eighteen riders 26 seconds behind Barguil. Chaves had won the Tour de l'Avenir – and Colombia Es Pasión could boast consecutive wins with different riders. It was clear now, if there had been any doubt in Europe, that the Colombians were coming.

◈

For all its success, Colombia Es Pasión's relationship with the sports authorities was astonishingly difficult. To a degree, it was because of the team's trenchant anti-doping stance, but it was also a simple matter of state inefficiency and late payments.

Luis Guillermo Plata told me, 'Even when I was in government, Coldeportes was shirking its commitments. We were late in making payroll for three months. Since a lot of the kids came from Boyacá and the steel mill Paz del Río is a big Boyacá company, I called the CEO and said, "Help me out here."

'He says, "I can't give you money, but I have *x*-many tons of *scoria*. If you come and pick it up, it's yours. You can sell that as fertiliser."

'So I call Ignacio. "There's *x*-many tons with a market value of *y*. If we can sell it, we make payroll."

'I don't know how, but he found a buyer. We loaded it into trucks, delivered it and paid everyone's salary.'

Under the Santos government, a new head of Coldeportes had been appointed: Jairo Clopatofsky, whose brother José, a prominent sports writer for the newspaper *El Tiempo*, was close to the Colombia Es Pasión rider Víctor Hugo Peña. As the first Colombian to wear the yellow jersey at the Tour de France, Peña – articulate, charismatic, well connected – was an important figure in Colombian sport, and his relations with the Colombia Es Pasión team management had become strained. This led him to contact José Clopatofsky and arrange a meeting with the new head of Coldeportes.

Peña wanted Vélez and Saldarriaga replaced by a European team manager who could secure invitations to top races, and contacted Claudio Corti, a former rider who had directed major teams in Italy, and, most recently the South African team Barloworld. The idea was that Corti would be shadowed by a prominent Colombian ex-rider, who would serve an apprenticeship in team management at his shoulder. Late in 2011 Corti flew to Colombia to meet Clopatofsky and agreed terms. Filling the shadow role proved more difficult. On 14 September 2011 a press release named Álvaro Mejía, fourth in the 1993 Tour de France and now a medical doctor, in the position, but Mejía had turned it down. On 12 October 2011 another communiqué announced Oliverio Rincón, a stage winner in all three Grand Tours during the 1990s, but he too had withdrawn his candidacy.

Oliverio Cárdenas told Peña that he should retire as a rider, work alongside Corti himself, then take over the team two or three years later. But Peña wanted to keep riding. When the new team, known as Colombia-Coldeportes, finally started functioning, every one of its staff was Italian, as if there were no Colombian sports directors, soigneurs or mechanics; as if to say, third-world muscle needed first-world intelligence to function.

Luis Guillermo Plata was furious:

> We win the Tour de l'Avenir twice, individually and as a team, we win the mountains, and what does Clopatofsky do but pull the rug from under our feet. He doesn't terminate the team because he can't, but he pulls his funding, starts Team Colombia and gives it an Italian coach and three million euros. At our peak we probably had a million.
>
> ProExport maintained its support for Colombia Es Pasión, so, instead of having one powerful team, we had a rich one and a poor one. I was no longer part of the government, and there was nothing I could do. I always had mixed feelings about Team Colombia. I didn't like what had happened, but I wanted the kids to win.

Through Luís Guillermo Plata and Ignacio Vélez, Saldarriaga and Rios had the promise of backing from the former state post office, 4-72, but they only had the budget to ride domestically. Fearing that, if their best riders left, the entire structure would collapse, they tried to convince them to stay. But, to the riders, the new initiative meant one thing: the opportunity to ride in Europe. Seven of them made the change, including Darwin Atapuma, Esteban Chaves and Jarlinson Pantano.

Nairo Quintana's contract ran until the end of 2012. He stayed loyal to Saldarriaga and Ríos anyway. In October 2011, he met them in Medellín.

Ríos told me, 'He said he trusted us and wanted to support us, and he didn't mind riding nationally, so he wanted to stay with the team for a third year. But we insisted: for Nairo, there was no going back. It was time to go to Europe.'

Saldarriaga added, 'I told him that he was ready and he should go, and not stay in Colombia, where doping would likely destroy him.'

Still representing Nairo, Vicente Belda fielded enquiries from Lance Armstrong's former sports director Johan Bruyneel, now at RadioShack-Nissan, and the Spanish team director Joxean 'Matxín' Fernández, of Geox-TMC. Belda took the initiative: 'I thought that Movistar was the best team for him because they spoke Spanish.'

Movistar belonged to Spain's former public telecommunications utility Telefónica, the country's largest company after its privatisation in 1997.

Telefónica had major interests in Colombia, as part of President Álvaro Uribe's efforts to improve foreign investment. Under Uribe, state holdings in regional energy companies, public banks like Granahorrar and Bancafé, and other public services, were sold to the private sector, contributing to a fourfold increase in foreign investment by the end of 2008.

In 2006 Telefónica had purchased a 51 per cent share of Colombia's former state telephone monopoly Colombia Telecomunicaciones and became at a stroke Colombia's largest land-line operator and a major broadband player. In May 2010 Telefónica rebranded its Spanish and Latin American products and services as Movistar. Three months later it was announced that, on 1 January 2011, Movistar would take over sponsorship of the cycling team formerly known as Reynolds, Banesto, Illes Balears and Caisse d'Épargne.

At the end of 2010 one of the team's two Colombians, Rigoberto Urán, had left to join Team Sky. In June 2011 the other, Mauricio Soler, from the village of Ramiriquí, 35 kilometres south-west of Tunja, was lying second overall in the Tour de Suisse when he hit the kerb at 80 kph. He hit a spectator and then a solid fence, suffering fractures to the cheekbone, collarbone, shoulder blade, seven ribs, the left ankle and the base of the skull on the left side. Placed in a medically induced coma, it would be four weeks before he could be moved to Spain, and six months before he would return home to Colombia. He would never ride again.

Suddenly, the team's general manager, Eusebio Unzué, had a sponsor with substantial Colombian interests, and no Colombian riders.

'In the end,' Belda tells me, 'without negotiating with the others, I pointed Nairo straight towards Eusebio. With Nairo's consent, we agreed a two-year contract.'

Saldarriaga says, 'Luisa called me and said that Movistar had contacted her. They were offering to buy out his contract. Nairo was still insisting that he had given us his word. I said, "Save yourself and go. In Europe you'll be a champion."'

Success came quickly.

Nairo won the Vuelta a Murcia in March, reacting to an attack on the Alto del Collado Bermejo, darting away alone, then keeping his advantage on the descent to the finish. The following day he defended his lead in the time trial, to win the race overall.

In June he added to his reputation at the Critérium du Dauphiné, on the notorious Col de Joux Plane, the penultimate climb of stage six. Five kilometres from the top, as Richie Porte, Chris Froome and Michael Rogers set a pace calibrated to discourage attacks and defend the race lead of Tour de France favourite Bradley Wiggins, Nairo eased out of the group. Over eighteen minutes of climbing he eked out a 22-second lead. Metres before the start of the descent, the 2011 Tour de France winner Cadel Evans attacked, powering after him. However, plummeting downhill, Nairo only added to his advantage, on his way to the most impressive win of his career so far. The cycling world duly took note.

The win offered him some consolation for a change in his schedule that meant he did not ride the Giro d'Italia, which he insists he was promised at the start of the year. Shy, silent, recently arrived in Europe, taking his first steps in professional cycling, Nairo made his anger clear to Unzué: 'I had already won a race or two, I had trained hard and I was ready. The team didn't have an established leader, and I knew I could do well, but at the last moment they said, "You're not going."'

Nairo's confidence, and his performances later in the year, suggest he might have done as well or even better than Rigoberto Urán and Sergio Luís Henao, who finished seventh and ninth overall, and first and second in the Best Young Rider competition.

The new era of Colombian cycling was still in its infancy. Colombia-Coldeportes had secured invitations to some of Italy's most important races: two one-day races – the Milano–Sanremo in mid-March, and the end-of-season Il Lombardia – and the week-long Tirreno–Adriatico at the start of March, and in April, Darwin Atapuma achieved Colombia-Coldeportes' first win at the mountainous Giro del Trentino, ascending one of Italy's most prestigious climbs, the Passo Pordoi, in the snow. Second was another Colombian, Carlos Betancur, riding for the Italian team Acqua & Sapone.

Even so, not one Colombian started the 2012 Tour de France, and the country had the right to just three riders at the Olympic Games road race on 28 July. The national coach Jenaro Leguízamo selected Rigoberto Urán, Sergio Luís Henao and Fabio Duarte, who had finished fifth overall in the Tour of California. He issued them with three simple instructions: 'One: don't go with the first breakaway. Two: get in the moves on the final lap. Three: finish alone, because, if one of us is sprinting against someone else, we'll finish second.'

It described the race perfectly.

Inside the final 15 kilometres, a crash reduced the lead group to around fifteen riders. With 8 kilometres to go, Rigoberto Urán attacked on the right. At the same instant, the Kazakh rider Alexander Vinokurov attacked on the left, then swung across the road to shelter in Urán's slipstream. They worked together until, with 300 metres to go, Urán, visibly weary, looked over his right shoulder at Vinokurov, then over his left shoulder at the chasing group. It was a long, lingering look – far too long – and, as he drifted left, the Kazakh seized the opportunity to launch his sprint. It won him the race.

Vinokurov had form: evidence had surfaced that in April 2010 he had paid the Russian rider Alexandr Kolobnev to throw the Liège–Bastogne–Liège. Rigoberto denies that he reached any similar agreement, and Leguízamo responded to my question with another: 'When could they have discussed it? There was no time. Rigo was simply too tired at the end, and made a mistake.'

At dinner in the hotel that night, the Colombian ambassador and his wife arrived with a tablet as a gift for Rigo.

Leguízamo told me, 'The ambassador said, "Rigo, why do you not bring your mum and sister to Europe to see you race?"

'Rigo said, "They need a visa."

'"I can help with that. I can call my counterpart in Spain to get the Schengen Area visa."

'And Rigo says to the ambassador, "Ah, you can now, *güevón*, now that they have given me this little medal!"'

☷

Esteban Chaves too was beginning to make waves. Three days before the Olympic road race, he had finished second to Gorka Izagirre in the hilly, one-day Prueba Villafranca-Ordiziako Klasika on 25 July 2012, with two more Colombians, Miguel Angel Rubiano and Jeffry Romero, third and fifth. At the Vuelta a Burgos on 5 August, he did even better.

A little over four kilometres from the top of the Lagunas de Neila, the decisive climb, Rigoberto Urán, working for his team-mate Sergio Luís Henao, accelerated. Esteban Chaves followed, and the three Colombians dropped the Spanish race leader, Dani Moreno. Henao and Chaves then worked together until the steep final metres, where Chaves moved easily ahead to take his first win as a professional cyclist. Moreno, who started the stage 32 seconds ahead of Henao, finished the stage 22 seconds later, to win the race overall, with Henao second and Chaves third.

Six days later, Chaves outsprinted his four breakaway companions to win the hilly, one-day GP Camaiore in Tuscany.

Suddenly, there seemed to be Colombian riders everywhere. Six of them started the 2012 Vuelta a España. Only one was a leader: the former Vuelta stage winner Leonardo Duque, lead sprinter for the Cofidis team. The rest were out-and-out domestiques: Sergio Luís Henao and Rigoberto Urán for Chris Froome, Nairo Quintana for Alejandro Valverde, his childhood friend Cayetano Sarmiento in support of Eros Capecchi, and Winner Anacona in favour of Damiano Cunego.

The race started in oppressive heat. Movistar won the opening team time trial in their home town, Pamplona, and Nairo emerged from stage two in second place overall, with the race leader's jersey within his grasp. But the following day he suffered dehydration and conceded over three minutes. All hope of wearing the red jersey gone, Nairo dedicated himself to working for Alejandro Valverde.

The sixteenth stage finished on a long and, towards the top, exceptionally steep climb called Cuitu Negru. With six kilometres to go, repeated accelerations by Alberto Contador dislodged Valverde from the leading group that included the race leader Joaquín Rodríguez and Nairo. Nairo dropped back, shepherded Valverde back to the group, then moved to the front. With 2.5 kilometres to go, on gradients exceeding 20 per cent, the group of four was in deadlock. To destabilise Contador and Rodríguez, Nairo launched a stunning acceleration. Contador took the bait and gave chase, with Rodríguez on his wheel. However, when the inevitable recovery period came, Valverde lacked the strength to take advantage. Nairo ended the race 36th overall, having helped Valverde finish second.

◈

Under cover of the Vuelta, the Tour de l'Avenir had taken place in France. Luís Fernando Saldarriaga had masterminded yet another brilliant campaign. At the end of stage four, on the Col du Télégraph, a twenty-year-old named Juan Ernesto Chamorro, from the village of Pupiales, eight kilometres from Ipiales on the Ecuadorean border, finished third and moved to within a second of the French race leader, Warren Barguil. In the 44-kilometre individual time trial the following day, Chamorro and Barguil finished in the same time.

On the final stage, over the Col des Aravis and the Col de la Croix Fry to Le Grand Bornand, Chamorro was unable to shake off his rival. One second separated him from a third consecutive Colombian victory in the Tour de l'Avenir.

Within a few years, a good ride at the Tour de l'Avenir by a Colombian would lead to immediate contract offers from World-Tour teams. Chamorro's 2012 Tour de l'Avenir performance led to none. Colombian cycling was still in the pupal stage, developing out of sight of the world. Colombian peace, too: on Tuesday 4 September 2012, three days after the Tour de l'Avenir had finished, and on the second rest day of the Vuelta a España, President Juan Manuel Santos revealed that the government had been holding secret talks with the FARC for six months, and that peace negotiations would begin in Oslo that October.

The season closed with more Colombian success. Rigoberto Urán won Gran Piemonte, a one-day appetiser to the Tour of Lombardy, with Henao and Betancur fourth and fifth, then finished third in Il Lombardia, with Henao fifth and Nairo, riding the first monument of his career, eleventh.

Nairo had three more race days before returning home to Colombia. Two of them saw Colombian victories. In the Coppa Sabatini around Pisa on 4 October, Nairo watched as former Colombia Es Pasión rider Fabio Duarte won, with Miguel Angel Rubiano in second place and Dalivier Ospina eighth. Two days later, on the climb up to the Madonna di San Luca, overlooking Bologna, Nairo darted away to win the gruelling Giro dell'Emilia. It was the perfect end to a brilliant first season as a professional cyclist, and underlined the threat he and the emerging legion of Colombian cyclists posed to their sport's hierarchy.

9

A Fortunate Man

Three days into the 2012 Vuelta a España, the leader of the Lampre-ISD team, Damiano Cunego, had a bad day. That left Winner Anacona as his team's best-placed rider. The perfect teammate, Cunego advised him and shepherded him to nineteenth place in his first Grand Tour. It was a morale-boosting achievement in the second attempt at a professional career by a rider who would play a significant part in some of Colombia's greatest results of the decade.

The son of a policeman who had the good fortune to survive postings in some of Colombia's most notorious regions, Winner's story starts with his father – and his name.

≡

Rodrigo Anacona Anacona told me, 'I'm a fortunate man. I saw many of my companions die. I was shot in the leg once by the paramilitaries in Muzo, but it was only a flesh wound. I made it to retirement age, received my pension and now I spend my time doing what I enjoy, which is cycling. I am grateful to God for it.'

He named his first born, a daughter, Angie Urany. For his son, born on 11 August 1988, he drew up a list of cycling names: 'I liked Johan. I settled on Jean-François. But, as we were leaving the house for the baptism, I said to Ednar, my wife, "He's going to be Winnen Andrew."'

They were topical names in cycling: the Dutchman Peter Winnen had just finished ninth in the Tour de France, while Andy Hampsten, from the United States, had won the Giro.

'I liked them because they were always on the attack, although the priest said, "What? What sort of names are these?"

'I wrote them down for him, although he still mistook the "n" for an "r", and when I collected the birth certificate, I noticed it said *Winner*. I was going to say, "No, this is wrong," and then I thought, "Hold on: Winner means champion, doesn't it? And at least they have got Andrew right."'

Winner Andrew Anacona Gómez was born in Coper, a village of 3,500 close to Colombia's famed emerald fields. His father continues, 'In my day, the roads were unsurfaced. When it rained, they were impassable. Even today, there's only one bus a day. It arrives at five in the afternoon and leaves at three in the morning. If you ever need a copy of your birth certificate from the parish records, it's an ordeal. So I spoke to a family friend who was a nurse, and she helped me have him registered as born in Bogotá.'

Winner tells me, 'So my documents say that I am from the capital, although I was born in Boyacá and I feel *boyacense*. I came to Tunja when I was five, and it has been my home for twenty-five years.'

Rodrigo had arrived in the emerald fields in 1984, fresh out of the police academy at El Espinal, Tolima, where he had trained as a Grenadier, a counter-insurgency role which qualified him to lead combat patrols. His first posting after graduation was at Pauna, ten kilometres east of Borbur, the gateway to the emerald mines at Peñas Blancas. The FARC had been trying to approach the mines through Pauna since the start of the 1980s.

'I had been there three months when the first guerrilla attack took place,' Rodrigo says. 'It must have been March 1984, at two o'clock in the morning, although it was only a skirmish, and I was soon sent to Muzo, forty kilometres to the south. There, the problem wasn't the guerrillas, it was the bosses from the mine at Coscuez, who wanted to take over.

'But the Muzo bosses had civilians with small arms, sometimes referred to as paramilitaries' – when he speaks of the violence, Rodrigo does so as a policeman – 'and, if anyone defied the bosses, they were sent in. It was very simple and efficient. The bosses' men had 9mm pistols, mostly Brownings and Berettas, adapted to carry thirty instead of fifteen slugs, which gave them more firepower in a gun fight. They carried AR-15 assault rifles too, customised to take magazines of thirty cartridges instead of the standard twenty. The guns were all legal. The murders weren't, and there were ten or fifteen a day.'

Everyday policing around the emerald mines included stopping and searching emerald miners and bodyguards for unlicensed firearms: 'If there were only one or two of them, they cooperated. But if there were five or more, you had to be smart about it. They were very ready to put hand on belt, as we called it. A lot of their people died. A lot of police too.

'I never had personal contact with the bosses, but we sometimes stopped their cars to check documents, and we saw them inside.'

Colombia has never worked out what to do with its emeralds. The first European to see them was a Spanish colonial administrator named Pedro Arias de Ávila, on the northern coast in 1514. It took twenty-five years to find their source, and twenty more to subjugate their miners, the Muzo people. The town of Villa de la Santísima Trinidad de los Muzos was founded in February 1560, twelve kilometres east of the mines. The Spanish began to exploit the mines seven years later.

The administration of the mines has been an insoluble conundrum ever since. For centuries the local populace, who had always depended on fealty to one overlord or another for their subsistence and position in the community, saw the state as a competitor seeking to deprive them of their way of life and income. The mines were entrusted to the Bank of the Republic in 1946. It responded with corruption and incompetence.

In 1961 a farmworker discovered a new seam in a cave on Hacienda Peñas Blancas, and the black market in green stones grew to dwarf the legal one. Between 1967 and 1972, conflict raged over control of the mines. Twelve hundred are said to have died.

The government tried privatising the mines, but the established bosses simply bought back their share on the black market, so the mines were temporarily closed while concessions were awarded to independent entrepreneurs. But the emerald mafias used political donations to protect their interests. In 1977 the mines at Muzo, celebrated for their rare and extraodinary *Gota de Aceite* (oil drop) emeralds, were ceded to companies owned by Víctor Carranza, known as the Emerald Czar. The territorial concessions granted him were a white flag raised by the state. As well as the right to self-enrichment, he was authorised to administer security and justice. His private army, the Carranceros, committed more than a thousand killings in 1985 and 1986 alone. His emerald fiefdom was the precursor of the informal states ruled over by Colombia's paramilitary warlords in the 1990s and 2000s.

Carranza had made *Forbes* magazine's list of dollar billionaires in 1992. Said to own a million hectares in eleven departments, a million head of cattle – 10 per cent of all the cows in Colombia – and colossal investments in every imaginable sector, he counted Colombian presidents among his friends, and funded the studies and careers of lawyers and state functionaries who rose to preside over the highest courts in the land. The survivor, down the years, of countless assassination attempts, Carranza's greatest achievement was to live to seventy-seven. He died of natural causes in April 2013.

The execution of an emerald dealer called Arsenio Acero and his bodyguards near Peñas Blancas in April 1984 had triggered a series of killings that eventually led to six years of ferocious violence. Rodrigo Anacona had reached the emerald fields at the start of the year.

He tells me, 'And I only joined the police force so I could afford a bike.'

Born in August 1961, the eldest of five children, Rodrigo Anacona grew up on Vereda El Alto, forty minutes by foot from the pretty colonial village of San Sebastián, 300 kilometres from the Ecuadorean border, with his parents Isaías Anacona Anacona and Ercilia Anacona Jiménez, peasant farmers who worked the land on two fincas. On the higher one, where the temperatures are lower, they grew potatoes and onions. On the lower one, they cultivated maize, cassava, plantain and coffee.

'My father was strict and hard-working, but he never made me labour in the fields. I helped him because I wanted to, not because he made me.'

Rodrigo Anacona grew up with a secret obsession: 'At primary school, when I was learning to read, I was fascinated by pictures of bicycles. I tried to imagine how you kept them upright on those narrow wheels.

'When we went to market, I used to see the sons of the richest families riding bikes, and I said to myself, "One day I'll have one of those."'

Aged thirteen, after finishing primary school on the vereda, Rodrigo went to live with an uncle in Ríopaila, near the coffee-growing capital of Armenia, to continue his schooling. By the time he was fifteen, he had moved on to another uncle, this time in San Agustín, in the department of El Huila, celebrated for the largest complex of pre-Columbian megalithic funerary monuments in the Americas, a UNESCO World Heritage site.

While there, he bought his first bike: 'It only had one rear cog, but it was enough to start me racing. The competitions were organised by a *Dragoneante*' – one step up from a Private, perhaps what the US Army calls a Private First Class – 'in the Police. I still remember his name: Ospina Noguera, from Pereira. He had married a girl from San Agustín, and one day he asked me to go home with him to collect some bottle cages, and we talked. He said that the countryside was fine, but it was no good working in it. He asked me what study grades I had, and explained how you get into the police force. I sat my exams in Neiva and joined up.'

Having survived the murderous emerald wars with just a gunshot wound to the leg, Rodrigo Anacona was given some more tranquil years. In August 1988 he was moved to Coper, just off the road to Muzo, where his wife Ednar gave birth to their second child. In April 1989, when Winner was eight months old, Rodrigo was sent to Tinjacá, a hundred kilometres east of the emerald mines and a world away.

'It was a quiet, peaceful village. Everyone said I looked on edge, but I wasn't used to places where you could sit and relax over a coffee. I was used to gunfire, and never knowing if they were killing each other, or your colleagues.'

Aged one and a half, Winner Andrew saw a little boy riding around Tinjacá. He took his Christmas tricycle into the village square, and joined him.

From Tinjacá, the Anaconas moved to Sutamarchán, a handful of kilometres away, and then to the departmental capital, Tunja. By then, peace was in the air: in July 1990, in the village of Quípama, the parties to the Emerald War signed an agreement ending a conflict that had cost 3,500 lives.

After the heat of western Boyacá, Tunja came as a shock to Winner Anacona: 'I remember the day we arrived. It was cold and shrouded in freezing fog. These days the temperatures reach thirty degrees Celsius. You never saw those temperatures when I was a child. At night it fell below freezing and there was frost in the mornings. Then, at about 9 a.m., the sun came out and the day went from cold to warm.'

He started racing when he was six, in the *Minipitufos* – the Mini-Smurfs! – category of the Santiago de Tunja Cycling School run by Lino Casas, a veteran of the 1988 Vuelta a España.

His father recalls, 'His first race was in Paipa,' forty kilometres north-east of Tunja. 'He came home with a bronze medal, enthused, and began to work at it. After that, he was regularly finishing first or second.

'To begin with, cycling was just a way of keeping the kids out of trouble in their free time.'

Winner, in turn, worried about his father: 'When he was stationed away, it was in dangerous areas. We stayed in Tunja, partly because of school, but also for our security.'

When Winner was eight, he took the bus with his father to meet his grandparents for the first time. He recalls, 'The journey took more than twenty-four hours. From the south of Tunja to the north of Bogotá takes an hour and forty minutes today. In those days it took three hours. We had to go over La Línea' – known to cyclists as one of Colombia's hardest climbs, reaching an altitude of 3,265 metres – 'to get to Popayán.'

In the capital of the Cauca department, they changed bus. Many of the remaining 145 kilometres to San Sebastián were on unsurfaced roads. The bus passed groups of FARC fighters. At a guerrilla roadblock, the bus was stopped and searched. As a policeman, Rodrigo would have made the perfect hostage. Winner simply says, 'Thankfully, nothing happened, and we made it to San Sebastián.'

The trip was a success: Winner was able to meet his grandparents, and perhaps even tell them about his life as a cyclist.

In 1998, as negotiations started between the Pastrana government and the FARC, the guerrillas continued to kill and kidnap in the far east and far north of Boyacá. These were Rodrigo Anacona's next postings.

Rodrigo left Ednar and their three children (Angie and Winner having been joined by Brian Estheinger, the latter another of Rodrigo's original appellations) in Tunja, and set off on an erratic moth's flight of postings through the FARC borderlands. He started in Chiscas, 240 kilometres to the north-east. After three weeks, he was moved thirty kilometres south to San Mateo. It was just as well: barely a month and a half after his move, Chiscas endured an eight-hour assault by 150 guerrillas. Three of Rodrigo's former colleagues were taken as hostages. Another was left with spinal injuries when a wall collapsed on him.

Two days later, at seven in the evening, Rodrigo Anacona was on duty in San Mateo when 200 FARC guerrillas sacked the village of El Espino, thirteen kilometres from Chiscas. Nine policemen were killed in the attack, several of whom had worked with Rodrigo elsewhere in Boyacá.

According to intelligence reports, San Mateo was next. The police station was an easy target, so the ten officers were withdrawn, the station closed, and Rodrigo returned to the peace of Tinjacá.

In 2001 and 2004, he spent three six-month postings in Pajarito, a village of 700 on the border between Boyacá and Casanare: guerrilla country. In September 1997 Pajarito had been sacked by the FARC, who attacked the police station with rockets and grenades and destroyed homesteads. Five policemen and the cook were killed.

There were occasional skirmishes without casualties, but after 2002 the waning of the guerrillas was palpable. Rodrigo Anacona retired in 2007. By a miracle, or a series of them, he had sidestepped every attack. A fortunate man indeed.

By 2006 Winner was a fixture in the departmental and national teams on road and track. At the 2006 Pan-American Games, he took silver in the individual time trial, and bronze in the individual pursuit. He was national champion in the points race, and finished twelfth in the Vuelta del Porvenir, won by Darwin Atapuma.

But Winner's progress was interrupted in 2007 by plica syndrome, an irritation of the membrane around the knee that seals in the synovial fluid lubricating the joint.

Winner says, 'It was the health system that was complicated, not the injury: a month to get an X-ray, another month for an appointment with the orthopaedic surgeon. Four or five months, all told – nearly the whole season. I didn't want to be a burden on my family, and I wasn't old, but I still thought, "The years are passing." I seriously considered giving up cycling.'

The knee operation finally took place in October: 'Then I had physio and started to train, and then to race, but without a team. Boyacá was interested, but they said I had to give up my Bogotá racing licence, otherwise they couldn't pay me, so I walked away.'

With the offer of food, transport and a bike on loan, Winner moved to Bogotá and, in May 2008, started the Vuelta a Colombia for the Instituto de Recreación y Deporte de Bogotá (IRDB)– Bogotá Positiva team.

Stage three finished in Tunja. His father was waiting for him in the Plaza de Bolívar, expecting his nineteen-year-old son to finish sometime after the group of favourites: 'I had a transistor radio in my ear. "At Agua Aruna, such-and-such is happening, on the Alto del Sote, it's so-and-so . . ."

'Suddenly, the winner comes in, and then the group of the best climbers, thirty-five or so, and Winner is among them.'

He seemed to grow stronger and stronger. In stage twelve he joined an eight-man breakaway group through the coffee groves from Quimbaya to Pereira.

Rodrigo says, 'In the final sprint, he let himself get boxed in and finished sixth. But he won the jersey as the *Pilsen Hero*' – a sort of most aggressive rider prize – 'and finished the Vuelta.'

Rodrigo says, 'He was spending more time in the capital than here. He was studying at the Santo Tomás University, which gave grants to medallists in the national championships.'

On 11 August 2008, the day of his twentieth birthday, his

father called him: 'Son, if you have time this week, come over for lunch.'

Winner said, 'Dad, something has come up. I have to go to Italy the day after tomorrow. I'm going to need money.'

The Colombian rider Miguel Ángel Rubiano was moving to Centri Della Calzatura-Partizan, a Continental team based in the region of Le Marche in south-central Italy, and had mentioned Winner. Nelson Javier Rodríguez Zea, whose family owned Confecciones Maria Elvira or CME, a Boyacá-based manufacturer of cycling clothes, had sent them Winner's CV, and the deal had been done. Rodrigo called Winner's coach, Marco Tulio Ruíz, who confirmed the news.

Winner recalls, 'The team gave me a chance, but I had to pay for the flights, which weren't cheap.'

Nelson Rodríguez helped, the IRDB made a contribution, his father collected donations from his friends and, on 13 August 2008, Winner flew to Italy.

Centri Della Calzatura-Partizan was registered in Serbia. With eighteen riders – Serbian, Uzbek, Russian, Polish, Kazakh, Italian and Colombian – half of them new professionals, it was, says Winner, 'a team of mercenaries'. The equipment was poor – 'If you're not riding a Tour, a Giro or a Vuelta, they don't give you the good stuff,' he says – but it was an opportunity.

Winner moved into a team house in Montegranaro, midway between Ancona and Ascoli Piceno in eastern Italy. The reality of European cycling at its lower levels soon hit him: 'I was a *stagiaire*' – an apprentice – 'for two months there. The fridge was always empty. There was nothing to eat except pasta, so I put on weight. And the speeds were very different from anything I was used to.'

His programme included the Trofeo Melinda, won by former Giro d'Italia winner Stefano Garzelli, the Tour of Slovenia, won by the Slovenian Jure Golčer ahead of Franco Pellizotti, who had finished fourth in the Giro d'Italia earlier that year, and the

Beghelli Grand Prix, won by one of the world's leading sprinters, Alessandro Petacchi.

'The team decided I was still young and it would be better to ride for a few years at Under-23 level. In the end Nelson, through a business contact in Italy, took me to a team in Tuscany for 2009.'

At G.S. Maltinti-Lampadari-BCC-Cambiano, Winner followed in the footsteps of another Colombian: Alex Cano, the winner of a stage at the 2006 GiroBio, the biggest Under-23 stage race in Italy, and two stages and the General Classification in the 2007 Giro del Valle de Aosta, Italy's most mountainous stage race.

'They thought I would win every race I started, just because I was Colombian.

'I moved into a team apartment with a collective dormitory at Ponte a Elsa, close to Empoli. The owner cooked for us in the evenings. For other meals, a team auxiliary brought us a bag of shopping once a week.'

All the same, a second place, a third, two fourths, an eighth and a tenth seem a respectable first season in Italy's competitive Under-23 category: 'But the team owner wanted a winner. Carlos Julián Quintero was riding for Bedogni-Grassi-Natalini-Gruppo Praga – alongside the Australian Richie Porte – and Maltinti wanted him.

'A friend spoke to Antonio Politano, the coach at a team called Danton-Caparrini-Le Village-Vibert, and introduced us. Politano said I had talent but I didn't know how to use it. He offered me a one-year contract. Maltinti was a good team, but you didn't learn anything there: you just used what you already knew.'

Under Politano, Winner used a heart rate monitor for the first time. He flourished, winning the prestigious Under-23 Trofeo Matteotti in May and the Giro del Montalbano in June: 'Politano lived at Navacchio, near Pisa. I was at Sant'Annunziate, four kilometres away. He picked me up every evening and I ate with him and his family. I still live close to them in Italy, and see them three or four times a week.'

Danton extended Anacona's contract and in 2011 Winner won seven races, including a stage win at June's GiroBio. He finished second overall: 'I was the strongest, but I lost time when I let a big breakaway get away on stage two, and the Italian Matteo Cattaneo gained two minutes. I made time up in the other stages, but I never caught him.'

On stages four and five, the two uphill finishes, Winner finished second and first (ahead of future Vuelta winner Fabio Aru), and reduced his rival's lead to 51 seconds. By the end of stage seven Cattaneo's advantage was down to 31 seconds; by the end of stage eight it was down to 26 seconds – Cattaneo's final winning margin.

Now well known to the professional teams, Winner made a plan for the rest of the year: 'It was important to be consistent. In Italy, you saw riders win four or five races in a month, then disappear. It created suspicion. I had to be up there every time, to inspire confidence. I don't know how many podiums I stood on – maybe twenty – and I was almost never outside the top ten.'

His 2011 results included seven wins, seven second places, four thirds, a fifth, two sixth places, three sevenths, three ninths and a tenth place.

Approaching the end of the year, Winner still had no contract for 2012. A friend of Nelson Rodríguez, a cycling coach named Sandro Lerici, made contact with Giuseppe Saronni, the general manager of the professional team Lampre-ISD, and showed him Winner's CV. Saronni offered him a one-year contract, and Winner moved into a flat owned by Lerici.

After his good Vuelta performance, with the help of two of Italy's top rider agents, Alex and Johnny Carera, he signed an improved and extended contract, and his life took on some stability. Never having ridden for departmental teams or Colombia Es Pasión, Anacona had made his own way. Some years later, towards the end of the 2016 Tour de France, after President Santos tweeted his congratulations to the Colombian riders, Winner Anacona quickly responded:

> **@JuanManSantos @NairoQuinCo @jarlinsonpantan**
> volveremos porque nos hemos hecho SOLOS en este bonito y duro deporte con la ayuda de pocos.
> **@JuanManSantos @NairoQuinCo @jarlinsonpantan**
> *we will be back because we have made it ALONE in this beautiful and hard sport with little help from anyone.*

10

Born Again

On 16 February 2013 Esteban Chaves started the second race of his second season as a professional cyclist: the Laigueglia Grand Prix, traditionally the first international race of the season in Italy, held over a succession of loops on the narrow, winding roads of coastal Liguria.

About a hundred kilometres into the race, at Villanova d'Albenga, 11.5 kilometres north and inland from Laigueglia, Jarlinson Pantano, riding two places behind him, watched as he missed the bend and collided with a rail.

'There was a traffic sign in front of him and he rode straight into the pole.'

Chaves was admitted to the Santa Corona Hospital in Pietra Ligure, 20 kilometres away, as a Code Red patient, denoting immediate danger of death. A CAT scan revealed fractures along the right side of his body: in the petrous bone (the dense part of the temporal bone that surrounds the inner ear); the sphenoid bone in the skull, close to the temple; the cheek bone; the maxillary sinuses near the nose, the collarbone and various ribs. There was bruising to the lungs associated with chest compression and bleeding in the space between the brain and the spinal cord that contains the cerebrospinal fluid. Forty-eight hours were wiped permanently from Esteban's recall, starting just before the accident.

In Colombia, his parents heard about the accident from a news bulletin. Then Claudio Corti called: 'He told us, "He's conscious. He's OK."'

Then, at about 2 p.m. Colombian time – 9 p.m. in Italy, perhaps seven hours after the accident – Esteban himself got through.

Jairo Chaves told me, 'He was awake and talking. He wanted to put our minds at rest.

'"I've had an accident. I've broken my collarbone, but I'm OK so don't worry."

'Then he called again.

'"I've had an accident. I've broken my collarbone, but I'm OK so don't worry."

'And again, and again: "I've had an accident . . ." each time thinking it was the first time we'd spoken. In Italy he was telling the hospital staff, "I have to call my parents and let them know I'm OK." Each time he called, I said, "Don't worry, my son."'

He stayed in hospital for a week. Then, unable to fly, he moved in with an Italian-Colombian couple who lived near him in Bergamo, Alessandro Belotti and Angélica María Cadavid. In Jairo's words, they treated him like a son.

Ten days after the crash, he had an operation to pin his collarbone. Two and a half weeks later, he flew to Bogotá.

In Colombia, he told his father, 'I can't move my arm.'

'Let's go and see Dr Castro.'

Dr Gustavo Castro had been a consultant orthopaedic surgeon for the Colombia Es Pasión team. He had operated on Sergio Luís Henao in 2007, and on Esteban in 2009.

Not even partial paralysis could dim Esteban's warmth. At Castro's clinic in Bogotá, he said, '*Quiubo* [What's up], Dr Castrico? They've sent me so that you can fix me up.'

'OK, sunshine. What happened?'

'Nothing much,' Esteban told him. 'Brain trauma. Collarbone. I need your help with rehabilitation.'

Dr Castro described the encounter. 'He removed the sling. I said, "Move the arm," but he couldn't.'

'I sent him for a scan, then said, "Tell your team you need a neurological examination of the brachial plexus."'

The brachial plexus – plexus comes from the Latin *plectere*, to braid – controls movement and sensation in the arm and hand. Its structure resembles a map of a major railway terminus, the lines being the lower four cervical nerves and the first thoracic nerve. Traumatic brachial plexus injury often involves impacts to the side of the head and shoulder, like the one Esteban had suffered.

He spoke to the team and returned to see Dr Castro for electromyography to evaluate the electrical activity in the muscles.

'The nerve is broken, Esteban. And when the nerve is broken, that's it. End of story.'

'So what do I do now, doc?'

'*Chino*, you can't be a cyclist any more.'

'It was a nightmare,' Jairo tells me. 'But I said, "Let's find a doctor who can put it right."'

Castro sent Esteban to see a hand and upper extremity specialist, Dr Julio Sandoval, who said, 'It may be possible to save the nerve but the operation will be long and difficult, and if we don't operate in six months, it will be too late.'

For insurance purposes, Esteban needed a second opinion in Italy. There, he was told to be patient.

Carolina recalls, 'They thought it was a stretch injury, not a break, and that physiotherapy alone would fix it.'

Jairo continues: 'I went back with Esteban to see Dr Sandoval, and I said, "We're not waiting." It meant forfeiting the insurance, but the doctor told us that if we could find enough money to pay for the operating theatre and the anaesthetist, we could worry about the rest later.'

At 10 a.m. on Friday 31 May, Esteban went for surgery. Carolina remembers, 'He was operated on face down, so his face, chest and legs were going to be swollen and bruised. We were told to expect him out at one or two in the afternoon. Two, three and four came and went. At six o'clock we went to reception. We were told, "They have asked for more time in theatre. The operation is going well, but there has been a complication."'

A four-centimetre breach in the nerve could only be repaired by a graft using a section of the sural nerve, close to the Achilles tendon. Normally they would have resuscitated the patient to ask for consent. But the surgeons knew the family's position and carried on.

The operation took eleven hours.

Physiotherapy began four weeks later. Sent for two sessions a day, Esteban insisted on three. The physio arrived each morning at seven. Esteban was there at 6.45. He continued the exercises between sessions.

Dr Castro assessed Esteban's improvement once a week. Carolina described it: 'He stood close to the wall and the doctor said, "Very good. Now, let's see: move your arm." Esteban tried but, if there was any movement, you couldn't see it. The doctor filmed each session, and every week he said, "Attaboy. You're getting there."'

Carolina told me, 'I never saw any improvement.'

In August 2013 Orica-GreenEdge sports director Neil Stephens called Esteban at home.

Esteban recalls, 'I thought it was a joke.'

Stephens explains, 'We were considering the idea of bringing through young riders who might one day be Grand Tour contenders.'

Stephens had been working with the Australian Under-23 team at the 2011 Tour de l'Avenir, with future stars in Michael Hepburn and Rohan Dennis, but he had been very taken with Chaves. The following year he saw him at the Clásica de Ordizia and the Vuelta a Burgos, and it was clear to him that the 22-year-old Colombian had a future.

'Esteban told me that he still had a year to go with Corti. I told him to count on us, and that we would speak later.'

Stephens called him regularly in Bogotá to ask about his progress: 'For me, they were routine calls,' the Australian says. 'Only later did I understand that the days I called were special for him.'

Esteban says that, with each call, 'My motivation grew by a factor of three. I'd go to therapy and do more than they were asking me to. I'd be screaming.'

Then, one day that August, six months after the accident, an EMG detected a barely perceptible response. It was the first sign of light in the tunnel.

In October Chaves flew to Catalunya for testing.

Jairo recalls, 'A month before his flight, he was riding, but he still had to pick up his right hand with his left and put it on the bars.'

In Spain, his teammates would tell him they were going out for two hours and stay out for four.

'They said, "Go back, if you want." He wouldn't, of course, and, back in the hotel, without washing or changing his clothes, he would collapse on the bed and sleep.'

On the day of the tests, Stephens says, 'I could see that, even if he was still weak, it was much better than before, and I could also see that he was totally committed. I didn't doubt him. We signed the contract then and there.'

Chaves was a cyclist again.

At his European home in Gerona, Esteban continued his rehabilitation. Jairo recalls, 'When we spoke, it was, "How are you, son?"

'"Not bad."

'"How is the arm?"

'"The same."'

Somehow he was able to race. At the 2014 Tour of Langkawi, Malaysia, in March, he was fourth on the climb to the Genting Highlands. Back in Europe, he finished two hard WorldTour stage races, the Volta a Catalunya and the Tour of the Basque Country.

In May he flew to the United States for the Tour of California. On the first mountain stage, finishing on Mount Diablo, he finished eighth. Three days later, stage six took the riders to Mountain High in the San Gabriel Mountains, Los Angeles County. At their home in Tenjo, north of Bogotá, his parents were watching, their hearts in their mouths.

With five kilometres to go, Esteban, seated, quickened the pace, then rose over the saddle and made a second acceleration. He glanced behind: the Spanish rider David De la Cruz was recovering some metres back. The American Tom Danielson was trying to close the gap, putting himself into oxygen debt. Each time Esteban Chaves stood on the pedals, his advantage increased.

On the finish line, his celebratory gesture intrigued the eye. He touched the front of his helmet, the abdomen just below the solar plexus, and the left shoulder, with two fingers, middle and fore, of his right hand. But as the hand moved across his torso to complete the sign, it changed shape. The forefinger alone touched the right shoulder. *He was pointing at it*. The hand continued the same careful action, vertically now, until the elbow extended fully, with a slight raising of the upper chest. The finger now pointed at the sky. It was the most literal of spiritual exercises: the devout profession of joint mobility in the upper limbs. And the smile broadened.

His mother, Carolina, remembers, 'I turned around so that I was facing the same way as the computer, just to be sure. Then I shouted, "Esteban is back! He is Esteban again!"'

Then he called them and said: 'The win doesn't matter. Nothing matters except my arm. I have been reborn today.'

'He has a birthday on 17 January and another on 16 May,' Carolina points out, 'the day he won the stage at the Tour of California.'

Later, Dr Castro said to Esteban, 'You had me frightened, kid.'

'Why's that, Doc?'

'Because there was no improvement in physio. I thought you'd lost the arm.'

Carolina explained, 'He [Castro] told me he looked at the physiotherapy videos and photographs, and never saw any improvement. None.'

But the doctor had always encouraged him. 'Boy, you've got some steel. I was looking at the video from a week ago, and you have a millimetre more movement this week. Keep it up, lad.'

Dr Castro raised his hands and told me, 'What was I supposed to say?'

11

Two Seconds

After a disastrous ride in the pouring rain, Bradley Wiggins lay 1 minute 22 seconds behind his rival Vincenzo Nibali. The 54.8km time trial was his big opportunity. Many expected him to make up that time, add a comfortable cushion, and lay the foundations for overall victory in the 2013 Giro d'Italia.

But that is not how things turned out. Wiggins came only second in the stage, and made up just 11 seconds on Nibali.

Two days later, in a tunnel eight kilometres from Altopiano del Montasio, Wiggins's teammate Rigoberto Urán rode off the front as the group of favourites marked each other. Urán took the stage win and moved into third place overall, nearly 90 seconds behind Cadel Evans, and a little over two minutes behind Nibali.

Wiggins lasted two more days before leaving the race, making Rigoberto the Team Sky leader.

Eight days after that, in the final mountain stage, as the snow fell on the Tre Cime di Lavaredo, Evans lost time and Urán secured second place overall. Another Colombian, Carlos Alberto Betancur, who had finished second in four stages, ended the Giro fifth overall and Best Young Rider. The new generation was beginning to fulfil its potential.

Nairo's career as a Grand Tour leader had equally fortuitous beginnings. It started among the wheatfields of central France on 12 July 2013, at the midpoint of a stage between Tours and Saint-Amand-Montrond that promised little, until, after sixty predictable kilometres, a complacent breeze mustered some unforeseen energy. The peloton quickly split into several groups, and flew through the feed zone at speeds that made collecting feedbags a liability. One rider tried, and ended up careering into Alejandro Valverde's rear wheel. Before it could disintegrate, the Movistar leader, second overall, screeched to a halt. Instead of swapping bikes, he took a teammate's rear wheel and fitted it himself. It ensured he would embark on the long chase on his own machine, but cost him precious seconds.

Bauke Mollema, 12 seconds behind Valverde overall, set his teammates to hold off the Spaniard's return. The entire Movistar team bar Rui Costa and Nairo dropped back to help their leader.

Nairo's directeur sportif, José Luís Arrieta, in the team car, faced a dilemma: 'We had two riders up front, we were only 15 seconds back, so I told Rui [Costa] to drop back and help. To Nairo, I said, loud and clear, "I need you right up front."'

But Valverde never closed the gap. Arrieta was philosophical: 'We were close, but we never made it, and we lost a chance of a high position overall with Rui. But that is what the big, decision-making moments are like. Nairo went from being Alejandro's support rider in the mountains, to having Alejandro working for him.'

Nairo says, 'I had prepared well, I was strong, and I knew I was capable. It was confirmation that when you work conscientiously and honestly, good things come – and at that moment they came to me.'

Two weeks earlier, at Porto-Vecchio in Corsica, Nairo had sat alongside Valverde to take questions from the media. I had asked Eusebio Unzué why he had brought the young Colombian to the press conference, rather than the twenty-five-year-old Rui Costa, who had won two stages in the previous year's Tour and, more recently, his second consecutive Tour de Suisse, or the outstanding Costa Rican Andrey Amador, a stage winner at the previous year's Giro d'Italia.

Unzué replied, 'In 1983 Pedro Delgado sat here next to Angel Arroyo. In 1988 [Miguel] Induráin sat next to Delgado. Now Nairo is sitting alongside Alejandro.' The current leader had each time been shadowed by his successor.

In February Nairo had helped Valverde win the Vuelta a Andalucia and Vuelta a Murcia, while finishing eighth and eleventh himself. He had started Paris–Nice in March as Rui Costa's domestique, but both riders had fallen and it was Nairo who finished best, fifteenth overall and third in the concluding mountain time trial behind Porte and Talansky.

A week later he started the Volta a Catalunya. At the ski station of Vallter 2000, Nairo had won in the falling snow. The following day the race leader, his teammate Valverde, crashed. It meant Movistar went to their home race, the Tour of the Basque Country, without a clear leader.

Arrieta says, 'One of the race organisers said to me, "That's a puny little team!"'

'I said, "Let's see who wins."'

Sergio Luís Henao won stage three and took the race lead, with Nairo second, eight seconds back. The following day, Nairo won at Eibar in stage four, shaving off two seconds of Henao's advantage. On the final day, in a rolling, 24km time trial around the Basque town of Beasain, Nairo finished second only to time trial world champion Tony Martin, and 40 seconds ahead of Henao. It brought him the first WorldTour stage race win of his career and established him as rather more than Valverde's mountain domestique.

He had returned home late in April, after his first taste of the Ardennes classics, then flown back to start the Tour de France.

Arrieta says, 'He was there to get a feeling for the Tour and to learn, although anything can happen at any time, so we always said, "Stay close to your teammates."'

Reflecting on his new status, Nairo says, 'It had taken time, but that was entirely logical. We Colombians were just beginning to arrive in Europe again, and I was one of the first: before me there was only Rigoberto, and maybe one or two more. We obviously had to make friends and show that, however strong we were, we were team players. I never felt uncomfortable about it. I did my job, and I learned all I could, and, when my chance came, my teammates, who had seen me working for them, were ready to do the same for me.'

The first stage of his first Tour, in Corsica, was unforgettable: 'I had done the Vuelta a España the year before, but the level in Corsica was incredible. Only the best were there. I never imagined cycling could be so fast and aggressive.'

After the third stage, a team time trial around Nice, he and Valverde trailed Chris Froome by 17 seconds. The deficit was unchanged at the start of stage eight, from Castres to the ski resort at Ax 3 Domaines, via the 2,001-metre Col de Pailhères.

With 36 kilometres remaining of the stage, on the slopes of the Pailhères, Nairo scampered out of the group. He glanced left and right, and quickly saw no one would be going with him. No matter: he climbed alone for seven kilometres and, as he crossed the summit, the highest point of the Tour, he led the stage.

Later, in his autobiography, Froome reflected:

So this was it. This young and very talented Colombian climber had been sent on a mission: go early, make the others chase, make them spend a lot of energy and create the opportunity for your leader, Alejandro Valverde. It felt like a tiny victory for me: Quintana was the unknown, the one who could be the dangerous dark horse. Valverde, I knew. I didn't fear him.

The group containing Froome and Contador passed 1 minute 5 seconds later. On the descent, Nairo's lead was brought back to 40 seconds. On the last climb, with something over five kilometres to go, Porte finally piloted Froome onto Nairo's wheel, shedding Cadel Evans, Andy Schleck, Andrew Talansky and Daniel Martin.

Then Froome attacked, ending the day with a stage win and the yellow jersey. Nairo's self-sacrifice had allowed Valverde to counterattack, take third place in the stage behind Froome and Porte, and move up to third overall behind the same two riders. Nairo was ninth that day, in the same time as Alberto Contador, 1 minute 45 seconds behind Froome.

But that was before the ride to Saint-Amand-Montrond left Nairo as team leader and eighth overall, 5 minutes 18 seconds behind Froome, and 2 minutes 33 seconds from Alberto Contador and the bottom step of the podium. And the next mountain stage took the riders to Mont Ventoux.

On the lower slopes, Froome's teammates moved to the head of the peloton. Behind them massed Omega Pharma-Quick-Step, the team of Michał Kwiatkowski, wearing the white jersey of the best young rider. Kwiatkowski's teammate Gert Steegmans told me, 'At a certain point, Movistar wanted to move into our position behind Team Sky. We said no. Nairo tried to bring me down.'

Steegmans, 23 kilos heavier and 23 centimetres taller, responded by aiming a punch at Nairo. He missed.

'Words were exchanged, and there was some jostling, but we were animals defending our territory,' Steegmans tells me. 'After that they calmed down and sat behind us. Froome laughed about it, but we had made our point: you don't mess with us. Sometimes you need to show shit like that for good position.'

The breakaway riders were caught one by one or in pairs, Fédrigo and Roy with 16.7 kilometres to go, Losada and Impey 1,500 metres higher up, Poels, the climber, after another 200 metres. Of the early breakaway, only Chavanel, trailed by Irizar and Riblon, remained ahead.

Meanwhile, Bakelands and Nieve attacked. They floated in the heat haze ahead of the peloton. Peter Kennaugh and Richie Porte sherpherded the yellow jersey, whose outward-pointing elbows, bowed head, and lowered eyes, the wiping of his brow on his shirt sleeve and the intermittent shaking of the head suggested bad acting rather than genuine discomfort. But you never knew with Froome.

☶

From the dappled penumbra of the canopy, a shadow seems to drift ahead of the group. But the pictures cut away, and for a while the move disappears into a sort of heat haze of unknowing. And then we are looking straight at him. Elbows tucked in, shoulders showing the slightest of pendulum motions, the head, still as a statue, the face, dark skinned and devoid of all expression, boyish and at the same time ageless. Nairo Quintana stands in the pedals and we lose sight of him again. The heat is unforgiving: the bitumen ripples and blisters, and it all takes place as if in a far-off dream.

The longest stage of the 2013 Tour was conceived to test the most robust of hearts. Even before the terminal spike of Mont Ventoux, the profile charted a worrying succession of peaks and troughs. The peloton showed its early defiance by devouring the first hundred kilometres in barely two hours. It is late afternoon now and the stage is five hours old.

For twenty minutes, as the young Colombian continues his attack, Chris Froome, in the yellow jersey of the Tour de France leader, directs his mountain protectors to sustain a pace that places his rivals at the physical limit.

Then, as they flag, he unleashes his own vicious acceleration. Even on his wheel, benefiting from the slight vacuum of his wake, Alberto Contador cannot match him.

Through clouds of red smoke and cheering fans on both sides, the yellow jersey hurtles upward, approaching his next quarry. Nairo slows, perhaps to recover before the coming duel.

Froome rushes past and gains five metres, but Quintana rides back up to him. Moments of fraught truce follow, interpersed with abrupt changes of rhythm by Froome, to each of which Nairo responds until, one and a half kilometres from the finish line, the Briton, out of the saddle and riding at the front, forces the pace once more.

For two hundred metres Nairo shadows him. But then he reaches a threshold or limit and relents, and another race starts. With nine wins in sixteen months, he has made a promising start to his career as a professional cyclist. But success or failure is achieved at the Tour de France. So, over the next kilometre, against every bodily impulse, Nairo tunnels deep into the pain.

On the final right-hand corner, he hauls himself out of the saddle and musters fifteen more seconds of discomfort, his face crumpled into a silent moan, each turn of the pedals an act of self-harm.

Beyond the finish line, he coasts down the slight descent with enough awareness to locate his soigneur, who helps him fall as Nairo surrenders to unconsciousness.

Not a victory, then, but a victory of sorts: Nairo *agonistes*, in all his remarkable strength and fragility.

◈

The mountain stages of the final week saw Nairo climb the General Classification as others faded. The final mountain stage fell on 20 July, Colombian Independence Day, five years to the day after Nairo had asked Jenaro Leguízamo to watch him race.

Nairo started the day third in the overall standings, still 5 minutes 32 seconds behind Froome, but just 21 seconds behind second-placed Alberto Contador. On the concluding climb of the Tour, the Semnoz, towering over Annecy, the collective work of Froome's teammates, followed by stinging attacks by Joaquím Rodríguez and Froome himself, left Contador lagging behind. Just outside the final kilometre, in a bid to win the stage, the Briton established a small lead. Nairo eased onto his wheel, then drifted past and sped away into the light.

Second overall in his first Tour de France, with a stage win, the white jersey of best young rider and the red polka dot jersey of the king of the mountains, Nairo had given Colombia a Grand Tour winner in waiting.

卅

It was raining hard when Nairo landed in Bogotá. Movistar Colombia had contracted a double-decker for a celebratory tour, protected by two thousand police officers.

'It wasn't nearly enough,' Karina Vélez, head of communication at Movistar Colombia, recalls. 'We thought there might be crowds, but we had no idea what awaited us. At the airport, we took Nairo to a secondary exit and forced a corridor through the crowds. He went upstairs and joined his parents and his wife Paula.

'We intended the itinerary to take three hours. It took six. When we went under bridges, the crowds threw rose petals. In Seventh Avenue the office workers threw ticker tape. In the Candelaria, close to Plaza de Bolívar, they threw roses from the balconies. Kids lifted their bikes up for Nairo to sign.'

At the Palacio de Nariño President Santos met him as he had in 2010. This time, Nairo was a national hero, and Santos duly awarded him the Cross of Boyacá, the highest honour the president can confer.

It was a moment of celebration for a nation in turmoil. In January the government had promised help to a far-off area near the Venezuelan border known as Catatumbo, notorious for paramilitary violence, coca plantations and smuggling.

The population demanded roads, schools, hospitals,

electrification, drinking water, social programmes, and the legalisation of four thousand homesteads and 250,000 hectares of land. The government had promised 1.7 billion pesos in funding. It had spent large sums on preliminary studies, but by June Catatumbo had seen no progress beyond crop eradication that left former coca farmers with no income.

Nairo had been training in Boyacá on 11 June when 17,000 Catatumbo peasants took to the streets. For fifty-three days, the region was paralysed.

The coffee sector was already in crisis. It cost farmers 650,000 to 700,000 Colombian pesos to produce a 125kg load of dry parchment coffee. On Friday 22 February, the market price had plummeted to 511,300 pesos. Even taking into account the state subsidy of 60,000 pesos per load, the coffee growers were working at a loss.

The following Monday 130,000 farmers in the coffee-growing departments staged mass demonstrations. On 4 March more than 40,000 protesters had brought road transport to a standstill all over the country. Service stations and markets, even in large towns, were left without fuel and food.

President Santos agreed to a substantial increase in subsidies and the protests ceased, only to resume in July. The coffee farmers claimed that fewer than half of the increased payments had been made, while the issue of soaring fertiliser costs, and of mining concessions that were destroying coffee plantations, had not even been addressed. Mobile phone footage showed riot squad officers unleashing violence on pregnant women, children and the elderly.

Cacao production, affected by disease but also by black market competition and cheap imports, was down by between 40 and 50 per cent. Rice yields were down by 35 per cent, again due in part to blight. Potato growers had worked hard to increase their yields, yet they too were selling at less than cost price, so, in August, on Nairo's return to Colombia, dairy and cacao farmers joined potato, maize, panela, fruit and rice producers in the protests.

Nairo, suddenly a national figure, had personal experience of rural hardship, and counted friends and neighbours among the protesters. At the same time, his brother Alfredo was in the military and Dayer was a policeman.

He told me, 'The peasant farmers supported me because I am a *campesino* too. I had been in their shoes. They opened the barricades to let me train. I was the only one they let pass.'

To thank them, he spoke out to the news media, condemning the use of violence by the authorities while asking the protesters to respect the police and urging the president to seek a 'dignified' agreement with the peasants.

'Many years ago my family lost land because we were growing potatoes at a loss,' he told the national newspaper *El Espectador*. 'It is very distressing to go to market and find that the sale price of a sack of potatoes does not even cover the transport.'

The crisis had deep roots. Under Uribe and Santos, Colombia figured in a group of emerging markets called the CIVETS, which included Indonesia, Vietnam, Egypt, Turkey and South Africa: all diverse, dynamic economies with young, growing populations. The economy, taken to be a thing in itself, flourished. Free Trade Agreements were the chosen way forward. Uribe had negotiated treaties with forty-five countries, including the USA, the European Union, Canada, Mercosur – the South American trade block, with Brazil as its major partner – and Switzerland, and started talks with Korea. The idea was that, like cycling, free trade would lead to integration into the wider world, and integration would guarantee future security. It seemed a perfect circle. Yet a long series of reports had forecast the subsequent slump in national food production and peasant income in the event of a Free Trade Agreement with the United States. With no lasting solution to be found, the protests recurred in 2014, and continued to resurface.

Concluding its interview with Nairo, *El Espectador* noted: 'Quintana is currently at home in Cómbita, where he is preparing for next month's World Cycling Championships in Florence.' But, on 29 September 2013, Nairo abandoned the World Championships road race early. His teammate Rigoberto Urán was far more competitive. Perfectly positioned on the descent from San Baronto with 9.2 kilometres to go, he was third in a line of five riders, just behind Vincenzo Nibali and Purito Rodríguez, with Rui Costa and Alejandro Valverde on his wheel. Swinging around a right-hand bend, on wet roads, he went too wide. He unclipped his left foot for balance, but it was too late. Suddenly, his bike flew into the air, and his bid to become Colombia's first world champion, like his bid to become its first Olympic champion thirteen months earlier, ended in defeat. The four riders either side of him – Costa, Rodríguez, Valverde and Nibali – ended the race first, second, third and fourth.

Meanwhile, Juan Chamorro had won the 2013 Ronde de l'Isard, and started the 2013 Tour de l'Avenir as favourite. On stage two, he fell badly, injuring a knee. He soldiered on for three stages, abandoning on the Col du Glandon on stage five, then spent months seeing specialists for knee pain. He returned to training, but the pain never subsided. Luís Fernando Saldarriaga invited him to join Manzana Postobón in 2015, but Juan Chamorro never recovered, and retired in 2016.

Saldarriaga says of him, 'He was a great rider: a fabulous climber, and an intuitive strategist – the champion Colombia would never have.'

12

Rules of Engagement

On 17 April 2014 Gabriel García Márquez passed away in Mexico City. The author of *One Hundred Years of Solitude* and *Love in the Time of Cholera*, among other masterpieces of a genre which came to be known as magic realism but was really just a concentration of all things Colombian, died aged eighty-seven. True, he had lived abroad since the 1960s, and Alzheimer's Disease had ravaged his extraordinary mind, but when President Santos called him 'the greatest Colombian who ever lived', no one disagreed. His death removed a unifying figure in a polarised nation.

Fourteen Colombian cyclists carried their nation's mourning to the Giro in May, and brought their country its greatest-ever stage race performance, even if fans were torn between Nairo Quintana and Rigoberto Urán. The country was divided at home too.

With Ecuador to the south and Venezuela to the east, Colombia was hemmed in by leftist regimes indulgent towards the FARC. Presidents Hugo Chávez and, after his death in 2013, Nicolás Maduro had managed to bring oil-rich Venezuela to its knees, but they remained potential FARC allies and rarely let an opportunity pass to add to Colombia's woes. When former president Uribe became a senator in March 2014, he began his first speech: 'We are here to confront the risk of *Castro-Chavismo*.'

As a teenager, Nairo Quintana kept his distance from the established teams, often riding single races for the highest bidder. As a result, there are photographs of him in many different team jerseys. (Rusbal Achagua)

Team director Luís Fernando Saldarriaga (left), general manager Luisa Fernanda Ríos (left front, dark glasses) and chairman Ignacio Vélez (centre, in the cap, beside Nairo), with their all-conquering 2010 Tour de l'Avenir team: (left to right) Darwin Atapuma, Esteban Chaves, Camilo Suárez, Jarlinson Pantano, Sebastián Salazar, and, in yellow, Nairo Quintana. (Gilberto Chocce)

Coach and team director Luís Fernando Saldarriaga with his protégé Esteban Chaves, the winner of the 2011 Tour de l'Avenir. (Gilberto Chocce)

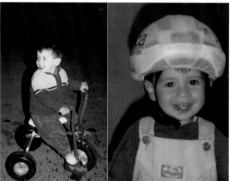

Son of passionate cycling fans, Esteban Chaves was riding – and flashing his infectious smile – from an early age. (Chaves family)

The best young climber in Colombia in his age group, Darwin Atapuma won the 2006 Vuelta del Porvenir in his hometown of Túquerres. (Atapuma family)

In stage 7 of the 2007 Tour of Switzerland, Rigoberto Urán took his first victory at the sport's highest level. He was still only twenty. (Getty Images)

Like many Colombian cyclists, Winner Anacona is from a military family. His father Rodrigo was a policeman trained in counter-subversion. But Rodrigo loved cycling and passed on his passion to his son. (Anacona family)

11 November 2011. Miguel Ángel López milks Rafael Acevedo's cow. Later that afternoon, he would fight off bicycle thieves. A Sogamoso radio reporter, John Henry Sarmiento, dubbed him Superman. The nickname stuck. (Rafael Acevedo)

In 2015 Richard Carapaz became the first non-Colombian to win the Vuelta de la Juventud or Under-23 Tour of Colombia, with stage victories at Riosucio and Concordia (shown here). (Movistar Colombia)

Wall-to-wall Colombians and an Ecuadorean: Daniel Martínez (pink helmet), Miguel Ángel López (light blue), Winner, Richard and Nairo with Egan Bernal visible between Richard and Nairo, Sebastián Molano over Nairo's shoulder (white and red helmet), Dayer Quintana behind Nairo, and Jhojan García (pink jersey) behind Dayer. (Bettiniphoto)

Richard Carapez is proudly indigenous through his father Antonio (*above*), and Afro-descendant through his mother, Ana Luisa (*left*). (Movistar Colombia/Fabio Cuttica)

Another brilliant youngster, Daniel Martínez, leads Miguel Angel Lopez on the Col de Turini in stage 7 of the 2019 Paris–Nice. (Bettiniphoto)

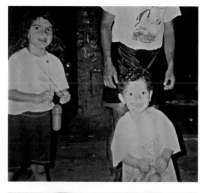

As a six-year-old, Fernando Gaviria followed his older sister Juliana into in-line skating. Aged twelve, he followed her into cycling. (Gaviria family) In 2018 Fernando became only the second Colombian (after Víctor Hugo Peña in 2003) to wear the yellow jersey. (Getty Images)

Pablo Mazuera in 2011, on his first day training with Egan Bernal, and in 2014, with his Junior World and Olumpic medallists Egan and Brandon Rivera. (Pablo Mazuera)

Egan's first trip to the beach, with his then agent Paolo Alberati, September 2015. (Paolo Alberati)

Ivan Ramiro Sosa joined Egan Bernal at Androni Giocattoli in 2017. Seen here at that year's Tour de Langkawi, their formidable double act promises to be a feature of WorldTour cycling for the coming decade. (Bettiniphoto)

Too often, sport is a vector for a mindless variety of cultural uniformity. Riders with indigenous backgrounds – Carapaz, Atapuma and, of course, Nairo, seen here visiting a Wayuu indigenous village in 2016 – use sport to strengthen the resilience of their community. (Libardo Leyton)

A member of the Misak indigenous people from the Guambía reservation near Silvia in the Colombian south, Jimy Esteven Morales Hurtado, seen with his family, rode for Jarlinson Pantano's foundation, then moved to Catalunya for Juniors and Under-23. (Morales family)

A wonderful year for Colombian cycling culminated on 4 December 2019 when Luís Fernando Saldarriaga (*second left*) received the Simón Bolívar medal for services to his country. With his parents Amparo and Fernando, who run the remarkable Nueva Generación cycling club, and (*far right*) Sports Minister Ernesto Lucena Barrero. (Matt Rendell)

The term, coined by the Venezuelan opposition, played to fears widespread in Colombia. Goaded by false reports on social media, some even came to believe that the leader of the blood-thirsty paramilitaries, Carlos Castaño, had been acting under President Uribe's direct command, or that President Santos was actually a guerrilla infiltrator known as 'Alias Santiago'.

卌

On 22 May Rigoberto won the rolling individual time trial from Bardonecchia to Barolo and became the first Colombian to wear the Giro leader's *Maglia Rosa*, or pink jersey. Nairo ended the stage in sixth place overall, a second shy of three and a half minutes off his compatriot's pace. He had been suffering flu and an ear infection although, over the penultimate weekend of the Giro, he showed signs of recovery. In stage fourteen to Oropa, he regained 25 seconds on Urán. The following day, at Montecampione, he clawed back 20 more. Even so, he started stage sixteen, from Ponte de Legno at the foot of the monumental Gavia Pass, to Val Martello in the Stelvio National Park, a distant fifth, 2 minutes 40 seconds back.

It was the stage Nairo had been waiting for: short at 139 kilometres, forbiddingly mountainous, and coming on the back of a rest day so cold and wet that many riders didn't go out. Nairo had spent much of the day in bed, recovering from his illness and a knock on the hip sustained the previous week.

A stage over the same route – north to the Gavia pass, eastwards and upwards to the towering Stelvio, 2,758 metres above sea level, before completing the horseshoe on a final, 22.35-kilometre climb up to the high-altitude valley of Val Martello or Martelltal – had been cancelled the previous year due to the cold. This time around it was again cold and wet at the stage start, and there was some uncertainty whether it would be able to go ahead as planned.

Nairo told his teammates, 'As far as I'm concerned, it's on,

I'm riding, and you are too. This is the day we win the Giro d'Italia. This is our stage.'

On the Gavia, three Colombians attacked: Chalapud, Pantano and Arredondo. Behind them, Nairo's teammates set the pace.

Seven kilometres before the top, Urán's teammates Thomas de Gendt and Serge Pauwels lost ground. His team was already crumbling.

At approximately 15.15, with the Maglia Rosa group six kilometres from the top of the Stelvio, race radio crackled into life. The top of the pass was smothered in thick, freezing fog, so race organisation motorbikes would signal the positions of the first six hairpins using red flags. While the red flags were out, there was to be no overtaking. The Italian message made no reference to neutralising the race; the English and French translations may have done, although no recording exists. The race Twitter feed certainly did, but it was not an official channel of information.

Snow began to fall on the riders 3.3 kilometres from the top. The cold became intense. As the peloton closed on the leaders, Team Sky's Dario Cataldo attacked out of the lead group. Arrieta had positioned his support staff a kilometre and a half before the pass, to equip his riders with warm clothing. Gorka Izagirre was charged with ensuring that Nairo was well fed and properly dressed for the descent.

At the summit, with 68.7 kilometres to go to the stage finish, Cataldo took the mountains points and pressed on. The French rider Alexandre Geniez stopped on the pass to don a thick winter jacket. The AG2R riders Alexis Vuillermoz and Hubert Dupont chased Cataldo, positioning themselves to help their teammate Domenico Pozzovivo, just two seconds behind Nairo in the General Classification, in the valley below, while Pantano caught Vuillermoz and Dupont on the descent and they rode on together.

The French climber Pierre Rolland, who had started the day eighth overall, four places and 2 minutes 27 seconds behind

Nairo, was ninth across, and plunged into the descent. Far ahead of him, Cataldo was sprinting out of each hairpin. For minutes there were no race pictures.

As Arrieta tells it, 'Gorka Izagirre stopped on the mountain to don warm clothing. He set off behind the group and described over the radio what he saw as he descended.

'"I've just passed so-and-so, he was frozen. I've just passed so-and-so, he was wrecked."

'"And where's Nairo?"

'"Up ahead."

'I told him, "You pull across the valley, and Nairo will do the climb alone."'

Halfway down the climb Gorka reached Nairo and told him, 'Let's go. They are all done for.'

The TV helicopters hovered beneath the clouds, waiting. Ten kilometres into the descent, a group appeared, seven riders strong. Nairo was there, with two teammates, Izagirre and Andrey Amador. There were no motorbikes and no red flags. If there was any kind of neutralisation, it was clearly over.

The helicopter camera pans upwards. The race leader, Rigoberto Urán – you can tell by his pink handlebar tape – is two hairpins, or just 45 seconds, behind. There are 57.5 kilometres left in the stage.

At 15.58, when the stage leader, Cataldo, has been descending for about 12 kilometres, the race Twitter feed issues a correction:

Comunicazione sbagliata: nessuna neutralizzazione della discesa dallo Stelvio. Scusateci per l'informazione sbagliata. Grazie. #giro 15:58 – 27 mag 2014
Mistaken communication: no neutralisation on the descent from the Stelvio. Excuse the erroneous information. Thank you. #giro 15:58 – 27 May 2014

Amador has been dropped on the descent. At its foot, with 44 kilometres remaining, Nairo and Gorka Izagirre forge ahead with the 2012 Giro winner Ryder Hesjedal – eleventh overall at 6 minutes 44 – the French Europcar teammates Pierre Rolland and Romain Sicard, and Matteo Rabottini, King of the Mountains two years ago.

With 40.5 kilometres still to go, Cataldo leads Vuillermoz, Dupont and Pantano by 44 seconds, with Nairo's six-man group 1 minute 21 seconds further back. The crucial gap, between Nairo and the Maglia Rosa, is exactly two minutes: Urán still leads overall by 40 seconds. Seven kilometres later, despite the work of the two domestiques, Izagirre and Sicard, the gap has come down to 1 minute 50. When Nairo's group catches Vuillermoz, Dupont and Pantano, there are 25 kilometres left in the stage. Sicard, spent, peels off. Izagirre takes over at the front for five more kilometres.

The final climb begins with 22.35 kilometres to go, at a shallow gradient of 3.4 per cent. With 21.8 kilometres to the finish, at the foot of the final climb, the gap is 1 minute 42.

With 20 kilometres to go, Gorka Izagirre has given all he can. Leaving him on the road, Pantano takes over at the front, riding for his old teammate. Meanwhile, at the front of the Maglia Rosa group, Urán has no more helpers, and Aru's domestique Mikel Landa is driving the pace.

Nairo moves to the front of his group with 18.9 kilometres left to ride. Apart from two brief intermissions, he will ride the rest of the stage at the front, knowing that his breakaway companions, smelling a stage win, will not cooperate. Expressionless, absorbed in his task, he advances as if alone. Cataldo is caught with 17 kilometres left in the stage.

With 13.7 kilometres to go, Nairo's lead over the Maglia Rosa is down to 1 minute 33 seconds. Urán is in a large chasing group that includes Pozzovivo and his colleagues Dupont and Vuillermoz, who are working at the head of the group. He still has 67 seconds of his race lead intact.

From that point on, Nairo gains around 10 seconds per kilometre on the Maglia Rosa group.

12km to go: 1m 53s.

11km: 2m 03s.

10km: 2m 16s.

9km: 2m 26s.

8km: 2m 35s.

Rigo moves to the front of his group, with Kelderman on his wheel.

7km: 2m 37s (although the switchbacks may have confused the automatic timing system).

6km: 3m 10s. For the first time, Nairo leads the race overall.

5.3km: on a steep, left-hand hairpin, Rolland, no longer able to follow Nairo's speed, loses contact.

5km: 3m 19s.

4.3km to go: on a flat section by a lake, for the first time, Hesjedal comes through and Nairo sits on his wheel.

4km: 2m 56s (again, the automatic timing system may not be working well at this point).

3km: 3m 15s.

2km: 3m 16s.

1km: 3m 18s.

On the hardest section of the climb, with the gradient at 11.2 per cent, Nairo stands on the pedals and rides away from Hesjedal. Head down, he sprints for the finish line.

Hesjedal finishes eight seconds after Nairo. Rolland crosses the line more than a minute later.

Then, for two minutes, nothing.

Then Kelderman, and Pozzovivo, and Aru.

Then, for half a minute, nothing.

Then Rafał Majka and, a couple of places behind him, Rigoberto Urán. He crosses the finish line 4 minutes 11 seconds after Nairo. The Maglia Rosa has lost 3 minutes 4 seconds in the final 13.7 kilometres of the stage, including 53 seconds in the final kilometre alone.

Adding the ten bonus seconds awarded to the stage winner, Nairo now led the race by 1 minute 41 seconds. Yet his brilliant ride was overshadowed and, by some, disparaged because of the neutralisation controversy.

After the stage, Arrieta went straight to the president of the commissaires: 'What did you say up there? You didn't say anything about neutralising the race. You said there were motorbikes, right? My riders didn't overtake a single motorbike.'

The following day, a delegation from the International Association of Professional Cycling Teams (AIGCP) met the race organisers and the commissaires to demand that Nairo's advantage be shortened by the time he gained on the descent from the Stelvio. The UCI rejected their request, observing, in a press release, that the race organisers' intent in positioning motorbikes ahead of each group on the descent was self-evidently to guarantee the riders' safety. 'The decision,' they said, 'should have been approved by the commissaires and communicated more efficiently to the teams,' but the results would stand. Talk of a boycott fizzled out: the AIGCP issued a press release to say, 'Out of respect for the fans and the world of cycling, the teams have decided to participate in today's stage.'

Nairo's comment was simple: 'The organisation said that the race was not neutralised. There were riders ahead of me and no one slowed down.'

His detractors, he said, were 'staging a story that isn't real'.

Arrieta wrings his hands and says, 'It angers me that people have tried to discredit what Nairo achieved.'

Stage nineteen, the uphill time trial from Bassano del Grappa to the Military Memorial on the summit of Monte Grappa, went to Nairo, who added 1 minute 26 seconds to his lead over Rigoberto. On 1 June 2014 Nairo became the first Colombian since Lucho Herrera to win a three-week tour, and the first to win the Giro d'Italia. Rigoberto Urán ensured that Colombian riders stood on the two highest steps on the final podium. Between them, Nairo, Rigo and Julián Arredondo had taken four stage wins. Fabio Duarte had finished second in two stages, with Jarlinson Pantano third in one.

The most Colombian of all Grand Tours provided some distraction for a nation mourning Gabo's loss, and torn between Santos and Uribe. And although some were discontented with the race organisation, Rigoberto Urán was, as always, graceful in defeat.

In the valley before the final climb to Val Martello, Rigoberto had been part of a chasing group containing Cadel Evans, Rafał Majka, Fabio Aru, Domenico Pozzovivo, Wilko Kelderman and Robert Kišerlovski, the second, third, fourth, sixth, seventh and ninth riders overall. Also there was Sergio Luís Henao's twenty-year-old cousin Sebastián: the ailing Urán rode much of the climb on his wheel. They finished the stage together, Henao eighth, Urán ninth.

Before stage nineteen's mountain time trial, Sebastián Henao lay twenty-fourth overall: 'That morning I said to my room-mate, Dario Cataldo, "I don't know how I'm going to ride today. Everything hurts." But, warming up on the rollers, I began to feel better. I started the stage on my time trial bike and changed to my road bike at the foot of the climb, but I didn't ride at top speed. I passed *País* [Jarlinson Pantano], Duarte and others, and over the radio my team car said I was on my way to a good time. Cataldo had the best split time but, over the radio, they told me I was beating it. I thought they had it wrong until I heard the helicopter overhead. When I finished, they took me to the hot seat.'

His lead lasted just eight minutes, but that time allowed a glimpse of a new generation of Colombian riders, even if

Sebastián Henao's childhood at the family finca near Rionegro was a traditional one:

> When I was nine or ten, I had school in the afternoon, so I used to get up at five, fix a spotlight on my hat and, rain or shine, go out and pick strawberries for four hours. My uncle Fernando used to rotate crops so that, when one was ready to pick, the next one was just beginning to come through.
>
> We had five or six hundred kilos of strawberries to pick and pack according to size: large, medium or small. We had to carry forty or fifty eleven-kilo boxes a day, two hundred metres to the truck, three at a time like this [he mimes carrying two on a shoulder and one in his hands].
>
> For four years I did it, earning four thousand pesos a day, or one and a half Euros. It paid my school expenses, and I enjoyed it. Sometimes I said to my uncle, 'Save up my money for a fortnight or a month and then pay me.'

It was not his cousin Sergio Luís Henao who inspired Sebastián Henao to start cycling, but Colombia's most successful Olympian, the BMX rider Mariana Pajón. The winner of three elite World Championship titles as well as two Olympic gold medals, Mariana Pajón Londoño, born in Medellín on 10 October 1991, achieved her first national title aged five, and her first world title at nine.

Sebastián recalls, 'I liked BMX, and I used to ride the nine kilometres to school on a BMX bike with a small ring. Mariana was already world champion. I was always doing wheelies and jumps with my cousin Julián, who was a year older than me. One day I tried to jump a creek, fell and damaged my knee. After that I lost my nerve.'

Sebastián's cousin, Julián Marín Henao, would finish second in Colombia's Under-23 national road race championships in 2013.

The whole family used to go and watch Sergio race, so one Sunday morning I took the bike Sergio had started on, and went out with Julián and another of my uncles, Uncle Wber. We rode two climbs, called the Hippodrome and Santa Elena. They rode hard and dropped me, but two weeks later, I went out training with Sergio, who was recovering from an injury. He encouraged me, and my uncles held a collection and bought me my first bike. In 2007 I joined the CICO Rionegro cycling club.

I was third in my first race, aged thirteen or fourteen, and I won my first hill climb. The Antioquia regional team took me to the national championships, which made me unofficially part of the Orgullo Paisa set-up.

We used to go out training at seven each morning. I had to study, so I could only train for two and a half or three hours. Then I would ride to school, study and ride home again. There were times when I was tired and sleepy in class, but that was how I passed that first year.

In 2009 Orgullo Paisa took him to his first national event, the Vuelta del Futuro for fifteen- and sixteen-year-olds. He was sixteenth. A year later, he won the mountains competition and finished fifth at the Vuelta del Porvenir for seventeen- and eighteen-year-olds. He took the mountains competition again the following year, and won the individual time trial on the way to second place in the 2011 Vuelta del Porvenir, before moving up to Under-23 level.

There he met Daniel Jaramillo, Rigoberto Urán's former colleague at the Centre for Sports Development (CEDEP), in Jardín: 'We shared everything: team, races, room. He had won the Vuelta de la Juventud in 2011, so he was team leader again in 2012, but he wasn't at his best, and I was the highest finisher, third overall.'

Still in his first year as an Under-23 rider, Sebastián was

selected for shorter stage races with elite riders: 'At the Clásica Girardot I was fourth against some of the country's top riders, and I was runner-up at the Clásica de Marinilla.'

In 2013 he joined Coldeportes-Claro, the domestic counterpart of the Colombia-Coldeportes team: 'They put it like this: "If you ride well for us this year, we'll send you to the team in Europe." So, obviously, you say, "I'm going there."'

Sebastián's father Alcides Henao had given up small farming and was driving a municipal bus in Rionegro: 'It meant long, stressful days so, when I moved to Coldeportes-Claro and started earning a little more, I told my father I'd put a bit more money into the house so that he could stop working. These days, he produces avocados – and rides his bike.'

At Coldeportes-Claro Sebastián joined Jaramillo and their former rivals Fernando Gaviria, Jhonatan Restrepo, Sebastián Molano and Felipe Laverde, nephew of Rigoberto's early coaches JL and Benjamín Laverde: 'It was a very strong team. In September we went back to the Vuelta de la Juventud, and I finished third again, with Daniel Jaramillo second this time. Then they took me to the 2013 Vuelta a Colombia.'

In a peloton studded with the best national riders and a number of former Tour de France riders, it would have been a forbidding challenge for most nineteen-year-olds: 'I had to draw on all my courage because at times I was yo-yoing off the back of the leaders.'

But he ended the race fifteenth overall, the winner of the Under-23 category. Selected for the 2013 World Championships in Florence, he finished in a group of seventeen riders thirteen seconds behind the winner, Slovenia's Matej Mohorič.

Team Sky had been monitoring Henao and Jaramillo since April. In 2012 Jaramillo had been invited to join a biological passport programme as a precondition for selection to the Tour de l'Avenir, but he had opted out. In 2013 he was close to signing for Orica-GreenEdge, but the move was never finalised.

In Florence, Sebastián met the riders' agent Giusappe Acquadro, who already represented his cousin Sergio Luís. After the championships, Acquadro took Sebastián Henao to Team Sky's house in Nice for three days of tests and examinations. They were sufficiently impressed to invite him to join the team. In December he travelled to Mallorca for his first training camp: 'I couldn't believe it. I was twenty, I was the youngest rider in the team, surrounded by riders who were at the top of the sport. I was, "What am I doing here? Maybe they have got the wrong guy."'

In Europe, Sebastián fielded questions from fellow riders who wanted to know all about Pablo Escobar: 'I didn't know anything about him. I was born the year they killed him, so I watched [the Netflix series] *Narcos* to find out what had happened.'

Sebastián's memories of the violence only emphasise the distance Colombia has travelled: 'When I was at primary school, which was in a house on the finca, I remember seeing helicopters, and hearing them shooting, *pa-pa-pa*, at whoever they were fighting. I could see the helicopter leaning in order to fire. But I was a child, wondering, "What are they doing over there? What game are they playing?"'

'And when we were on the finca, there were cars that passed at high speed' – it is the same memory that Sergio Luís mentioned – 'and then, fifteen minutes later, they came back, and then the news would filter through that they had left someone dead down there.'

But whereas his cousin, five and a half years older, lay in bed afraid, Sebastián was too young to understand: 'I was just a boy and all I cared about was playing.'

13

The Agricultural Ambassador

Nairo sat out the 2014 Tour de France, and started the Vuelta as favourite. Winner Anacona won stage nine, at the ski station of Valdelinares in Aragón, and Nairo took the race lead. The following day, at high speed just before a tight, right-hand bend on the descent from the category three Alto del Moncayo, twenty minutes into the time trial, he reached down to tighten his shoe straps, drifted wide – and crashed. Minutes later, he emerged from a scrum of team staff, doctors, race officials and photographers, and rejoined the race. But the Vuelta was lost. Nairo took the start the following morning but, after 20 kilometres, he came down in another crash and abandoned the race.

At hospital in Pamplona, a fracture was detected to a small hook-like bone called the coracoid process, an attachment for a number of important muscles on the left shoulder blade. Two screws were inserted, and Nairo was released.

◈

Six weeks later he appeared on *Pregunta Yamid* – 'Yamid asks the questions' – an influential talk show hosted by Yamid Amat, a prominent political interviewer. After discussing Nairo's brilliant season, Amat moved the discussion on to more controversial areas.

Amat: There is no leadership in Colombian cycling, is there?

Quintana: It hurts me to say so, and I don't want to get into trouble saying this, but the truth is, there is still a lot to be desired. [. . .]

Amat: What is to be done, in your view? Change the current leaders? [. . .]

Quintana: I don't have all the answers. The only thing we know is that it's very bad. It's not how it seems from the outside. Something has to be done.

Amat: Are the cyclists happy with the leadership that Colombian cycling has, and with the way the state treats cycling, or do you think it is time for radical change?

Quintana: Yes, I think there should be radical change in Colombian cycling. We should sit down and cold-bloodedly look at what we have and where it has come from, and at the leadership we have, and what we could have.

The following day, to clear the air, Nairo's manager Libardo Leyton went with him to Coldeportes, the Olympic Committee and the Cycling Federation. Their conversation was cordial, but when the federation president sought to take credit for the country's recent success, Nairo cut him short: it was clear to him that much of that success had been achieved not thanks to the federation but despite it. From then on, it was clear that Nairo would not remain silent over the federation's deficiencies. He became the de facto leader of a movement to reform the institutions of Colombian cycling.

Since the Pastrana years, much of the Colombian state had been revolutionised by honest, efficient technocrats, but there remained vast areas that existed as modern feudal fiefdoms run as sinecures by more or less absent landlords. The Colombian Cycling Federation was one: it had allowed the domestic sport to be corrupted to the core.

On Saturday 7 March 2012, at Barajas airport in Madrid, Spanish police approached Dr Alberto Beltrán Niño, a medical practitioner well known in Colombian cycling circles, who was waiting for a flight home to join his team, EPM-Une. They asked to open his hand luggage, knowing that inside they would find banned performance-enhancing drugs known as AICAR and TB-500.

'They are for horses,' he explained. 'I am a veterinary surgeon.'

They responded, 'We know.'

At the same moment, ten other sports scientists, coaches and dealers in banned substances were being arrested across Spain. Later, police described the group as 'the most important distribution network for next-generation doping products', adding, 'The Colombian is the boss.'

Highly regarded by the private patients at his clinic in well-to-do north Bogotá, Beltrán was described in the Colombian press as a graduate of the city's Universidad Javeriana who had studied sports medicine at the Hôpital Cochin in Paris. He was a member of the Colombian Olympic Committee's Medical Commission, and he had been the team doctor with Café de Colombia and the national team when the UCI World Championships were held at Duitama in 1995. He had worked with various manifestations of the Colombia-backed cycling team co-sponsored by the saddle manufacturer Selle Italia, although the Colombian press was more reticent about Beltrán's association with Colombia's most successful domestic team, variously Orbitel-EPM, Une-Orbitel, Une-EPM and EPM-Une. He also worked privately with a number of Colombian cyclists who raced in Europe, to whom he provided off-season dry-out treatments after months of heavy EPO use.

It was not the first time he had been arrested. On 22 March 2001, near Modena, Italy, two journalists out for a ride had passed a team car belonging to Selle Italia and witnessed Beltrán receiving a suspect package. They had called a police contact working on anti-doping, and, minutes later, police had stopped the car and found it packed with steroids. Beltrán's arrest ended the careers of a number of riders, although for him it meant no more than momentary inconvenience. In 2004 he was back, treating a series of small Spanish teams: first Baqué, then Kaiku, where one of his riders, Ricardo Serrano, was briefly suspended in 2006 with suspect blood values. Over the same period he was also working for the elite-level Phonak team.

By 2009, alongside his EPM-Une activities, Beltrán was working for the Portuguese team Liberty Seguros Continental. Soon after the Tour of Portugal, three of his riders tested positive for CERA, the latest version of EPO. One of them, the race winner Nuno Ribeiro, told the newspaper *O Jogo*, 'I took what the team doctor [Alberto Beltrán] told me to. Until I received the test result, I thought they were recovery products.'

Ribeiro's confession came in October 2009, but by then Beltrán had moved on. In the middle of the Vuelta a España, Álvaro Pino, formerly at Kelme and Phonak, now at Xacobeo-Galicia, had dismissed the team doctor, Xoan Manuel Rodríguez Bastida, and Beltrán had stepped in. The team ended the race with a stage win, fifth place overall and victory in the team competition. The sacked doctor claimed that he had been removed because he refused to dope the riders.

At the end of 2009, Beltrán had emigrated to Bahrain, although he continued to work with Xacobeo-Galicia. During the 2010 Vuelta a España, the Xacobeo-Galicia rider David García, who went on to finish eleventh overall, returned positive results for a form of EPO called Retacrit and another prohibited substance, a blood plasma volume expander called Hydroxyethyl Starch (HES), thought to disguise the increase in red blood cells that occurs with EPO use. Another rider on the team, Ezequiel Mosquera, finished runner-up in the same Vuelta before he too tested positive for HES.

García cooperated with investigators and named his supplier: Beltrán. The police began monitoring the doctor. The checks became more rigorous before the 2012 Olympics, with the Gulf

States said to be obsessed with winning medals. Illegal products arrived in amounts the police called 'alarming'.

At the time of his detention, Beltrán was being considered for the position of head of anti-doping at the Colombian sports ministry, Coldeportes. His appointment would surely have led to the creation of a full-scale national doping system.

During Beltrán's detention in 2012, the products he had been touting quickly found other conduits to Colombia. Marlon Pérez, then riding for the team Colombia-Claro, tested positive for an experimental compound called GW501516. In public he denied ever having used illegal substances, but later on he privately confessed to the UCI's Anti-Doping Commission that he had obtained the substance, in the form of an orange spray, from his team. He had been told it was a legal fat burner.

The authorities had been aware of these experimental substances for some time. In 2010 the Doping Control Laboratory at Cologne in Germany had obtained AICAR, GW501516 and another product labelled MK-2866 from Internet suppliers. The packaging identified them as amino acids and green tea extract. Tests showed that the active ingredients were genuine, although the products contained considerably smaller amounts than suggested on the label. GW501516 was an orange-yellow suspension in water and glycerol, just as Pérez described it.

In October 2012, bereft of their long-time team doctor, the EPM-Une team signed up the Spanish rider Óscar Sevilla. Already thirty-six, Sevilla had recently completed a six-month suspension for HES, having tested positive during the 2010 Vuelta a Colombia, won by his teammate Sergio Luís Henao. Whether or not Henao won the race clean is one of the open questions of Colombian sport. When I put this to him, Henao simply said that his doubters find him guilty by association.

In 2013 a number of Colombian national riders told me that the domestic peloton was divided into those using AICAR and those not using it. The suppliers, riders who had formerly ridden in Europe, charged their teammates twice: a fee for the products and a percentage of their salaries. The substance, I was told, cost a million Colombian pesos (US$500) per dose: the majority of riders were earning the minimum wage of US$140 per month. Being competitive in this poorest, most humble of sports, was becoming extremely costly.

In 2013 the federation's president Ramiro Valencia Cossio seemed to repudiate any sort of defence of clean cyclists by the federation: 'When they talk to me about doping, I tell them I have to start from the basis that the control of doping and illegal drugs is not my goal. It is absolutely not the objective of the federation. Why is it not a goal? Because we make an assumption of propriety. I cannot conceive of practising a sport while doped. So if that's the base level, knowing it's free of drugs, and of course you have to fight against those things, the objective is the cyclist as a human being.'

Whatever he really meant, if anything, his words must have given reassurance to those using illegal products and practices.

The most influential voice in the Colombian media was Hector Urrego of RCN Radio and the magazine *Mundo Ciclístico*. Urrego had been the press officer for Colombia Es Pasión in 2006 but had subsequently become a trenchant critic. In February 2013 he published an interview on the biological passport with UCI Scientific Commission member Dr Mario Zorzoli. There was certainly a lot to talk about: Colombia's doping problem was an open secret, while the biological passport programme had well-known deficiencies: potential manipulation through micro-dosing, huge problems in turning suspicious readings into legal proceedings, the absence of hormone values from its protocols, and so on.

But Urrego's questions had a very different orientation:

Urrego: The biological passport programme can be implemented in any country, but can any team or institution do so?

If they do, what validity does it have? Or can only the UCI carry it out?

Zorzoli: No. The biological passport is a tool in the fight against doping and can only be implemented by anti-doping organisations recognised by the World Anti-Doping Agency. The analyses can only be carried out in WADA-accredited laboratories, and those laboratories are not permitted to carry out analyses which are not supplied by an officially recognised anti-doping body.

[. . .]

Urrego: In Colombia or in any other country, is any team or individual authorised to create or utilise the biological passport?

Zorzoli: . . . No team or private athlete can claim to use WADA's biological passport. Athletes and teams can only undergo anti-doping examinations in accredited laboratories.

[. . .]

Urrego: Do you know of any Colombian team that is part of the biological passport programme?

Zorzoli: The second-division team Colombia-Coldeportes, I believe.

Urrego: Anyone else in Colombia?

Zorzoli: Not that I know of.

The sole point of the exchange was to discredit 4-72 Colombia's anti-doping programme. Ignacio Vélez used an interview with the American journalist Joe Lindsay to defend it: 'The UCI's Biological Passport includes blood tests but it still stops short of measuring hormone values,' he said. 'Our programme includes 38 different blood and hormone values . . .'

However, with Urrego and the federation set against the team, it was close to impossible to explain its anti-doping philosophy to the public.

In March 2014, 4-72 Colombia and two other national teams,

Orgullo Antioqueño and GW, published a manifesto entitled 'Towards an Ethical Cycling' to protect their riders' health and safeguard their right to compete in honest, legal and transparent sport. The scheme included a Code of Commitment to which all three teams had subscribed, which made whistleblowing obligatory and provided for education in anti-doping and sporting transparency.

By coincidence, soon after the publication of the manifesto, the Italian sports daily *La Gazzetta dello Sport* learned that, sometime after the Tour of Oman in late February, Team Sky had suspended Sergio Luis Henao from competition after irregularities were noted in his blood values. The precise nature of the irregularities was never made public, although Henao returned to racing on 14 June at the Tour de Suisse, mystery solved, apparently, and scandal averted.

In the meantime, Henao had returned to Colombia for intensive testing. In a press release composed after the story had broken, the team explained, confusingly, 'We are commissioning independent scientific research to better understand the effects of prolonged periods at altitude after returning from sea level, specifically on altitude natives.'

The real scandal was that such research did not already exist in Colombia. With its distinguished cycling tradition and an emerging generation of sports scientists, the country should lead the world in altitude training data and techniques for cyclists. But Colombian cycling, with its own laws and practices, not least medical, was disconnected from the national universities, the world of science, national health policy, even honest, scrupulous journalism.

The riders succeeding in Europe, almost without exception, had either developed in the protected, anti-doping precincts of Colombia Es Pasión, or left Colombia young. Proudly Colombian, brilliant exponents of cycling, they had neither emerged from, nor reflected, elite-level Colombian cycling at all.

Nairo was unique among his generation in Colombia, in that his horizons had always extended beyond sport. In October 2014, ten months after the birth of his first child, Mariana, he became a Friend of the United Nations International Children's Emergency Fund (UNICEF). At a press conference in Bogotá, he said, 'I do not come from a wealthy family, and I went through difficult moments as a child. Child abuse is most visible in the poorer social groups, whose language I speak.'

He also began a social-media campaign against violence directed towards women, while also becoming a rare voice for small agricultural producers, in the face of the governmental focus on large-scale, industrial agriculture. In January 2018, sitting opposite the wholesale fruit and vegetable market in Tunja, he had told me, as animatedly as if we had been talking about the Tour de France: 'Right now there is a glut of cassava. The prices are so low, it isn't worth harvesting. But cassava starch is used to produce tapioca, which sells at good prices. Given the right machinery, the cassava could be processed into tapioca and exported. But the government has no industrial or commercial strategy for small producers.'

In May 2015, he was named Goodwill Ambassador for Colombian Agriculture to represent Colombian produce abroad and, said the press release, 'develop public policies to improve food production among small farmers'.

'First we launched a campaign encouraging peasant farmers to sow,' he told me. 'Then we launched another, inviting Colombian consumers to eat locally produced cassava or potato, at competitive prices, instead of expensive, imported pasta.'

In 2016, fresh from his Vuelta win, Nairo visited the Wayuu indigenous community in La Guajira on behalf of UNICEF. He told them, 'I am just like you. I wasn't born competing in Europe. I worked hard for it.'

Nairo asked who owned the grassland and cattle encroaching on Wayuu land. The community representatives told him, 'Such-and-such a politician.'

'And the lake?'

'It's ours, but the animals use it as a toilet.'

'And the trash?'

They admitted that the piles of rotting waste were their own.

Nairo's to-do list came straight from his childhood experience: fence in the lake to keep the animals out, dig a channel and a smaller pond lower down for the animals, clear up the litter, separate the metal, the plastic and the flammable material, sell the metal and put the plastic in a metal bin over a bonfire of all the flammable waste, then pour the melted plastic on the floor of the shower block.

'Then you'll be able to wash without standing ankle deep in mud.'

Nairo gave them a month to send him a video showing the whole area transformed: 'If you do everything I've said, I promise to help you with the politics.'

To the media, Nairo was scathing about the child hunger. He spoke of a passive government of overweight politicians gorging on dinners while kids were dying of hunger: 'It doesn't all come down to money. Much of it can be resolved by the community themselves. Children are the future of our country, and we should be looking out for them. I come from the countryside too, and there is child malnutrition in Boyacá as well. We need to educate the adults so that the children don't have to suffer hardship.'

I asked him if they had ever sent him the video. He shook his head. Nairo's was a philosophy of efficient, compassionate institutions, but also of honest self-reliance and individual responsibility. Among those used to handouts, it had little resonance. And Nairo was soon being criticised for looking beyond the tip of his nose, when he should have been thinking of nothing but cycling.

14

Everyday Pain

On 27 August 2014, stage four of the Tour de l'Avenir saw the first mountain finish at Plateau de Solaison, just north of Le Grand Bornand in the French Alps. Two riders, the Kazakh Ilya Davidenok and the Dutchman Sam Oomen, gained 42 seconds on Colombia's Miguel Ángel López, although third place in the stage was enough to propel López into the race lead overall, six seconds ahead of Oomen. Two days later, over the Col des Saisies, the Cormet de Roselend and the Montée de La Rosière, Oomen cracked, losing more than six minutes. López won the stage, consolidating his lead overall. On 30 August 2014 he became the fifth Colombian to stand on the Tour de l'Avenir podium in as many years, and the third winner.

His friend, coach and future father-in-law Rafael Acevedo raved, 'He has never raced outside Colombia, he goes to the Tour de l'Avenir aged twenty, and he wins the Tour, the mountains competition and the queen stage. Pretty good, eh?'

◈

Miguel Ángel's father, Santiago López López, is a practical man. On a small farm outside Pesca, Boyacá, he grows potatoes, onions, sweetcorn, peas, beans, fava and haricot. He keeps five cows, operates a sawmill, makes fencing posts and does construction work. A community leader who has represented Vereda El Hato

– *hato* means herd or flock – on the municipal council, he speaks clearly and methodically of tangible things. His conversation leads you into the landscapes of peasant speech, with its preference for the concrete over the abstract, factual description over abstruse ideas, the what of things over the why.

Among his favourite words is a clipped, assertive *ejemplo* – 'for example' without the 'for' – followed by concrete instantiation. 'The village is a dead end,' he tells me, 'so prices are low here. *Ejemplo:* in Sogamoso' – 25 kilometres away – 'a bottle of milk goes at between a thousand and twelve hundred pesos [between 23 and 28 pence, in UK prices]. Here they collect it at 650 pesos [15 pence].

'*Ejemplo:* for a pound of cheese here in Pesca, they pay 3,000, 3,300, 3,500 pesos. Go to Sogamoso and they pay 5,000. Isn't that right, Don Rafael?'

Sitting beside us, Rafael Acevedo, known to all as Don Rafa or Rafico, twelfth in the 1984 Tour de France and a long-time town councillor in nearby Sogamoso – a man whose detailed recall of every time, date, corner and climb must have made him an invaluable teammate to Lucho Herrera, in the days before miniature radios and satnavs entered the peloton – nods in assent. We are in the dining room of the bungalow Santiago built ('There wasn't much money, so I left it low,' he says) on land he bought when his fifth child, Miguel Ángel, was one. Around us, lush green vegetation blankets gentle, rolling hills, although, if the setting suggests a rural idyll, the conversation paints a more ambivalent picture: 'Fifteen years ago, seventy per cent of the land in this valley was cultivated. Now' – our interview took place in January 2018 – 'it is about ten per cent. We used to live from wheat and barley. Now wheat costs more than its sale price to grow. They bring in, *ejemplo*, barley from elsewhere to make beer, then they take the beer back there to sell it. If only we Colombians had *analysed* this . . .'

It is another of his favourite words, and with his rolling

sequence of examples and analyses, he paints a precise picture of life's practicalities in rural Colombia.

From the age of four, Miguel Ángel López walked the two or three kilometres to primary school on the steep hills of Vereda El Hato. Aged thirteen he transferred to the school in the village to prepare for his school certificate. Pesca lay five kilometres away along a rustic track through the hills, so his father took him to Rafael Acevedo's bicycle shop in Sogamoso and bought him a mountain bike.

Rafael says, 'He was just another customer at the time.'

His rides to school and back enthused the young Miguel with an idea: 'There was an annual fête on the Vereda to raise funds for the chapel and the school. One of the events was a bicycle race. I wanted to take part.'

As long as he was at school, his father refused to let him: 'I was in class until one in the afternoon, then I went to work in the fields, so I didn't have time to train until I left school. The first two years my father said it was better not to enter. I would only get beaten. The third year, 2010, I said, "This year, I'm riding."'

He was sixteen. Dressed in a tracksuit and training shoes, Miguel joined fifteen other competitors, and won: 'It made my father happy, and spurred me on to compete more.'

It was, of course, the year that Nairo won the Tour de l'Avenir. But that was in the outside world – even if Cómbita is only about thirty kilometres away as the crow flies. Like Nairo at the same age, Miguel knew nothing of professional cycling, and had never heard the words Giro d'Italia or Tour de France: 'It was only in 2011 that I started training and began to understand what it was all about.'

He earned the cash to buy his first road bike by helping his neighbours with their harvest, but only when he had finished his work on the family land. He met Rafael Acevedo again at the end of September 2011, at a mountain time trial on the climb above Sogamoso called the Alto El Crucero, 16.5 kilometres up to Lake Tota, at an altitude of 3,200 metres. Rafico tells me, 'His bike was very heavy, his cycling shoes were worn out and he had no technique, but he beat all the boys in my club, and everyone else too. His time was 37 minutes 25 seconds. I asked him how old he was and where he lived, and invited him to join the club.'

Miguel Ángel's father remembers the moment his son told him he wanted to be a cyclist: 'I said, "Look, my son: when you analyse where we come from, and whether a boy from here can make it out there, it doesn't look easy. You can win in the village, and you might be one of the top ten in the department, but what about nationally? There are people out there who can afford the best bicycles."'

When Fredy Alexander, his eldest, was in grade eleven or twelve, Santiago had bought him a bicycle to get to and from Pesca: 'But,' he says, 'no one analysed the situation. No one thought that it could be a future for them' – 'them' meaning Fredy and the next three, Leonardo, Mónica and Yoana.

Then Miguel came along, and Rafico, and the balance changed between what was and what could be, and Santiago's speech takes on another tone: 'I think he was born to be a cyclist.'

Another strict peasant father had been converted to the idea that cycling might provide his children with the future the countryside no longer could.

'And that,' says Rafael, in the classic phrase, 'was when the process started.'

Miguel Ángel López had his first crash in 2011. Rafael Acevedo volunteers, 'It was the third day we worked together.'

Miguel responds, 'We were training behind a motorbike for the 2011 Vuelta del Porvenir. I was on a teammate's wheel, but he was tired. A gap opened between him and the motorbike, we overlapped wheels and I went down. I was just a beginner.'

When I enquire after his injuries, he brushes off the question.

'Lots of little things. But we carried on,' he says. 'When you have been working in the fields since childhood like us, pain is a small, everyday thing. You put up with worse when you were small, cutting yourself with a machete or getting kicked by cattle. You learn when you are very small that life is hard and you stop worrying about it.'

Five hundred kilometres west of here, in a very different part of Colombia, Sergio Luís Henao had told me something very similar: 'The city and the country are very different. In the countryside, you learn to live with blisters and chafing. Life is more precarious. Hospitals are often a long way away, and you probably can't afford medical treatment anyway, so if you have an accident, you pour water on it and carry on.'

Miguel says of himself and his siblings, 'We had to pay our way when we were still very small, so by the time we were fifteen or sixteen, we were independent. We had to face life head on.'

In Western Europe and the United States, where teenagers were invented in the 1950s, and adolescence long ago stretched into early middle age and beyond, such precocious responsibility might be seen as a form of abuse. In these hills it is a simple fact of life. I ask Miguel how conscious the Colombian riders in the international peloton are of their peasant roots: 'Very, all of us,' he answers. 'We have all been eating food we have grown ourselves, and drinking the milk from our own cows. It is very healthy, very natural. As kids, we always had to be doing something practical, learning new things, not lying around playing video games or watching television. All this makes us different from the other riders.'

It occurs to me to ask Rafael Acevedo if any of his teammates all those years ago had an urban background. He seems fairly sure of the answer: 'No, no, no, no. No. No, no, no. In those days we were all *campesinos*. Everyone.'

Don Rafa himself is the fourth of five children of peasant farmers from Vereda de Vanegas, six kilometres from Sogamoso.

'When I was a child, I worked. I sowed potatoes and sweetcorn, and cut the barley,' he says, and adds, 'Daddy's and Mummy's boys are good for golf or tennis, but riding a bike at that level? Impossible. If you haven't had to fight for everything you have, you won't have the mettle for it.'

I repeat to him something that Jarlinson Pantano had said: 'Cycling is the only sport where the athletes say, "I don't want my son . . ."'

He finishes the sentence for me – '". . . to be a cyclist"' – and laughs.

☰

Rafael installed Miguel Ángel in a smallholding three or four kilometres outside Sogamoso with another promising cyclist, the 2010 Vuelta de la Juventud winner Javier Gómez, who lived there with his mother. Miguel Ángel had only been at the finca for three days when his cycling career nearly came to a violent end, before it had even started.

On Friday 11 November 2011, Rafico visited to see a calf newly born to a cow he kept there. The rider's mother told him the cow wasn't giving any milk: '*El Mono*' – the dark-skinned Acevedo's nickname for his blond-haired protégé – 'said, "What do you mean it's not giving any milk?" He took a bucket out and milked it. I told him if his riding was as good as his milking, his future was assured.'

At ten to six that evening, Rafico and his family left for Sogamoso. Miguel Ángel set off behind them on his mountain bike to go and buy credit for his mobile phone. Rafico went home, showered, changed into his pyjamas and put the news on. At five past seven, the phone rang.

'Don Rafa, I've been mugged.'

'What did they do to you? Take your bike? Are you OK?'

'They didn't get away with anything but they stabbed me twice in the leg.'

Acevedo got dressed and headed straight to the finca.

López had reached Eleventh Avenue (*Carrera Once*) and First Street (*Calle Primera*) when his assailants appeared, two of them, both armed with knives. He wrestled the knife off the bigger one, but the smaller one stabbed him twice in the leg. Then he faced the nightmare of being a peasant's son seeking medical care in Colombia. He made his way to a clinic with an emergency ward six blocks away, but he only had 8,000 pesos on him and they turned him away. He took a taxi as far as his cash would allow, to the fuel station at the fork at Tres Esquinas, then walked the kilometre and a half back to the finca and called Rafico, who arrived twenty-five minutes later.

'I saw two violent bruises covered in blood. The boy had insurance under the Subsidized Health Regime' – a mechanism supposedly allowing the poorest section of the population access to health services – 'so we put him in the car and took him to the El Laguito Clinic, but they turned him away too. Eventually we found a hospital that would accept his insurance. In the operating theatre, they applied pressure to the wounds and blood spurted out, splattering the overhead lamp. I was there until half past one in the morning. I took him food then left him in the hospital.'

The following day, Rafico was leaving for a race, the Clásica Ciudad de Aguazul, in the department of Casanare, three hours away. Before setting off, he called a doctor friend, who visited his protégé and prescribed no training for a week.

Although Rafico knew the doctor's orders, he called him half-way through the race and asked, 'How's the leg? What did the doctor say?'

Miguel Ángel told him, 'I went to Everest today.' Everest is a two-kilometre climb with gradients at 26 per cent.

'What are you doing riding when the doctor said, "No bike"?'

Miguel Ángel simply said, 'The leg stings like fuck, Rafa, but I have to train.'

Rafael Acevedo tells me, 'The blade missed the sciatic nerve by millimetres. God knows what he's doing, eh? I'm telling you, there is no evil but good comes of it.'

In Rafico's version of the concrete, there is space for the divine to intervene.

The 2011 Vuelta del Porvenir, for seventeen- and eighteen-year-olds, started in Chiquinquirá on 23 November. It meant that, after the injury, they only had twelve days to prepare. Four days before the race, there was a qualifier at the village of Ramiriquí. Miguel Ángel finished sixth, riding in a field of thirty for the first time. At the Vuelta del Porvenir, the peloton was 220 strong. Rafael gave the boy a red helmet so that he could keep an eye on him: 'I told him to keep to the side and stay close to the Paisas.'

'I had no idea who they were,' Miguel Ángel recalls. 'I was nervous on day one, but I got through it without any problems. I felt more confident each day.'

So fearless was he that, on stage two, from Moniquirá to Duitama, taking in the Alto De La Cumbre, he went on the attack. The Ecuadorean rider Richard Carapaz, riding for the Bogotá-based team Canapro-Bogotá, went with him. Carapaz and López crossed the pass fourth and seventh, and finished the stage safely in the same time as the winner.

Sebastián Henao won stage three, an individual time trial from Paipa to Pantano de Vargas, with Carapaz sixth, 36 seconds behind him, and Miguel Ángel twelfth, 49 seconds back, in the same time as Henao's teammate Fernando Gaviria.

Stage four, from Sogamoso to Aquitania, included the Alto de Crucero, which Miguel Ángel knew by heart. A small group attacked, including Miguel Ángel, Carapaz, Sebastián Henao and Roller Diagama, a close friend of Nairo Quintana. They were caught one kilometre from the finish.

Overall, Miguel Ángel finished thirteenth, 2 minutes 30 seconds behind the winner.

Rafael Acevedo tells me, 'At Miguel Ángel's next race, we told some journalists how he took the knife off one of his attackers. One of them called him Superman, and it stuck.' Just weeks into the adventure of cycling, he had passed from the straitjacket of peasant realism to the cape and mask of comic-book heroism.

He approached the 2012 Vuelta del Porvenir with high ambitions: 'After my 2011 experiences I thought that, with more preparation and by polishing one or two things, I could finish on the podium.'

But it was not to be. After rampaging through stage one and taking the mountains and the intermediate sprints jerseys, and taking points at the first two intermediate sprints of stage two, he crashed on a descent, fractured a hand and abandoned. Months of frustration followed. A pre-season knee injury sidelined him for 2013. Acevedo arranged for his pupil to see Dr Gustavo Castro in Bogotá.

Castro diagnosed cartilage damage and patella hyperpressure, and López began three months of treatment. Rafael Acevedo says, 'He wanted to give up cycling. I wouldn't let him. I told him he was destined for great things.'

Castro agreed. He told me, 'Of all the cyclists I've seen, Egan Bernal has the best brain, but Miguel Ángel López has the best cycling physique.'

In 2014 Miguel Ángel went to Cómbita, Nairo's village, to compete in a mountain time trial from the main avenue to the Alto del Sote. He set a new record, beating Nairo's time. Rafael says, 'Claro-Coldeportes and Orgullo Paisa wanted him, but I told him he was better off staying with us at Boyacá, Raza de Campeones, which had the governor's support, and then, when he left, going straight to a WorldTour team.'

Miguel Ángel never questioned Acevedo's judgement: 'I have always had faith in Don Rafa. He helped me when I was nobody. He lent me a bike; he gave me everything I needed. With him, I had training, races, planning, and it all worked, and I felt at ease.

So I decided to stay until the opportunity came to join one of the big teams.'

Miguel Ángel finished fourth in the national Under-23 time trial championship in April, then, on 2 June, he was second in the prologue to the Vuelta de la Juventud, the Under-23 version of the Tour of Colombia.

Stage four started at Villa de Leyva, crossed three category two climbs, the Alto de Samacá, the Alto de Cucaita and the Alto de Villa Rosita, and finished atop El Crucero after 125 kilometres. Miguel Ángel crossed the Alto de Villa Rosita in first place, then won alone on El Crucero by 45 seconds. It gave him a 42-second lead over his nearest rival. Fourth place in stage five and fifth in stage six secured him victory overall by the same margin. On 3 July, he won the opening 26-kilometre time trial at the Clásica de Fusagasugá. Those results earned him leadership of the Colombia team to dispute the Tour de l'Avenir in August.

Rafael Acevedo fielded a call from Claudio Corti, offering what Rafael calls a pittance to join Team Colombia: 'He said, "It's a chance to show himself."'

'I told him, "Riders like Miguel Ángel don't need to show themselves. The world is waiting for them." I told him he was going to win the Tour de l'Avenir. He said, "Let's talk when he has."'

Victory opened the door to the WorldTour contract Acevedo had foreseen. Acevedo contacted an old friend from his riding days: 'When I first met Miguel Ángel, I told Vicente Belda that I had a young rider who was going to be spectacularly good. After the Tour de l'Avenir win, I told Belda I wanted Miguel Ángel to do the same as Nairo and Rigoberto, compete in Europe but train in Colombia.'

Belda spoke to the Kazakh team Astana, who gave him the assurances they were asking for, and, in September 2014, it was announced that Miguel Ángel López would be joining the team.

Inspired by their brother's progress, his younger siblings

followed in his footsteps. Miguel says, 'There are eight of us. I'm the fifth, and the first cyclist. The younger three, all boys, have started training now.'

Rafael Acevedo says, 'They have something genetic. Luís, known as *Lucho*, Diego and Juan Carlos all have big futures.'

While we were talking on the family finca, Juan Carlos arrived back from training. He told me he had recently finished sixth in a mountain bike race called the Floresta, and third in the Vereda de Otengá in Betéitiva, beating riders in higher age brackets.

Just as Miguel Ángel inspired his brothers to try out the sport, so his successes added to the sport's popularity, as more and more rural families, the peasant economy collapsing around them, encouraged their children to try cycling as an alternative.

15

Fast Feet

The reports from stage one of the 2015 Tour de San Luís in Argentina mention swirling gusts of wind, although the foliage on the roadside trees seems still, even if the television images are low resolution and neither confirm nor refute the claims. After the stage the losers spoke of metre markers too small to see, or missing entirely. Again, they may have been right. All that is certain is that Fernando Gaviria Rendón went all out with something like three hundred metres to go. Mark Cavendish, with twenty-five Tour de France stages behind him, dived into his wake, even gaining his rear wheel as Gaviria slowed, but too late. The poor Argentinian commentators, who attributed the win to Gaviria's madison partner, Juan Esteban Arango, probably did better than most. Even Cavendish admitted he had never heard of Gaviria.

Two days later, the Colombian launched another, almost impossibly long sprint, leaving Cavendish and the Italian Sacha Modolo fighting for second place, metres behind. In the post-stage press conference, Gaviria said, 'When I won on day one, you could have said it was a fluke. But this time everyone knew I was there and I still won.'

Fernando Gaviria had only joined the Colombian national road team in Argentina with February's Track World Championships in mind. In December 2014 he had won the omnium at the London leg of the UCI Track World Cup. On 19 and 20 February 2015 at the Saint-Quentin-en-Yvelines velodrome, he wanted to become world champion. Third in the scratch race, second in the individual pursuit, third in the elimination race, fourth in the time trial, and eighth in the flying lap, he secured the world title with victory in the final points race.

His first encounter with top European sprinters was not his first exposure to greatness. In his beginnings at the Medellín velodrome, he was coached by Efraín Domínguez, who, in 1985, set six track world records at altitude, for the flying 200m and 500m time trials and the 1km time trial: 'He had been the best in the world, but I've never felt dumbfounded by other people's achievements. If I did, I might feel intimidated.'

◈

Fernando Gaviria was brought up in La Ceja del Tambo, a small town 45 kilometres south-east of Medellín, less than 20 kilometres from Rionegro. It is a town with a history – one that Fernando witnessed before he was old enough to understand it.

It was 1 December 2006, and La Ceja was at lunch when the sky turned black. The five Black Hawk helicopters overhead were part of a massive military operation. Three hundred regular army and Special Forces troops supported by rooftop snipers, riot control vehicles and several dozen police officers descended on the old Jesuit monastery, redesignated the National Centre for Peace and Coexistence.

At approximately 5.30 p.m., the monastery gates opened and a convoy of at least thirty vehicles emerged. Fifty-nine leaders of the demobilised United Self-Defense Forces of Colombia were being moved 45 kilometres to the maximum security prison at Itagüí, just south of Medellín. The operation paralysed traffic in much of Medellín. Thirty-six of them were then transferred to maximum security penitentiaries at Cómbita, Boyacá and in Bogotá.

The first laying down of arms of the paramilitary demobilisation had taken place on Tuesday 25 November 2003, when 868 paramilitary gunmen of the so-called Cacique Nutibara Battalion, active in Medellín, surrendered their weapons. To speed their reintegration into civil society, they were transferred to a holding area in La Ceja. There they attended three weeks of so-called re-education before returning to civilian life.

One other paramilitary group demobilised in 2003. Five followed in 2004. Seventeen did so in 2005 and fourteen more in 2006.

From August 2006 the centre in La Ceja had filled with paramilitary leaders, many of whom – Salvatore Mancuso, Ramón Isaza, Fredy Rendón, 'El Alemán', 'Monoleche', 'Jorge 40' – were household names in Colombia, and notorious for their sadistic violence. By November, all fifty-nine of them were living in the centre. Fantastically rich from drugs trafficking, contraband petrol, the extortion and appropriation of legitimate businesses, not to mention disbursements by central government to regional politicians allied to the gunmen, they distorted the economy in their operational heartlands with their buying power, and did the same in La Ceja.

An ex-PE teacher at a local school, José Hernando Gaviria López, told me, 'They had deep pockets, so prices rose. They'd give fifty thousand peso notes to the guys in the street who keep an eye on your car. You didn't feel their presence at every moment, but they were always in the back of your mind.'

On one of the national news bulletins, an electronics store owner described a rush on televisions, DVD players and coffee machines. In the next shop along, the property agent said that sales and rents were up. The mayor commented that the town's new residents were expected to remain there for five years. Meanwhile, in their former territories, their lieutenants were killing and being killed in purges apparently directed from La Ceja.

On 30 November 2006 President Uribe said of the killings, 'If they were murdered by people who are taking part in the peace process, then those people must lose the benefits of transitional justice. If someone accused of these crimes has had an extradition order suspended, I will lift the suspension.'

When the intelligence services learned that some paramilitary leaders had thought twice about demobilisation and decided to return to their fiefdoms, the police and army stepped in. The former PE teacher's son, Fernando Gaviria, was twelve years old when they did – too young to be afraid as he watched from his school playground: 'We saw five helicopters, flying really low. They landed and took off again. It attracted a lot of attention. I was only a child, and I had no understanding of the situation, and the first thing I thought was, "They can't fly over the town. Only the Governor of Antioquia can do that when he pays a visit." But, yes, I saw them.'

José Hernando Gaviria told me, 'It was always hard here, mostly to the south of the town. There were battles between the guerrillas and the paramilitaries, and massacres.'

In 1992, a guerrilla campaign of bank bombings across the country reached La Ceja, killing two and injuring sixteen, two of whom lost their legs. In February 1998 responsibility for the murders of seven peasant farmers was claimed by the Peasant Self-Defense Forces of Córdoba and Urabá (ACCU), and sixty coffee and blackberry growers took refuge in La Ceja for fear of continued attacks. But those were different times. Fernando Gaviria was three years old in February 1998.

Years later, one of the town's many cyclists, Rafael Infantino – second in the Under-23 Vuelta a Colombia in 2004, behind Mauricio Soler – was training near Guayaquil, forty kilometres south-east of La Ceja, when he was stopped by armed men and held for four or five hours while he was background checked. 'But while he waited they gave him *Sancocho*,' a traditional local broth, José Hernando told me with a laugh.

ⵌ

José Hernando Gaviria had been sent to La Ceja by his father. One of eight children, Antonio José Gaviria was a peasant farmer who broke horses and cultivated maize, potatoes, beans, peas, tamarillo and *arracacha* – a root crop, halfway between carrot and celery – at Finca Buenos Aires, near the village of Aguas Claras, nine kilometres from La Ceja. As a child, José Hernando helped his father work the heavy land with a hoe. But Antonio José wanted his children to have an education, so, after primary school at Aguas Claras, José Hernando and his brothers were dispatched to La Ceja, where his father owned a property, to continue their studies.

'During term time we spent Monday to Friday at La Ceja and Saturdays and Sundays at the finca. I spent my holidays working there. Then I went to university and studied industrial technology and physical education. I taught mathematics, electronics and PE for 34 years.'

But he was a competitive cyclist too: 'When I started working, I used to go to bed at 7 p.m. and get up at 3 a.m. to go training: one circuit in the dark, then the road to Llano Grande as day broke.'

His cycling career stalled after he finished only 48th in the 1980 RCN Classic stage race, riding as an independent. His wife, María del Carmen Rendón, played basketball and taught in the primary school on Vereda San Miguel, six kilometres from La Ceja. Their daughter Juliana was born in March 1991. When she was five, her father was making a call from the telephone box when a boy rode past on a bike. Juliana was captivated by the machine. Her father bought her one the same week. Juliana and her brother Fernando, born in August 1994, both learned to ride on it.

When Juliana was nine, she informed her father she wanted to try inline skating. He enrolled Juliana and Fernando, who can't have been any more than six, in the *Halcones* ('Falcons') club at Rionegro, sponsored by the Colombian Armed Forces.

José Hernando tells me, 'I never tried to push them into cycling, even though I had been a cyclist. I told them when they were very young, "Do what you want to do, but try to be the best in the world. In any field: if you want to study and be doctors or engineers, or if you want to be athletes, try to be the best in the world. And the same if you want to shine shoes: be the best shoeshine boy in the world." That was the mentality I brought them up with. After that, they made up their own minds.'

They became good skaters, and, in 2003, the year Juliana turned twelve and Fernando nine, they were selected to go to Miami for an international competition between clubs, although their future cycling coach, Jhon Jaime Rodríguez, remembers Fernando as more interested in extreme skating than in track racing.

Fernando disputes this: 'I liked elimination races, which are the same in inline skating as they are in cycling. I've always done well in them. But I was never especially fast. I always wanted to be a cyclist, although it never occurred to me that I would become a sprinter.'

To stir his children's curiosity, José Hernando would drop offhand hints – 'They're racing bicycles at such-and-such a place' – then make a family outing of the event, going a day early and staying overnight somewhere with a swimming pool.

Aged about nine, Fernando saw the Tour de France on television and told his father, matter of factly, 'I'll have to go and ride the Tour one day.'

'My sister didn't want to be a cyclist,' Fernando says, 'until one day when we went to the track in Medellín and she started training. They took her to the national track championships, and she decided she liked it.'

Their father's account takes in the way stations of her early career: 'Juliana began to take an interest in cycling in 2007. The following year she rode the departmental championships on the road and earned selection for the nationals in Popayán. Then, at the departmental track championships, she discovered where her talent lay.'

For the next two years José Hernando drove the 90-kilometre round trip between La Ceja and the Martín Emilio Cochise Rodríguez Velodrome in Medellín every Tuesday, Thursday and Saturday. 'We never missed a session,' he says.

At the 2008 junior national track championships in Duitama, Juliana took bronze in the 500 metres time trial and made the national squad for the junior Pan-American championships in Cuenca, Ecuador, where she won another time trial bronze, her first international medal. Second in the 500 metres time trial at the elite national championships 2010, she won five consecutive national titles starting in 2011, three individual and seven team sprint gold medals, plus two national keirin titles. She would be Pan-American team sprint champion with her partner Martha Bayona, in 2013, and South American keirin champion in 2014.

In 2008 her brother Fernando made the switch from inline skating to cycling. The bulk of Fernando's training and racing was on the road. He rode for a team sponsored by a mattress manufacturer called Ramguiflex, alongside a rider named Jhonatan Restrepo, from the far-off, coffee-growing town of Pácora. The two boys became close friends: 'We are the same age. We started riding together, and we have always got on. We rode together for four years, two as juniors for Ramguiflex, then I went to Orgullo Paisa, then we met again at Coldeportes-Claro and spent two more years together.'

Sebastián Henao told me, 'Gaviria was quite a climber too.'

José Hernando remembers, 'Fernando won circuit races and stages. In a Clásica al Suroeste in 2011 he finished third in Concordia, at the top of a 22-kilometre climb. He put the Orgullo Paisa team to the sword.'

But the young Fernando was difficult at school, where his

father was on the teaching staff: 'Every so often I was called by the school office because Fernando was being a nuisance. In the office, I said, "Fernando, behave yourself," but afterwards I didn't say anything. The way I saw it, that part of his make-up would help him as a cyclist.'

One day in 2012, Jhon Jaime González, the national sprint coach and the coach to the Antioquian track team, was in a La Ceja café when Fernando walked in and approached him.

'Profe, will you help me to see how far I can go?'

'What do you want to achieve?'

'I want to be national champion.'

'You don't have to worry about that.'

'All right, what about world champion?'

'That's more like it. And Olympic champion. And making history.'

'OK. Tell me how to train tomorrow.'

They started working together the next day.

Fernando remembers it well: 'I was still a junior, and I wanted to go to the Track World Championships in New Zealand.'

For the first time, he started to use technology-based training. Jhon Jaime González recalls, 'The thing that impressed me about Fernando was that he invested every peso he could find in things that would make him a better rider: a Garmin, a power meter, Tacx rollers.'

Fernando told me, 'I started using a power meter and studying how to use it. I liked it because I could see myself getting stronger.'

The national championships at Pereira that June were happy ones for the Gaviria family. Juliana won the elite women's individual sprint, the 500m time trial and the keirin, and took silver in team sprint. Her boyfriend, Fabian Puerta, won the elite men's 1km time trial, keirin and team sprint, and silver in the individual sprint. Among the juniors, Fernando won the points race, team pursuit and madison on the track, then, on 26 June, took gold in the time trial over a 20-kilometre course.

With no candidate to ride the omnium at the approaching World Championships, the national coach, Absolón Rincón, called up Fernando, whose father told me, 'Absolón called me one Friday and said, "I need him for training in Bogotá on Monday." I bought the ticket and sent him off with my bank card and wages, to keep him for July and August.'

On Thursday 23 August 2012, the first night of competition at the Invercargill track on South Island, Gaviria got up from two heavy falls to finish second in the flying lap, first in the points race, and second in the elimination race. He began the following day with a practice session to see if he could compete with his injuries. Despite the bandages on one knee and both elbows, he took third in the individual pursuit, fourth in the scratch race and third in the 1000m time trial, to become the junior world omnium champion. Two days later, partnering Jordan Parra, he took gold in the madison. He completed his season with the points title and victory in the final stage of the Vuelta del Porvenir on 25 November.

In February 2013 he won the omnium at the Pan-American Games. At the Bolivarian Games in Peru on 20 November, the Gaviria family had another unforgettable day: Juliana and her future husband Fabián Puerta won their respective keirin titles, then Fernando won the madison with Juan Esteban Arango. Four days later Fernando won the Bolivarian Games road race around Lima.

And the crescendo only continued: on 11 May 2014, two weeks after Juliana married Fabio, Fernando celebrated with the Under-23 Pan-American road race title. In November, he added the omnium title at the Central American and Caribbean Games, and a silver medal in the individual time trial.

On 24 February 2015, a month after his two stage wins in San Luís – four days after taking his first world omnium title – it was reported that he had signed a two-year contract with the Etixx–Quick-Step team, with another former Coldeportes-Claro rider, Rodrigo Contreras, who had won the youth classification in San Luis.

Fernando Gaviria's old friend Jhonatan Restrepo joined Katusha as a *stagiaire* in August, meaning that twelve of the seventeen WorldTour teams had at least one Colombian rider. If the future looked bright, the present looked even brighter, as Nairo Quintana prepared for his country's most serious bid yet for victory in the Tour de France.

16

Closer

In March 2014, to build form for the Giro d'Italia, Nairo had gone to the Tirreno–Adriatico stage race and encountered Alberto Contador. Thirty-two kilometres remained in stage five when, on the forbidding Lanciano pass, Contador darted away and gained twenty lengths. He cast long taunting looks back, seemingly inviting Nairo to join him without ever relaxing the pace, as the race footage showed a TV motorbike close enough to offer Contador precious cover from the wind.

Nairo chased for several kilometres, then relented. José Luís Arrieta protested so vigorously to the race judges that his team car was relegated to last place the following day for 'failure to respect instructions concerning a vehicle'.

Contador won the stage and the race overall. For Nairo, second overall, it felt like a humiliation.

At the 2015 Tirreno–Adriatico, Nairo and Contador met again. This time, their roles were reversed: Contador was targeting a Giro–Tour double, and was using the race to hone his condition. Nairo, focused on the Tour, could afford an early peak and arrived in excellent condition.

On the major mountain stage, finishing in the snow on Mount Terminillo, Nairo turned Contador's tactics against him. He darted away alone, gained a few bike lengths, then waited. A helicopter shot showed him several bike lengths ahead of Contador on a long right-hand bend, apparently unable to continue the attack as the Spaniard closed in on him. Then, in a flash of speed, Nairo had gone, a second acceleration launching him upwards and away. In falling snow, he took the stage win and the race.

In the car on the way to the post-stage press conference, he said, 'Last year they were laughing at me. They're not laughing now.'

Nairo's training for his second Tour de France was carefully calibrated: 'My first podium finish was a surprise. Not that anyone gave me any presents: I had to suffer for it. But I wasn't conscious of what I was doing at the time. Afterwards, my preparation became much more meticulous. It is very different. It means you achieve things with much more effort.'

But his Tour bid went awry as early as stage two. Between Utrecht and Neeltje Jans on the Dutch coast, crosswinds caused a series of collisions and crashes. Held up behind one of them, Nairo was forced into a long and frustrating chase that ended in the concession of 1 minute 28 seconds to the favourite, Chris Froome.

On stage ten, the day after the first rest day, his predicament worsened. Fifteen kilometres before the foot of the final climb up to La Pierre Saint-Martin, Nairo asked his team to set a high pace. On the first five kilometres of the climb, the previous year's podium finishers Vincenzo Nibali, Jean-Christophe Pérault and Thibaut Pinot were dropped from the leading group, soon to be followed by Joaquím Rodríguez.

Then Froome's teammates moved to the front. With eight kilometres to go, Valverde made two accelerations to tempt them into chasing, but Geraint Thomas and Richie Porte held their nerve and let Valverde ride himself out. Suddenly, inside the final seven kilometres, an acceleration by Porte, with his leader Froome on his wheel, saw Contador and Valverde drop back. Only Nairo could follow.

Then, on a right-hand bend 6.4 kilometres from the finish,

Froome ducked inside Porte and, out of the saddle, launched a devastating sprint. Nairo gave chase, but the acceleration was unanswerable, and gave Froome a one-minute lead which he maintained to the finish. Adding insult to the time Nairo was losing, Porte chased him down inside the final kilometre, beating him to the time bonus for second place.

Nairo told me, 'I set my team to work mid-stage because I wanted the race to be very fast. It was very hot, and it was the first day of climbing in the Tour, so I thought people would pay the price, and that is what happened. The only thing was that the Sky riders, and Froome in particular, were enormously superior to all of us.'

To the 1 minute 28 seconds Nairo had conceded on stage two, Froome added another 1 minute 9 seconds.

Still, Nairo withstood the accumulated fatigue of stage racing better than most. Before the final stage around Paris, the 2015 Tour ended with two decisive mountain stages: from St-Jean-de-Maurienne to La Toussuire, and from Modane to Alpe d'Huez, where Lucho Herrera had won Colombia's first Tour stage in 1984, and where Nairo Quintana hoped to secure its first win overall.

With 5.1 kilometres left in the first of those two stages, Nairo pulled to the side, took a considered look at the line of riders in the yellow jersey group, then sprinted away.

For a moment, as Froome sped after him, Nairo appeared to stall, tempting the Briton to chase him down, before riding clear. Froome, in clear difficulty, wisely rode on at his own pace. By finishing the stage second to Vincenzo Nibali, Nairo cut his deficit from 3 minutes 10 seconds to 2 minutes 38. With one mountain stage to go, 158 seconds stood between him and the greatest prize in cycling.

The final mountain stage covered just 110.5 kilometres. Nairo had reconnoitred the stage just before the Tour in the company of his directeur sportif, José Luis Arrieta, who told me, 'We looked at the stage knowing that we might come into it with a couple of minutes to make up.'

First, Winner Anacona made an early breakaway group. Then, on the Col de la Croix de Fer, still some sixty kilometres from the finish, Alejandro Valverde sprang out of the yellow jersey group. Minutes later, Nairo made his move, bridging across to Valverde who, his teammate in tow, raised the pace. It was all executed to perfection – until the air itself turned against them. Headwinds on the descent from the Col de la Croix de Fer made the attack impossible. For the second time in the Tour, Nairo's ambitions had been thwarted by the elements. By the foot of the final climb up to Alpe d'Huez, the yellow jersey group was thirty strong, with three of Froome's teammates leading.

Then they reached Alpe d'Huez.

12.4km to go: wasting no time, Nairo attacks, then waits ahead of the group. Porte moves onto his wheel, Froome slowly crosses the gap, and Nairo relents.

11.9km: he flashes away again. Again, he holds it there, tempting Froome's helpers. Wouter Poels speeds across and passes him, showing off Team Sky's strength in depth.

11.7km: Nairo goes again. Again, Poels follows. Nairo tows him for a few hundred metres, then relents.

9.9km: Valverde attacks. Poels looks around at his leader, Froome, and lets the Spaniard go.

9.4km: this time, Nairo flashes out of the group. He looks over his shoulder, an invitation to Poels and Porte. They bridge across. Then, the second acceleration. Poels and Porte stay with him. Behind them, Froome drops Contador, but a gap appears ahead of him. He is on his own.

9.1km: Nairo launches yet another acceleration. Poels nods in breathless defeat, and Nairo bridges across to Valverde.

8km: Nairo and Valverde reach their teammate Winner Anacona, a survivor of the early breakaway. Valverde's job is done: it is up to the two kids from Tunja now to win the Tour de France.

7km: Nairo has gained 27 seconds on Froome. That leaves 131 seconds to make up in seven kilometres, meaning he needs to gain nearly 19 seconds per kilometre – a near-impossible task.

6km: Nairo leads Froome by 34 seconds. He has gained 7 seconds in the last kilometre. He needs to gain 124 more in six kilometres – just under 20 seconds per kilometre.

5km: Froome is holding Nairo at 33 seconds.

4.5km: 35 seconds. Nairo has clawed back two more seconds: it is not enough. He flashes past Winner, whose job is done. Behind him, Porte leads Froome, with Valverde and Pierre Rolland on their wheel.

4km: 54 seconds. Nairo has gained 19 more seconds, but Froome still leads the Tour de France by 104 seconds. Nairo now has to gain 26 seconds per kilometre.

3km: Nairo leads by 62 seconds. He has gained 6 seconds in the last kilometre. He needs to gain over half a minute in each of the final three kilometres.

2.5km: Nairo flies past Ryder Hesjedal. He is now second in the stage.

2km: Nairo leads by 74 seconds. Even if he wins the stage and gains the ten-second time bonus, he will need to gain 32 seconds in each of the final two kilometres.

1km: Nairo leads Froome by 58 seconds. The stage leader, Thibaut Pinot, is 21 seconds ahead of him. Porte has been dropped. Froome has Valverde on his wheel.

Eighteen seconds after Pinot has crossed the finish line, Nairo finishes in second place, with, 1 minute 20 seconds later, Froome coming in fifth. With the time bonus for finishing second in the stage, Nairo has gained 1 minute 26 seconds on Froome. Put another way, he has lost the Tour de France by 1 minute and 12 seconds.

Had there been one more mountain stage, or just one more climb, or if Nairo hadn't conceded 1 minute 28 seconds in the wind on stage two, or been put to the sword on La

Pierre-Saint-Martin, the result could have been different. But the Tour had slipped from his grasp.

One fact remained: Nairo was still just twenty-five. Froome was thirty. Long term, time was on Nairo's side. The order of succession seemed clear.

≣

Meanwhile, as Nairo grew ever closer to winning the Tour, his former Colombia Es Pasión teammate Esteban Chaves set his sights on the 2016 Giro d'Italia. His challenge began, in a sense, on the climb to Abetone on stage five of the 2015 Giro. It was his turn in pink. His team had won the team time trial on stage one in Sanremo and held the race leader's jersey for four days. He had started stages two and three in the same time as the race leader, and stages four and five just ten seconds away, working selflessly to help teammates Simon Gerrans, Michael Matthews and Simon Clarke take or defend the race lead.

Then they hit the climb to Abetone. There were 4.5 kilometres left of the stage when Alberto Contador rocketed out of the group. Then, having opened a significant gap, he seemed to pause and look around, to see who was capable of following. There were four volunteers: Fabio Aru, Richie Porte, Mikel Landa – and Esteban Chaves, but only for a few hundred metres. For the moment, he was not up to the task.

'They were so fast, it was unbelievable,' he told me after the race. 'But getting through that Giro was incredibly important. My body matured, and I became stronger mentally too. Afterwards, I could train longer and at greater intensities.'

The pay-off came five months later at the Vuelta a España. Esteban won two stages, led the race for six days, and finished fifth overall, one place behind Nairo, whose own efforts had been frustrated by illness.

Then, at Abu Dhabi in October, with Esteban on his wheel, Team Sky's Wout Poels went into the tight final left-hand bend of the climb up to Jebel Hafeet with too much speed and went down. Esteban won the stage and the first stage race of his career. In Chaves, Colombia had a radiant English-speaking star, and another Grand Tour contender.

◈

The protagonists in stage fourteen of the 2016 Giro, near the Austrian border in Italy's far north, included two former Colombia Es Pasión riders. Darwin Atapuma joined an early breakaway, then attacked alone on the category two Passo Valparola, the last of six recognised climbs. At the top, he led by 35 seconds. Fifteen kilometres later, five kilometres from the ski resort of Alta Badia, Steven Kruiswijk, fifth overall, and Esteban Chaves, eighth, were just 21 seconds behind him. On the lower, steeper slopes Atapuma maintained his advantage, but as the gradient relaxed he began to lose ground. 1.8 kilometres from the finish line, he was caught.

Esteban Chaves's greatest assets, his explosive sprint and impeccable sense of timing, won him the stage. Kruijswijk, second, took the Maglia Rosa. Chaves lay third now, behind Kruisjwijk and Vincenzo Nibali. Darwin Atapuma crossed the line fourth, his head bowed down in bitter disappointment.

The following day, a poor ride by Nibali in the Alpe di Siusi mountain time trial, and his own sixth place, allowed Chaves to move up to second place overall, 2 minutes 12 seconds behind Kruijswijk. But on stage sixteen the Dutchman finished second to Valverde and stretched his overall lead to three minutes exactly. The Giro was his, or as good as. Until stage nineteen.

The route took the towering Colle dell'Agnello to Risoul, where Nairo had won the 2010 Avenir. Climbing the Agnello, swaddled in thick fog, Nibali, Chaves and Kruijswijk led between two-metre snowbanks, then plummeted into the descent. A gentle left-hand curve tightened and Kruijswijk touched the snow wall. Suddenly bike and rider were spiralling through the air.

Sufficiently intact to remount and restart, Kruijswijk joined a group of chasers, but none of its members saw fit to relay the Maglia Rosa, and he haemorrhaged time as, minutes ahead of him, Vincenzo Nibali launched repeated accelerations to shake off Chaves. With something over five kilometres to go, the Colombian could no longer respond. He tracked the Sicilian to the finish line, conceding 59 seconds but taking the Maglia Rosa.

At the press conference post-stage, a dry throat and hoarse voice betrayed the beginnings of illness. One mountain stage, with four cruel ascents, stood between Esteban and victory. But would his 44-second lead be enough?

The next day, Nibali made his attack on the penultimate climb, the Colle della Lombarda. Chaves had no choice but to let him go. Rigoberto Urán invited him onto his wheel, but Esteban lacked the strength to benefit from the gesture. Nibali's lead soon exceeded his deficit. At the top of the climb, he was the virtual race leader by seventeen seconds. On the descent he only added to his advantage.

Ahead of the battle for the Maglia Rosa, Darwin Atapuma, by responding in kind to attacks by Mikel Nieve and Joe Dombrowski, both declared and sabotaged his intent to win the stage. On the steep final climb, the Estonian Rein Taaramae led. Atapuma seemed to be closing in on him, but the finish came too soon.

Behind him, Nibali sprinted to the line. Chaves rode limply home 1 minute 36 seconds later, as distraught as Atapuma.

Jairo and Carolina, Esteban's parents, were waiting for him on the finish line. He joined them in the riders' area, shed his tears, then joined me for the flash interview for international TV:

Q: Esteban, you are still smiling, which is a good sign.
A: Yes, I'm tired but that's life. It's not such a big thing. It's only a bicycle race. I tried. I did my best. The team did its best. Three years ago, I would have been happy just to be racing for

the Giro d'Italia podium. I can hardly believe it. So now I'm here and I'm happy, I have done my best, and this is just the beginning.

Q: You've never made excuses. You sounded ill in yesterday's press conference. How are you in terms of your health?

A: I'm OK. I have no excuses. I just didn't have the legs. You have to take it straight. Everyone is a little bit sick, but it's one race for 80 hours, 3,000 kilometres, there are no excuses. It's simple. I didn't have the legs.

Q: And, as far as you are concerned, this is not the end of something, this is the beginning?

A: That's right. It's a beginning and, for sure, better things will come along.

Afterwards, Jairo told me, 'I've never wanted sport to be a war. We wept with our son, but we also congratulated Nibali. To see him take away the Giro, honestly, in an equal fight, is the essence of sport.'

Carolina added, 'Those are the values we have always believed in. You do your best, but with humility, with both feet on the ground.'

⚎

At the 2016 Tour de France, Colombian hopes again rested on Nairo. His Tour started without misadventures. For a week, not a second separated him from Chris Froome. Then, on the third climb of stage eight, the category one Col de Val Louron-Azet, Froome seemed to show an interest in the mountains competition and inched forward to take second place on the col. Twenty kilometres later, after an animated climb of the Col de Peyresourde, he made a similar move. Nairo, on his wheel, reached out for a water bottle on the line, and a tiny gap appeared. At that moment Froome pitched himself into the chasm. Descending on the very limits of control over 15 precarious kilometres, he eked out a 13-second lead. The stage winner's 10-second bonus gave him a 23-second advantage over Nairo, conjured out of nothing.

Four days later, with the stage finish at Montpellier still 12 kilometres away, and sidewinds buffeting the peloton, teammates Maciej Bodnar and Peter Sagan darted clear of the leading echelon. Froome and Geraint Thomas, providentially located in the widening angle of the front echelon, gave chase. In seconds, the four were away. Nairo, boxed in just behind, could only watch. The quartet's advantage contracted from 25 seconds to just six by the finish line. Still, with another time bonus for finishing second, Froome extended his lead over Nairo to 35 seconds.

The next day, in a stage shortened due to high winds on Mont Ventoux, Nairo, bereft of climbers to support him, launched three terse accelerations, breaking up the group. Each time, Froome's teammates Wout Poels and Sergio Luís Henao cushioned Nairo's jolting changes of pace for the yellow jersey, ensuring that Froome did not have to burn crucial energy by matching them. Then, Froome posted his own attack. Nairo and Richie Porte, once Froome's helper but now his rival, went with him. The yellow jersey changed pace repeatedly, sprinting, slowing, then darting away again. Suddenly, Nairo could no longer follow.

The Dutch climber Bauke Mollema darted past and rode up to Froome and Porte. Then as they neared the new, improvised stage finish at Chalet Reynard, they encountered the fans who had trekked down the mountain from the higher slopes, met the spectators already in place, and spilled out into the race route. A TV motorbike hit the brakes. Porte slapped into it from behind, and Froome and Mollema rode into him. Mollema quickly remounted and sped away. Porte was delayed by a problem with his chain. Froome, his bike unusable, started to run.

Mollema was the first of them to finish. Nineteen seconds passed, and five more riders – Yates, Aru, Meintjes, Bardet and Purito Rodríguez – crossed the line. Nairo, on Valverde's wheel, conceded another eight seconds. Footage emerged of him holding a motorbike: he had to make a statement to explain that he was merely trying to stay upright in the melee. Porte finished nearly 29 seconds behind him, with Froome, finally reunited with a usable bike, 44 seconds further back.

The first set of post-stage results showed Nairo third overall, 1 minute 14 seconds ahead of Froome, but, ignoring the rulebook, the commissaires awarded the time gaps that held at the time of the incident. Froome, who had already proven himself far superior to his rivals, lost the chance to overcome outrageous fortune with a heroic comeback.

Jarlinson Pantano's victory at Culoz, where he outsprinted the Polish climber Rafał Majka to win stage fifteen, was a sideshow, but took him back ten years to the final stage of the 2006 Vuelta del Porvenir in Túquerres, where he had joined Darwin Atapuma in a two-man attack. Pantano had sprinted too early, allowing Atapuma to come back at him to win the stage. At Culoz, against Majka, he made sure he got it right.

Two stages later, Pantano and Majka joined the breakaway again, and finished second and third behind the Russian Ilnur Zakarin near the dam at Finhaut-Émosson in Switzerland. Behind them Nairo, in crisis, had to let the best climbers go, and conceded 28 seconds to Froome and Porte. Then, in the rolling time trial between Sallanches and Megève, he lost more than a minute to Froome and nearly 30 seconds to his old rival Romain Bardet.

Nairo's stunning change of pace and rocklike toughness had deserted him. He had no explanation and no excuses. All he could say was 'The legs don't work.'

On stage nineteen, through the Alps from Albertville to Saint-Gervais, on the slopes of Mont Blanc, a crash moved Bauke Mollema from second place overall to tenth. A mechanical problem cost the Englishman Adam Yates time, and Nairo, however out of sorts, slotted into third place in the general classification. Two days later he made the podium of the Tour de France for the third time in four years.

In 2015 he had been threatening to win the Tour. Twelve months on, Nairo puzzled over his performance issues. For the first time, it no longer seemed inevitable that he would win a future Tour.

The team owner, Eusebio Unzué, was giving journalists private briefings to say that the problem was poor preparation. It was not the first sign of tension between Nairo and his Spanish team. In 2013 Nairo's Tour performance had been decisive to the renewal of the three-year contract between Telefónica and Eusebio Unzué's management company. At the end of 2015, Nairo had been unhappy with the team composition, the technical equipment, the small team staff – meaning bike builds by tired mechanics and massages from tired soigneurs – not to mention the treatment meted out to his brother Dayer, a stage winner at the 2014 Tour of Austria, but now cannon fodder dispatched, via circuitous itineraries, to races where he had no hope of competing. Nairo had been ready to leave the team. Movistar Colombia, to whom he was a major asset, promised that, if he stayed, his issues would be resolved. He stayed, but the promise was never fulfilled.

Where other teams published beautiful, considered images by cycling's best photographers on their social media feeds, Movistar published mobile phone pictures of Nairo with his mouth full, eating his post-stage snack. Indeed, by 2016 the team were seeking to minimise his public exposure. In February that year, as part of its fortieth anniversary celebrations, the Spanish daily *El País* had asked Nairo to participate in one of a series of televised conversations bringing together participants of some heft: the footballers Diego Maradona and Michel Platini, the Brazilian singer Caetano Veloso and his country's President 'Lula' da Silva, the Nobel Prize-winning novelist Mario Vargas Llosa and the Spanish singer-songwriter Joaquín Sabina, the political activists

Noam Chomsky and Tariq Ali. The goal was to pair Nairo with either the MotoGP pilot Valentino Rossi, perhaps, or the Oscar-winning bike lover Daniel Day-Lewis. But Nairo's team explained that the event did not fall within its global strategy. When the Spanish national press agency EFE asked to interview him for a volume called *Eminent Ibero-Americans*, to be sent to the embassies of Spanish-speaking countries around the world, the team said it was not team policy.

After the Olympic road race in London four years earlier, Sergio Luís Henao had finished sixteenth and thrown his bike down in frustration. 'I'm still fresh,' he told Jenaro Leguízamo. 'My powder is still dry.'

On the decisive climb in Rio de Janeiro, he joined Vincenzo Nibali and Rafał Majka in what looked like the winning move. He seemed certain of at least a bronze medal until, on the final descent, with just 11 kilometres left to ride, he slipped on a damp corner and slid at high speed into the kerb, fracturing a hip.

Colombia's Olympic disappointment continued on the track, where Fernando Gaviria finished no better than fourth overall and announced his immediate retirement from track cycling. From now on, he would compete exclusively on the road.

At the 2016 Vuelta a España, Miguel Ángel López started his first three-week tour. Much was expected of him until, late in stage three, he fell face first into the road and knocked out three teeth. He abandoned three days later.

Then, at San Andrés de Teixido, a hundred kilometres north along the coast from A Coruña, Darwin Atapuma finished second in stage four and took over the race lead, with his former Colombia Es Pasión teammates Nairo Quintana and Esteban Chaves fourth and fifth.

Four days on, Nairo took the jersey from Atapuma, as he had from Urán at the 2014 Giro. On the final, eight-kilometre climb up to La Camperona, Froome accelerated, with Contador and Quintana on his wheel. A second acceleration saw Contador lose contact and Nairo move through onto Froome's wheel. Then, as Froome slowed, Nairo darted past. Over the final 1,100 metres, he gained 35 seconds on the race leader and took the race lead by 27 seconds over his eternal rival.

The following day, a breakaway gained nearly three minutes on the group of favourites, allowing the Spaniard David de la Cruz to take the leader's jersey overnight, but on the climb to Lagos de Covadonga, Nairo took his second stage win in three days and recovered the leader's jersey. He led Froome by 58 seconds.

Stage eleven followed a rest day. It ended in a steep ascent on Peña Cabarga, overlooking the city of Santander. With 1.8 kilometres to go, Esteban Chaves attacked, opening a 21-second lead. By the *flamme rouge*, his lead had contracted to 17 seconds. Behind him, Valverde had dragged Froome and Nairo to within 12 seconds of Chaves when Nairo flashed past, Froome on his wheel.

They passed Chaves with 500 metres still to climb. At that instant, Froome attacked. Nairo gradually regained his wheel and they rode side by side for 150 metres, before Froome inched ahead, then sprinted away. The commissaires credited Nairo with the same time: Froome now lay 54 seconds back.

The early mountain stages were ridden with foreknowledge of stage nineteen, a mostly flat individual time trial over a 37-kilometre route between Xàbia and Calp, where Froome was expected to make important time gains. Nairo's 54-second lead was unlikely to be enough, and it was hard to see where he could add to it before the time trial. Climbing the Aubisque on stage fourteen, the two leaders cancelled each other out.

Meanwhile, Alberto Contador had faded to sixth place, nearly three and a half minutes behind Nairo. Stage fifteen took in gruelling roads through the Pyrenean foothills of Aragon on which a fractured peloton might never regroup, and finished at the ski station of Formigal, close to the French border, atop a category one climb.

The stage was only 118 kilometres long, and started with a 30-kilometre loop around Sabiñánigo. Before the stage start, Nairo and his teammates rode the loop and saw it was full of potential traps. As the race started, they made sure their leader was well positioned at the front of the peloton.

Early in the stage, Nairo's teammate José Herrada had a mechanical problem. As he waited at the roadside, he noticed that Froome's teammates were bunched towards the back of the group and informed Arrieta in the team car. Before they had time to regroup, the attacks started, first through the Italian Gianluca Brambilla, and then Contador himself. Forewarned of Froome's predicament, Nairo joined the fourteen-man attack which had quickly formed, in which he and Contador had two teammates each.

Half an hour into the stage, Froome was in a second group, a minute behind the leaders, with the Spaniard David López alone among his team helpers to hand. The rest of his team was a further two minutes behind. Nairo's teammates played a delicate game at the front of the Froome group, sustaining the pace to keep Froome's support riders from joining him, while ensuring that no ground was made up on the leaders.

Five and a half kilometres up the Sallent de Gállego, the final climb, Quintana and Contador had both run out of team support. No one was willing to work with the race leader, so, with nine kilometres left to ride, Nairo moved to the front.

Two minutes behind him, Froome was in the same situation. Attacks by Valverde, then Chaves, forced him to respond. The accelerations only sapped his energy.

At the front, Brambilla, who had ridden the climb on Nairo's wheel, darted away to win the stage, with Nairo second. Esteban Chaves came in 1 minute 19 seconds behind Contador, retaining third place overall by five seconds. Froome finished 47 seconds after Chaves. He still lay second, but his deficit to Nairo had ballooned. It was impossible to imagine even Froome making up 3 minutes 37 seconds in the following day's time trial. Nairo duly rode the stage safely, avoiding errors on the narrow, twisting roads and finishing eleventh, 2 minutes 16 seconds behind Froome.

The final mountain stage from Benidorm to the military radar station Alto de Aitana was an exhibition by the former Colombia Es Pasión riders, in all their strength and weakness. Nairo went into it with a lead over Froome of 81 seconds. Esteban Chaves started 1 minute 11 seconds behind Contador and a place on the podium. Darwin Atapuma, faced with his last chance for a stage win, duly joined the early breakaway. Far behind him, on the penultimate climb, Esteban Chaves' teammates thinned out the chasing group. Three kilometres from the top of the climb, with all of 44.7 kilometres to go, Esteban attacked alone.

Contador, denuded of his teammates, moved to the front but, lacking the legs to chase, he dropped back into the body of the group. After 11 kilometres, Chaves reached his teammate Damien Howson, who had dropped out of the breakaway to wait for him. Howson forged on, with Chaves in his slipstream, for 18 kilometres. By the time Howson peeled away exhausted, Chaves led Contador by 1 minute 40 seconds. With fewer than 16 kilometres left, the tactic had worked. Alone now, Chaves increased his lead to within a few seconds of two minutes.

In the final seven kilometres, Darwin Atapuma darted out of the leading group and chased down the stage leader, Luís León Sánchez. The elusive stage win was in sight. But with 2.4 kilometres to go, the young Frenchman Pierre Latour reached him and attacked. Atapuma and Latour took turns sprinting and countering, each testing the other, each draining himself of energy.

Behind them, some hundred metres before the '5km to go' sign, Froome attacked. Nairo darted into his slipstream. After a moment of calm, Froome, out of the saddle, sprinted hard for fifteen seconds. Nairo did not cede an inch. Just before the '3km to go sign,' Froome made another fifteen-second effort, out of the saddle. Again, Nairo stayed close. After a brief respite, Froome stood on the pedals again and made a less intense, twenty-second effort, suggesting fatigue. Then, he sat. Thirteen seconds passed. Then, he rose again and made an all-out, ten-second sprint. Nairo shadowed him all the way.

Latour led Atapuma under the *flamme rouge* marking one kilometre to go and held his position for 500 metres. Then Atapuma sprinted past, gained twenty metres, and passed beneath a red banner. But it was not the finish line.

At the '300m to go' marker, Latour regained Atapuma's wheel and surged past. Darwin had no more to offer. For the fifth time of the season, he had finished in the top four of a Grand Tour stage, without winning one. He crossed the finish line a second back and burst into tears.

Esteban Chaves finished 3 minutes 17 seconds after Latour. With 200 metres to go, Froome made a final sprint. Nairo danced past and crossed the line 46 seconds after Chaves, and three seconds ahead of Froome. The Englishman applauded his rival.

Then 4 minutes 41 seconds after Latour, and 1 minute 24 seconds after Chaves, Contador arrived alone. Esteban had made the podium by 13 seconds. Nairo, Esteban and Darwin, the three former members of Colombia Es Pasión, had given their nation remarkable visibility.

Madrid was Colombian for a day. The Paseo del Prado and the Plaza de Cibeles were lined with Colombian flags and fans in yellow football shirts. Nairo and Darwin Atapuma had worn the race leader's red jersey for sixteen of the twenty-one stages. Nairo and Esteban Chaves then occupied two of the three steps on the podium. Of the year's nine Grand Tour podium places,

Colombians had filled four. To even the most casual followers of cycling, Colombia had become a familiar and prestigious name. Its integration into cycling's global community of nations had been secured.

卌

Those huge Colombian crowds in Madrid were celebrating more than victory in the Vuelta. Since Nairo's successful Tour de l'Avenir, Colombian cycling had come a long way. So had the peace process, now drawing to its successful conclusion. It was in September 2010, during Nairo's Tour de l'Avenir, that President Juan Manuel Santos had sent his first, exploratory message to the FARC, expressing his readiness to talk peace. Then, on 24 August 2016, in the middle of Nairo's Vuelta, the peace negotiators announced that they had reached 'a full, final and definitive agreement on all the items on the agenda'.

The peace process and the cycling success had more in common than mere timing. Both were major international undertakings. From the start, Santos had involved the international community, from UN General Secretary Ban Ki-moon, who attended the promulgation of the Law of Victims and Land Restitution in 2011, to the four facilitator and guarantor countries – Cuba, Norway, Venezuela and Chile – assembled to host and observe the peace process. Then, to freshen up, unclog, enliven and refocus the talks over their six-year course, he had brought in international lawyers, diplomats, negotiators and non-governmental organisations from dozens of nations.

Since 1990, when a number of illegal armed groups had demobilised, international law had changed beyond all recognition. The 1990 Amnesty and Clemency Law, regulating the demobilisation, had made no mention of victims or of atrocities committed by the state. The entire text was thirty sentences long – not even 1,200 words. By contrast, the 310 pages, 140,000 words and sheer complexity of the 'New Final Agreement to End the

Armed Conflict and Build a Stable and Lasting Peace' were proof that national conflicts were no longer purely national affairs. The world had become a vastly more integrated place. Thanks to the peace and its cyclists, Colombia was part of it.

Peace and its conditions were as much part of the global system as sport. Amnesties handed out too lightly in El Salvador, Peru, Chile, Brazil and Uruguay had fallen foul of the Inter-American Court of Human Rights. The court's rulings, as well as precedents in conflict resolution from such places as Guatemala, South Africa, Rwanda, Burundi, Mali and the former Yugoslavia, all had to be incorporated into the 'New Final Agreement'.

As well as requiring that applicants for clemency provide a full and truthful account, seek their victims' forgiveness, pay reparations and contribute to projects to ensure there would be no backsliding into violence, the 'New Final Agreement' established an Integrated System for Truth, Justice, Reparations and Non-Repetition, a Commission for Truth, Co-existence and Non-Repetition, and a Special Search Unit for Persons deemed Missing in the Conflict – the latter to start its work in 2018.

The Vuelta finished on 11 September. Two weeks later, in the presence of representatives of the international community, President Santos and FARC leader Alias Timochenko signed the peace agreement in a formal ceremony in Cartagena, using a pen fashioned from a spent bullet casing. The ceremony may have had the unintended consequence of suggesting to those in favour of the peace that it was a fait accompli, and that there was no need to vote in the 2 October referendum, while giving its opponents conviction that it had been agreed without consultation, and that voting was of paramount importance.

On the eve of the referendum, Esteban Chaves out-thought both Rigoberto Urán and the Italian rider Diego Rosa to win Il Lombardia – formerly the Giro di Lombardia – and became the first Colombian to win one of cycling's one-day Monuments. It meant Colombia finished the 2016 season as the fourth-ranked nation in cycling's world rankings after France, Belgium and Italy. Together with the peace process, its cyclists were softening Colombia's international image.

The next day, Colombians were asked to ratify the Agreement in a referendum on the question: 'Do you support the New Final Agreement to End the Armed Conflict and Build a Stable and Lasting Peace?'

With the polls showing 'Yes' at 70 per cent, President Santos insisted that there was no 'Plan B' for peace. The Constitutional Court had already ruled that peace was a fundamental constitutional right and, as such, 'immune to counter-majoritarian decisions'. Colombia was polarised. Earlier that year, in a Bogotá restaurant, my dining partner, the Spanish journalist Carlos Arribas, asked the waiter how he would be voting: 'The FARC kidnapped my father and sent us his body parts in parcels.' To our stunned silence, he told us, 'I'll be voting no.'

Just 37.41 per cent of the electorate bothered turning out. By 6,431,376 votes against 6,377,482 – 50.21 per cent against 49.78 per cent of votes cast – 'No' won the day. According to some analysts, the regions most affected by the violence voted 'Yes', while 'No' prevailed in urban areas, where the conflict was a far-off reality. Four days after the referendum, perhaps to keep the peace process from stalling, Santos was awarded the Nobel peace prize.

A revised deal was signed on 24 November. Santos did not take it back to the people. The Senate and the House of Representatives approved it without dissent. Uribe's supporters boycotted the session. Santos declared, triumphantly, 'In 150 days all of the FARC's weapons will be in the hands of the United Nations. As an armed group, the FARC will cease to exist.'

17

The Boy Who Grew Up Too Fast

In March 2017, while Sergio Luís Henao was in France winning Paris–Nice, Nairo constructed his second Tirreno–Adriatico win as he had his first, around the climb of Monte Terminillo in Abruzzo. An acceleration by Thibaut Pinot with five kilometres to go split the peloton. Only a handful of the world's best climbers could respond: Nairo, Geraint Thomas, Adam Yates, Tom Dumoulin and, on his wheel, a twenty-year-old ex-mountain biker with next to no experience on the road, riding his first WorldTour race for the Androni Sidermec Bottecchia team: Egan Arley Bernal Gómez.

A series of accelerations, the last of them with 2.2 kilometres to go, took Nairo clear, and he won the stage by 18 seconds from Geraint Thomas. But Bernal's thirteenth place, 61 seconds behind his compatriot, spoke of genuine talent.

Six weeks later, in the Monte Bondone stage of April's Tour of the Alps, Egan was there again, matching Landa, Pinot, Pozzovivo, Rolland, Michele Scarponi and Thomas over a climb that, in all, extended to 35 kilometres.

In September 2015, aged eighteen, Egan Bernal had gone to a junior road race in Tuscany called the Monte Pisano Autumn Trophy, also known as *Sognando il Giro delle Fiandre* – literally, 'Dreaming of the Tour of Flanders'. There, he had split up the group, orchestrated a two-man attack and won. The evening after the race he had driven the hundred miles from Navacchio, just east of Pisa, to a restaurant in Bolzaneto, just outside Genoa, where he had signed a four-year contract with a Professional-Continental cycling team. It was, in every way, an unusual contract for someone so young and untested. But Egan Bernal was an unusual talent.

≣

He had been hyperactive even in the womb. His mother, Flor Marina, was twenty-three when she had him: 'None of the other mothers had babies who kicked as much as mine. One day he didn't move for four hours. I was so worried I went to accident and emergency.'

Soon after birth Egan suffered repeated bouts of illness. 'I had lung problems and I was often ill,' he told me, 'and she was always taking me to the doctor. My mother says it was serious.'

Longer term, the family malaise was not ill-health but financial anxiety. The Bernals had lived in Los Cámbulos, part of Bolívar 83, known as Zipaquirá's most insecure barrio but founded in September 1982 when a group of radical students and trade unionists campaigning on behalf of the town's poor organised an occupation on a patch of waste land owned by the church. Between classes, the students divided the area into lots and helped the occupiers build basic shelters. Despite attempts by the police to clear the area, the residents were issued home-spun deeds in June 1983. The students held workshops to teach the new homeowners their rights, and instructed them how to defend their newly won properties.

In April 1984, the leader of the student activists, Gustavo Francisco Petro Urrego, announced his allegiance to the guerrilla group M-19, joining the other founders of Bolívar 83. It is said that, in those days, the inhabitants of the neighbourhood decided to raise the M-19 flag every day at seven in the morning.

Eighteen months later, Petro was arrested in Bolívar 83 with a stash of arms and improvised explosive devices.

The area was a deprived one, lacking public services and plagued by drug pushing and addiction. It was only in December 2016, thirty-three years after its creation, that the town authorities finally connected Bolívar 83 to the water main and provided it with drinking water on tap. By then, Gustavo Petro was a left-wing senator, soon to be the mayor of Bogotá. In the 2018 elections he would be the left-wing candidate for the presidency, losing only in the final round.

◈

Flor told me, 'When Egan was five, we would sit down just as we are sitting here, and I would ask his opinion. "What are we going to do, my son?"

'And he would say, "Don't worry, Mummy, don't be sad. We'll get through." He was only five, but he talked like an adult.'

His remarkable precocity is something Flor regrets: 'I have always said that Egan grew up too soon. I sometimes feel sad because of it. He never had a childhood. There was no time for one. To achieve all his goals, his childhood was sacrificed. That's why I'm sometimes guilty of pampering [his brother] Ronald [eight years Egan's junior].'

In 2008 the collapse of an immense, country-wide series of illegal pyramid schemes hit Zipaquirá hard. In its wake, Bolívar 83 was targeted by drug pushers, with the accompanying violence. In 2009 the Bernals left the area and moved into social housing in another barrio called El Porvenir. The roads were still unpaved, and their house lacked a roof and floors, but the move represented a small but significant step up.

▥

Germán Bernal and Flor Marina Gómez had both been born into peasant farming families. Egan's father grew up at La Fuente, a rural area in Zipaquirá's outskirts, his mother at Pasuncha, an outcrop of dwellings in the countryside near Pacho. Theirs were working, peasant childhoods.

'I started doing little jobs when I was five or six,' Flor tells me. 'Before going to school I had to bring water and do my chores. When I got home, I had outdoor work to do before I could start my homework.'

There was no electricity so she did her schoolwork by candlelight, in the days before it was obligatory to pass your school certificate. She never took hers. Germán took his as an adult.

Aged eighteen Flor moved in with an older, married sister who lived in Zipaquirá, and found work in the cut flower industry. Its huge greenhouses, beneath the flight path of the planes coming in to land at El Dorado International airport, offered long hours of repetitive, low-paid work, exposure to the chemicals used in intensive cultivation, and constant pressure. Flor Marina started with sowing and cutting, later sorting roses into export blooms and inferior flowers for the national market. She rose at four to catch the five o'clock bus and finished at three in the afternoon to collect Egan from the crèche.

Germán Bernal was Flor's sister's husband's cousin. He too worked in the rose houses, although when he and Flor moved in together and started a family, even their combined wages left little to spare. Germán moved into construction, then security, working for a firm that rotated him between various sites around Zipaquirá, including the colossal underground cathedral, carved in the 1990s out of what is left of the rock salt, an obligatory day trip for foreign visitors to Bogotá.

Employees in the rose houses were allowed to buy bouquets at a discount. Flor Marina would buy ten bouquets at 3,000 pesos (about a Euro) each. Egan would then take them from door to door around El Porvenir and sell them for 5,000 pesos each.

He recalls, 'I gave her a thousand pesos and kept a thousand pesos for myself, and that paid some of my school expenses: photocopies, elevenses, that sort of thing. I was ten, eleven, twelve years old. The first few times I felt ashamed, so she came with me. I do not know if that kind of thing makes you mature faster, in inverted commas, but I've never had any problem choosing between teams and agents and contracts.'

Egan Bernal's first bike had been passed around his cousins for twenty years before it reached him. The dream of racing professionally came from his father. Germán Bernal had ridden an Under-23 Tour of Colombia, but, after years of striving with no financial support, he had given up.

Egan tells me, 'I'm a cyclist because of my father,' then adds, 'although, because of the ordeal he went through, he didn't actually want me to be one.'

One Sunday in 2005, when Egan was eight, a kids' cycling event was being held in a park in Zipaquirá by a former professional rider named Fabio Rodríguez. Germán Bernal knew Fabio Rodríguez – they had trained together – and they fell into conversation.

'My father didn't want me to take part,' Egan told me, 'so he said he didn't have enough change to pay the entry fee, even if it was only 2,000 pesos [about 50 pence]. One of his friends, a man named César Bermúdez, was also in the park, so I asked him to pay for me, and he did.'

Fabio Rodríguez recalls, 'He was tiny, and we didn't have a helmet for him. He found one somewhere, and even though it was way too big for him, he was able to race.'

As Egan remembers it, 'I couldn't see much so I didn't realise I had won until someone told me. The prize was a proper cycling uniform. I always wore football shorts and a sweatshirt, so I was really happy.'

The five best riders also received free membership of the

Zipaquirá Institute of Recreation and Sports and coaching from Fabio Rodríguez.

Fabio told me, 'I always told the director of the Institute, "Give scholarships to the riders who win. Don't charge the good ones: they are the ones we want to keep. They are the ones who will become champions."

'And that's the way it stayed: Egan never had to pay his monthly subs. We started to work together, and from the beginning he was a winner.'

Egan concludes, 'And that is how the process began.'

Egan's good fortune was to meet a coach like Fabio Rodríguez, whose vision encompassed both the local mountain biking scene and the highest reaches of global road racing. In the 1960s the milk marketing board in the northern Spanish region of Asturias – the Central Lechera Asturiana, to give it its full Spanish title – had sponsored an amateur cycling team whose most celebrated pupil, José Manuel Fuentes, went on to turn professional and win the Vuelta a España in 1972 and 1974. In 1988 Fuentes returned as the director of a professional team with the same sponsor, now known by the more digestible acronym CLAS – although the milk cartons still bore the old legend 'Central Lechera Asturiana', meaning that there was no way for consumers enthused by the aura of sports sponsorship to connect the team with the product. In 1992 CLAS-Cajastur took on a Swiss leader, Tony Rominger, who immediately won the Vuelta a España. He repeated the feat the following year, and the year after that.

Fabio Hernán Rodríguez Hernández, the only Colombian on the team's books, was one of Rominger's key mountain helpers. From Cogua, Cundinamarca, a rural community just outside Zipaquirá, he was the son of a peasant dairy farmer and a primary school teacher. Born with a cleft lip and widely known as *Besolindo* – 'Pretty kiss' – he entered the world of cycling, like many Colombian cyclists from the 1950s to the 1990s, as a delivery boy.

In a café in Zipaquirá, he told me, 'I found a job at a bakery, distributing bread on a pig-iron bike. I had friends who were already racing, and one Sunday they invited me to join them. They lent me a more suitable machine, and I began to go out with them and beat them. They said, "You are good on the climbs," and encouraged me to buy a bike.'

Soon he was matching Lucho Herrera in the mountains. Then came the move to CLAS in Spain, although Fabio always suffered homesickness: 'A telephone call cost an arm and a leg in those days, and there were no social media, so it was impossible to know what was going on in your home village. You had to forget this world. I was there three years, and that was enough. I missed the land that is my home.'

In 1995 Fabio returned to Cogua. He rode on until the 1998 economic crisis then retired because there were no more teams. His road career behind him, he took up mountain biking: 'These days the mountain bike scene in Colombia is strong. Back then it was just beginning, and there wasn't much support. There weren't enough races for you to stay in condition, so after a few years I gave up.'

Within months of the Uribe government coming to power, there were military operations in the hills at Neusa, fifteen kilometres to the north of Zipaquirá.

'The guerrillas never entered Zipaquirá,' says Fabio Rodríguez, 'but they occupied the hills near the Neusa Dam, one of the places where Germán Bernal worked. Early in Uribe's first term, in 2002 or 2003, helicopters and land troops moved in and eliminated them from the area. They killed two hundred guerrillas in a night. Nothing was ever said in public, it never made the newspapers, but the local people knew what had happened.'

Neusa is now a favourite tourist spot for the people of Bogotá, with boating on the reservoir, picnics in the park and cycling. The climb up to the dam, known as Las Margaritas, is ten kilometres long. Egan calls it his gymnasium. Fabio says, 'On Saturdays and Sundays it is thick with cyclists.'

In 2003 Zipaquirá's new mayor, José Edilberto Caicedo Sastoque, gave Fabio Rodríguez a call: 'He told me I had knowledge and experience from my years competing in Europe, and he wanted to put it to use in the community.'

Under the Instituto de Recreación y Deporte de Zipaquirá – the town's Institute of Recreation and Sports – Fabio Rodríguez opened a mountain bike school and organised cycling festivals in the local parks with races for children of all ages: 'And I began to study the theory behind what I had been doing as a professional athlete. We assembled a group of kids and started working with them. We got them racing, and we took them to events all over the country.'

When Mayor Caicedo's term came to an end, his successor, Jorge Enrique González Garnica, embraced the school with the same enthusiasm. 'The athletic potential here is enormous, and they could see that,' Fabio told me.

In 2011 a new administration with new priorities closed down Fabio's project. But the school's eight-year window had produced a long list of riders good enough to ride internationally: the future Team Illuminate rider Camilo Castiblanco; Diego Vásquez, who joined the Spanish team PCM Team Kuota in 2018; international mountain bikers Holman Villarraga and Yosiana Quintero Pineda; Wilson Peña, who graduated to the Fundación Alberto Contador team Polartec-Kometa; Brandon Rivera, who joined Team Ineos late in 2019; and Egan.

For a while, when he was ten or eleven, Egan was donning a tiny policeman's uniform and going to the Cuidapalos ('Tree Guardians'), an environmental association run by the police, along the lines of the Cub Scouts. His mother, Flor Marina, explained, 'I always worried about the dangers that lurk on the street corners where children play, so I wanted to keep the boys' – meaning Egan and, later, his brother Ronald – 'occupied. Anyway, he was beautiful in his uniform, all neat and tidy! Maybe that was where he learned his sense of responsibility and discipline.'

Egan laughed fondly when I mention the Cuidapalos, although, he says, 'I only went for six months. I had already started training and there wasn't time for both.'

In any case, his coach recalled, 'He began to win. He won in all categories, although he had a rival, Jhonatan Sotelo, who was also talented. When they closed the school, Jhonatan concentrated on his studies, put on weight and we lost him. But he was one of many good young athletes whose ability went to waste when the school closed.'

Flor Marina told me, 'When Egan had the opportunity to start cycling, and started on the right foot by winning his first race, Fabio told us the boy was good. That was the motivation we needed to support him, with Fabio's assistance and help from the Institute, which took the kids with good results to the national and departmental races. Egan always stood out. He was always among the best, so they paid the race registration, transport and expenses.'

In 2008 the eleven-year-old Egan Bernal won two departmental races and finished second in the Cundinamarca Cup. His schedule for the following year shows the extent of his commitment at the tender age of twelve:

15 February: Cundinamarca Cup, Round 1 (Zipaquirá): 1st
22 February: Colombia Cup, Round 1 (Sevilla): Valle: 2nd
15 March: Cundinamarca Cup, Round 2 (Cogua): 1st
26 March: Colombia Cup, Round 2 (La Tebaida): 1st
12 April: Cundinamarca Cup, Round 3 (Guatavita): 2nd
17 May: Cundinamarca Cup, Round 4 (Chía): 2nd
24 May: Colombia Cup, Round 3 (Chiquinquirá): 2nd
28 June: Colombia Cup, Round 4 (Jericó): 3rd
29 June: Cundinamarca Cup, Round 4 (location unknown): 1st
19 July: Colombia Cup, Round 5 (Zipaquirá): 3rd
16 August: Cundinamarca Cup, Round 6 (Cogua): 1st

20 September: Cundinamarca Cup, Round 7 (Mesitas del
  Colegio): 1st
27 September: Colombia Cup, Round 7 (Palestina): 2nd

Victory in five of the seven Cundinamarca Cup events, and
second place in the other two, brought him first place in the
series overall. One win, three second places and two third places
in the national Colombia Cup series, with one round missed
for reasons now forgotten, brought him second place overall.
Then, in November, came victory in the national championships
in Sevilla, in the Valle del Cauca. And Egan, undoubtedly the
flower of the Cundinamarca mountain biking scene, was not
alone. All told, the team won 185 medals that year. It was a formidable structure, and provided a support system in case of an
emergency, like the one that happened when Egan was about
twelve, perhaps during that busy 2009 season. On the way to
school, he stopped at some traffic lights and was approached
by a man supposedly selling puppies. Drawn in by his spiel,
Egan let him borrow his bike for a moment and never saw it
again.

  To replace it, Egan's parents gave what they could, and Fabio
Rodríguez mobilised the Institute of Recreation and Sport and
the other riders. Camilo Castiblanco, another rider named
Holman Villazaga, and their parents all made contributions.
Fabio provided the rest.

◈

While Egan was standing on his first podiums as a tiny mountain biker, Pablo Mazuera was struggling through Business
Administration at the University of La Sabana in Chía, north
of Bogotá. When he finished, he decided he needed something
more enjoyable to do and, having worked as a DJ when he was
a teenager, became a sound engineer. He took himself to Full
Sail University in Florida to study for a year, spent another year

working at Telemundo Television in Miami, then went back to Colombia and founded Mezuena Producciones, which, when we spoke, had been producing audio for advertising and for films for thirteen years.

In 2010 Mazuera was commissioned to make a video of the Pan-American mountain bike championships in Guatemala. There, he befriended one of the Colombian riders, a sixteen-year-old cross-country specialist from Ubaté named Hilvar Yamith Malaver. It was then that he formed the idea of sponsoring a small mountain bike team as a kind of charitable project.

After returning home to Colombia, he said to Hilvar Malaver, '"Find me four kids, and we will help them any way we can: uniforms, travel expenses, whatever." He brought me four skinny, dark-skinned twelve-year-olds. They were tiny, but they had already been competing for four years, and they already had great Cundinamarca Cup and National Cup results. Their names were Brandon Rivera, Diego Vázquez, Jhonatan Sotelo and Egan Bernal.'

To establish his cycling project, Pablo searched for extra sponsorship and support. He found them in a furniture showroom called Tugó, and in the importer to Colombia of Specialized bikes. The owner of Tugó was Santiago De Angulo, who, by coincidence, had gone to the same high school as Mazuera: 'We hit it off immediately. Santiago was crazy about cycling and madly impulsive. The moment he heard about the project, he said, "Count me in. How much do you need?" and pulled out his wallet. He gave me 500,000 pesos. It wasn't a huge sum, but we made it go a long way.'

In 2011 the team was born. Pablo called it *Pura Actitud* – Pure Attitude: 'For three years, I poured my own money into the team. As soon as my salary from the company arrived, it went in journeys and competitions. We drove to races in my minibus. To start off with we could only offer uniforms, travel and entry fees, although, as time went by, the sponsors increased their contributions, and the riders had racing and training bikes, better clothing, and so on.'

They went to compete abroad for the first time in April 2013. The Junior Pan-American championships were being held in Tucumán Province, Argentina. But before they had even left, disaster struck: 'Three weeks before the trip, while training in Neusa, Egan fell and broke his right collarbone. He still had the injury when we left. He was supposed to ride an Argentinian national championship event a few days before the Pan-American championships, but I didn't let him start. I only let him on the course two days before the race.

'In the race, he took an early lead, but his rear shifter went into the spokes and he had to abandon. He was deeply frustrated, although, in a way, it was the best thing that could have happened. It left him hungry for success.'.

The gregarious Mazuera made contacts everywhere. In July that year, he accepted an invitation from friends in Cuenca, Ecuador, to ride the national championships there. On 14 July Egan won the race, although not, of course, the title of Ecuadorean champion. In September 2013, at Balcarce, in Buenos Aires Province, Argentina, he became Latin American Champion. The next month, in Palmira, Valle, he won his fifth national MTB title.

Egan did not definitively leave Fabio Rodríguez until 2014, although relations between the coach who had launched Egan's career and the philanthropist who would help him develop on the international stage were understandably difficult. Rodríguez felt that Mazuera was stealing his riders.

Egan says today that he always preferred road racing to mountain biking. In late 2013 he had pressed Pablo Mazuera into helping him ride the Vuelta del Futuro in December. He had entered the qualifying races with Brandon Rivera and Wilson Peña, and won the heat at Sibaté, south-east of Bogotá, on a notorious climb called the Romeral. Of the Vuelta del Futuro itself he has little to say, except that he rode with little preparation. The result sheets suggest that he raced aggressively – he was fifth over the first categorised climb of the race in stage one, fourth in the first intermediate sprint two days later, when he crested the category one Alto de Guacáica seventh. He finished the stage ninth, 16 seconds behind the Ecuadorean Jhonatan Narváez who won the stage and the race overall. Egan completed the course 22nd overall, 3 minutes 14 seconds behind the winner. It was less than he was used to.

Meanwhile, he faced his school leaving exams. He was told that his patchy attendance record meant that any kind of financial assistance for a college career depended on an outstanding final mark. He turned his mind to his books and passed with a result that put him among the top 10 per cent in the department.

The result allowed him to start journalism studies at the Universidad de La Sabana north of Bogotá. He loved his studies, which he sandwiched between his morning time trial to university and his evening time trial home again.

Working now with the departmental mountain bike coach John Sergio Avellaneda Carranza, Egan began preparations for his first Junior World Championships at Hafjell, Norway. In August 2014 his close friend Brandon Rivera went to the Youth Olympic Games in Nanjing, China, and won a gold and two silver medals. It only spurred Egan on.

But the Norway trip required a considerable investment. 'To have a chance of winning, you need to start near the front,' Pablo Mazuera told me. 'To do so, you need championship points. So, even before travelling halfway across the world to Norway, we had to go to Brazil and Costa Rica, and then, five weeks before the Worlds, the United States. It was just as well. At the race in Vermont, Egan was only fourth. It was a wake-up call. We came home, and he trained hard.'

As the team prepared to leave for Europe, the Foundation ran out of money. The Colombian Cycling Federation let Mazuera take some national uniforms but offered no financial help: after all, they said, Colombia had never won anything in mountain biking.

If they had consulted Coldeportes' High Performance Centre in Bogotá, they might have seen that Egan was worth supporting. In 2006 Pablo Mazuera took Egan there for physiological testing. The results can only have been impressive ones, despite the altitude, but neither Egan nor his mentor ever received them.

Mazuera refused to give up: 'We held a raffle to raise funds. My father paid about half the costs. Santiago De Angulo made a contribution, and I paid the rest. We were as frugal as possible.'

On 4 September in Hafjell, Egan started on the second row in the cross-country event. He finished 37 seconds behind Denmark's Simon Andreassen and took the silver medal.

Andrea Bianco, an Italian coach, who was at the time the Colombian national MTB coach, says that the mountain bike team sponsored by the Colombian importers of GW bikes offered Egan €500 a month to join them: 'I encouraged him to accept. I said, "It's not a lot, but it's five times what you're earning now." But Egan felt he had more chance of winning the world title on a Specialized bike, so he stayed with Specialized-Tugó, earning €100 a month.'

At the start of March 2015, in a national race on the course to be used in the American Continental Championships three weeks later, Egan had a fall. Pablo Mazuera saw it: 'There was a tree trunk across the road, and he jumped it badly and fell. He broke the same collarbone as before.'

Mazuera sent him to Dr Gustavo Castro, who recalled: 'We operated the same day. I told him to take his time coming back, but his powers of recovery were astonishing.'

On the morning of the race, wearing a brace and strapping to immobilise the shoulder, he rode a few practice laps to prove he was OK, then rode the race to victory.

After qualifiers in Brazil, the United States and Costa Rica,

Egan prepared for the 2015 World Championships in Andorra. This time, the Colombian federation contributed to his travel and accommodation. In Europe, Mazuera took him to a race at Montgenèvre in the French Alps to monitor his form. He finished second, despite conceding 2 minutes 21 seconds to the French rider Antoine Philipp.

From Montgenèvre they crossed the Alps to Aigle, the home of the UCI's World Cycling Centre, where Mazuera took his UCI Directeur Sportif exam and arranged for Wilson Peña to attend the centre as a trainee. While they were there, road coach Alejandro González Tablas suggested that Egan take a VO_2 Max or oxygen uptake test.

'Let's do it now,' said Egan straight away.

He told me, 'They didn't want to because I had already been out training that morning, but it was our only day there, so I told them, "It was a very light session," and in the end they let me take the stress test.'

Egan says simply that it went well. Pablo Mazuera says, 'He put on a show.'

Alejandro González Tablas told me, 'We have reference figures, because a lot of cyclists have passed through here. A lot of Eritreans who are in the WorldTour have been here. So have people like [the Argentinian rider] Eduardo Sepúlveda. Froome was a little earlier, so we don't have his test results for comparison. But we have a data set, and when Egan took the test, it really was . . .' He was lost for words.

Egan's oxygen uptake was 88.8ml/kg/min, the highest value recorded at the centre since 2011. 'But,' he says, 'it's only a number – a tiny picture of the rider's potential, although when you see his results, and his world-class performances on a mountain bike . . . the one confirms the other, if you see what I mean.'

On 3 September Egan tested his unusual aerobic power at his second Junior World Cross-Country MTB Championships. Andrea Bianco watched the race:

The Andorran route seemed to favour him: the altitude and the climbs, so Egan was the favourite, or felt he was. But half an hour before the start, the skies opened and the route turned to mud. Egan was a good jumper, and rode well in the wet, but he was no Nino Schurter [the eight-time world cross country champion from Switzerland].

So, on the first climb, Egan took the lead and gained ten seconds, but on the descent, Simon Andreassen rode back to him and passed him. On the second lap, the same thing: Egan drops him on the climb, Andreassen passes him on the descent. Egan stayed with him and kept hydrated, but didn't eat. In the end, he began to get hungry, Andreassen escaped, and the German rider Maximilian Brandl caught Egan on the last lap, and pushed him down into third place.

After the race, in the hope of finding Egan a professional contract for 2016, Mazuera and Egan wandered the service area talking to the managers of the big professional teams.

'They all said the same thing: they had no money,' Pablo Mazuera recalls, 'they couldn't sign any more riders, they were even having to get rid of them. Team Specialized were taking Andreassen, but he already had three world titles to his name' – two in mountain biking and one in cyclo-cross – 'so we couldn't compete. They offered Egan bikes and technical support, but no money.'

Andrea Bianco was loading the van when Egan and his girlfriend, the women's Under-23 mountain biker Xiomara Guerrero, approached him. 'He came close and said, "Andrea, can I talk to you?"

'"Of course. Go ahead."

'"Let's go over there."'

They moved somewhere more private.

'"Andrea, I can't compete for nothing. I'm thinking of going back to university and studying journalism."

242

'I knew what riders earned,' Bianco told me, 'so I told him, "I can help you find an Italian team. We can speak to Massimo Ghirotto at Bianchi, or a smaller team for ten or twelve thousand euros."

'Egan just said, "That's not what I'm looking for."'

Bianco says he then tried another tack: 'We could look for a contract on the road.'

Egan pricked up his ears. He told me, 'I was going to switch to the road after my first World Championships, but by then I knew I had a realistic chance of winning the gold medal, so I held back.'

An old friend of Andrea Bianco in Italy named Paolo Alberati had ridden professionally on and off road, and then qualified as a rider agent. Bianco remembers telling Egan in Andorra, 'Go and see Alberati. I'll pay for the ticket.'

But this cannot be right. Juniors with foreign licences are allowed to ride three races in Italy, provided the two federations agree. Bianco cannot have first mentioned Paolo Alberati in Andorra on 3 September. Egan's stay at Alberati's must have been made well before the missive dated 28 August.

As Alberati remembers it, Bianco had called him before the federation booked the flights to Andorra, at the start of August or earlier: 'He said, "I'm taking a youngster to the World Championships and he's a phenomenon. We're booking the tickets now. I can book the return flights for the end of September. Why don't you invite him to your place in Sicily and take a look at him?"

'"Who is it?"

'"Bernal."'

Alberati told me, 'I have always followed the mountain bike scene, and Bernal had impressed me in Norway the previous year. I went back to look at his results, and we firmed up our agreement.'

The timing matters because, when Pablo Mazuera and Egan

were talking to team managers at Andorra in the afternoon of 3 September, Mazuera believed that he was Bernal's manager, and had a contract to that effect.

Egan flew from Barcelona to Trapani and stayed with Paolo Alberati, who lived in Sicily, on the slopes of Mount Etna. The following day, they trained in light rain on road bikes. Egan recalls, 'We left the house, and we were immediately descending. I took the corners the way you do on a mountain bike, went into a roundabout and fell. We were only 200 metres from his house!'

Four years later, the local cyclists were still calling it 'Bernal's roundabout'.

If Egan had broken a bone in the fall, the following years of cycling history could well have been very different. But he was unhurt, and after another training ride to the coast, which allowed Egan to stand on a beach for the first time in his life, he won the junior category of the Megaliti Gran Fondo, nearly winning the elite race at the same time.

Then he and Alberati flew to Monaco to follow up an offer made to Pablo Mazuera in Aigle by Guido Possetto, the director of the Unione Ciclistica Monaco. The club had road and mountain bike teams, and could allow Egan to do both. But Alberati told me the accommodation was not to their liking. In any case, he had already spoken to Gianni Savio, the manager of the Androni Giocattoli-Sidermec Professional-Continental team and a man with long links to Colombian and Venezuelan sport. They had arranged to meet at the Coppa Agostoni on Wednesday 16 September, in Lissone, 20 kilometres north of Milan, to talk about another rider who Alberati represented.

Before their meeting, Alberati took Egan to a laboratory in Perugia, where Egan underwent an oxygen consumption test. The result, a VO$_2$ Max of 89.4, was astounding.

At Lissone, Alberati walked around the team buses with Egan, who was enchanted. 'He could barely imagine that one day he would end up inside one.'

Egan stood at the barriers watching the race while Alberati and Savio talked in a bar: 'Savio told me, "I already have riders of your boy's characteristics. I'm looking for a Colombian climber, someone young I can develop."

'I said, "I have the rider you are looking for right here." I called Egan. "Here he is."'

Suddenly, Alberati was representing Bernal as his agent.

Savio said, 'He's just a child.'

'He's eighteen. But he's strong.'

That evening, Alberati sent Savio the results of the tests Egan had taken in Perugia. Savio's directeur sportif, Giovanni Ellena, looked at the test results and persuaded Savio to sign Egan up immediately.

The following morning, Alberati's phone rang. It was Savio: 'I want him for five years.'

'Too long, Gianni. Three.'

'Let's meet halfway: four years.'

On Sunday 20 September, three days after their verbal agreement, Alberati took Egan and another rider the same age, Federico Rosati, to Navacchio, near Pisa, for the *Trofeo di Autunno del Monte Pisano-Sognando il Giro delle Fiandre*. The route consisted of a long loop followed by a circuit with 700 metres of dirt track at a 5 per cent gradient, to be ridden four times.

Alberati told Egan not to attack until the last lap.

'But,' Egan told me, 'I started feeling anxious on lap two, so I accelerated and took about fifteen riders with me. Then, with about eighty kilometres to go, I attacked again and Federico went with me.'

According to Alberati, Egan rode away on each climb, then paused at the top for Rosati. Egan confirms this: 'He was a good guy, so I waited for him.'

Approaching the finish, Rosati said, 'You go on. Win it alone. It'll be a better photo.'

Rosati crossed the finish line three seconds after Egan. The next rider was 1 minute 18 seconds back.

After the race, Savio called Alberati: 'Something has come up. I have to go to Milan.'

'Gianni, we go back to Catania tomorrow. It's tonight or who knows when?'

'Can you come straight away?'

Alberati and Bernal drove to Genoa, a hundred miles away, and signed the contract in a restaurant in Bolzaneto: 'It wasn't for the minimum wage either. Gianni understood immediately that this was no normal rider.'

Egan was tied into a contract with no buy-out clause until the fourth year. But he knew what he was doing:

It's true that four years is a long time, but when you think about it, signing me was a big risk. I was coming from Colombia to Europe. I didn't speak the language. I came from mountain biking, a different sport, and my success was as a junior. I had been riding against kids: now I was going to be riding against Nibali, Froome, Nairo, Chaves, Rigo and the rest.

If I signed for two years, the minimum term, and I didn't achieve anything in the first year, which is what I was expecting, I would have been under enormous pressure in year two. I would have had to do something or face being thrown out of the team, or going back to mountain biking. I would have been happy just finishing the races. So, no: four years didn't seem excessive to me.

He joined Androni Giocattoli-Sidermec for an initial wage of €42,000. For Egan's family, his new earning power was transformative. The first thing he did was tell his mother she could give up work. Flor Marina simply says, 'It was a very good salary. It changed our lives. It changed all our lives.'

But the contract negotiations led to a temporary loosening

of the bonds uniting Pablo Mazuera and Egan Bernal, and a permanent falling out between Mazuera and the two Italians. Bianco, who had a 1 per cent slice of Egan's contract with Savio, was accused by the Cycling Federation of selling off the cream of Colombian mountain biking and dismissed.

卅

Savio sent Egan to Michele Bartoli, the winner, either side of the year 2000, of two Liège–Bastogne–Lièges, two Tours of Lombardy and a Tour of Flanders, for coaching. Bartoli put Egan through another oxygen consumption test in November 2015, and told me, 'I think, speaking objectively, you see values like his once every twenty or thirty years.'

Bartoli and Egan worked together throughout Egan's two seasons at Androni Giocattoli. His first race as an elite professional was the 2016 La Méditerranéenne, a four-stage tour of the Mediterranean coast from Catalunya, through France to Liguria in Italy. It started with a team time trial. Egan had never ridden a time trial bike in his life: the first time was during training the day before the race. To make matters worse, on race day it was raining.

'With six kilometres to go, I messed up a curve and my team dropped me. Stage two was long, cold and wet, and I suffered more than I care to remember, but I wasn't dropped until the final five kilometres. I was in the top thirty in stage three, and the top ten in stage four. It was my first race, and I was really happy with it.'

In March he was the best young rider at the Settimana Internazionale Coppi e Bartali. The following month he won the same title at the Giro del Trentino, drawing attention to himself by climbing alongside riders like Landa, Pozzovivo, Bardet, the Dane Jakob Fuglsang, and Jean-Christophe Peraud.

Five months into his first professional season, Alberati renegotiated his wages to €65,000 and brought the buy-out clause forward twelve months to the end of year two. In June he was the best young rider at the Tour of Slovenia, and in August, fourth in the Tour de l'Avenir. And he was not yet twenty.

At the start of his second season with the team, now earning €100,000 a year, he rode his first WorldTour race, Tirreno–Adriatico, and finished second in the young rider standings, just 27 seconds behind Bob Jungels, four and a half years his senior, and sixteenth overall, 3 minutes 20 seconds behind the winner, Nairo Quintana.

Many people in Italy became aware of him for the first time at the 2016 Settimana Internazionale Coppi e Bartali, where he finished fourth overall and was best young rider for the second time. Internationally he made his mark at April's Tour of the Alps, climbing the 35-kilometre Monte Bondone with Landa, Scarponi, Thomas, Pinot, Pozzovivo and Rolland, confirming the abilities he had shown in Trentino the previous year. He was not yet considered the future of Colombian cycling, nor yet the leader of the world's richest and most successful team, but he was on his way.

His enduring friendship with Pablo Mazuera illustrated Colombia's evolution. A generation earlier, encounters between children of radical *barrios* like Bolívar 83 and men like Mazuera – the great-grandson of Laureano Gómez, President of the Republic from 1950 to 1953, an opponent of universal suffrage and an admirer of the Axis powers – were invariably violent. Their meeting late in 2010 led to the best possible news for Colombia: that of great sporting achievement.

18

Double Trouble

The vote for the new president of the Colombian Cycling Federation took place on 24 January 2017. A former president, Jorge Ovidio González, had announced his candidature. Of the top Colombian cyclists, only Nairo took an interest, and he wanted change. He told me, 'People brought me complaints and grievances, and I can see for myself the way cyclists are played by the system. When I spoke to the [departmental cycling] leagues, they agreed with me.'

One of many common issues was that, as funding filtered down from central government to the grass roots, the intermediary institutions imposed such heavy transaction costs that little or nothing ever reached the young athletes.

With backing from Hyundai, Telefónica and other major national industries, Nairo threw in his lot with a former mayor of Tunja, Fernando Flórez, and a modernising, technocratic platform of transparent resource management, open accounting, professionalisation, more races and support for juniors, and an end to cronyism and favours.

Nairo's manager, Libardo Leyton, told me, 'We held talks with the leagues to present our proposals, but it kept coming back to one thing. With a leadership so limited in its aspirations, the leagues could either vote for a great change in the way Colombian cycling worked, or stay safe and receive their twenty or thirty uniforms, four or five bikes, a computer or a trip abroad. And that was how they voted.'

It later leaked out that the González campaign had promised a new race, the Vuelta a la Guajira, to the department on the Venezuelan border noted for having barely any roads, and no cyclists at all. It was presumably one such promise among many.

Votes were cast not by secret ballot but by show of hands, meaning that voting against the winning candidate carried political costs, and in alphabetical order – Amazonas, Antioquia, Arauca, Atlántico, Bolívar . . . – which gave Jorge Ovidio González the early momentum. He was eventually supported by twenty-two of the twenty-five departmental leagues. After the vote, the Vuelta a la Guajira was never heard of again.

Nairo told me, 'After all their complaining, they let themselves be persuaded. I gave them the opportunity for change, and they made their choice. I lost the battle. Prising cycling out of their hands is not easy. To them it is a business, and they are very experienced. If ten more top riders emerge, then fine, but if they don't, it's no longer my affair.'

Looking back, he regretted taking on the federation. 'As a sportsman, and as a leader,' he says, 'I've sometimes put myself in an exposed position. I've got involved in things that really—'

But he can't bring himself to say 'don't concern me'.

Within days of the election, the World Anti-Doping Agency (WADA) suspended Bogotá's Doping Control Laboratory, identifying thirty-eight failures to comply with its regulations, including outdated technology, high staff turnover, delays in process validations, and lack of research, training, transparency and laboratory support. They were, in a sense, the least of Colombia's anti-doping issues: a number of independent informants told me that an Adverse Analytical Finding could be suppressed on payment of 30 to 40 million pesos (£7,000 to £9,500). Perhaps this was why there had been only one positive anti-doping test in the previous six Vueltas a Colombia.

It was a critical situation. Corruption in sport was no longer a purely national matter. Like the peace process – like sport itself – doping and the fight against it were both now international affairs. The UCI and the Colombian Olympic Committee were signatories to the WADA Code, which determined the rights and responsibilities of athletes, antidoping agencies, sport governing bodies and governments. WADA published an annual list of prohibited substances and practices, and laid down mandatory international standards for laboratory and testing practices, therapeutic use exemptions and the protection of privacy and personal information. The Colombian government was a signatory to the 2005 UNESCO International Convention against Doping in Sport, according to which it agreed to support the WADA Code in national law. If the institutions of Colombian cycling were incapable of reforming themselves, they were heading for a confrontation with the international authorities.

At the August 2017 Vuelta a Colombia, the Cycling Anti-Doping Foundation (CADF), the independent body mandated by the UCI to take charge of defining and implementing the anti-doping strategy in cycling, turned up in Colombia unannounced and conducted what it termed 'intelligence-led doping controls'. Seven riders tested positive for the EPO-related product CERA.

The state of domestic cycling was an embarrassment for Nairo and his WorldTour colleagues, and government support was about to contract even more. On 9 August 2017 President Santos announced that, due to the drop in international petroleum prices, it was cutting the sports budget from 530,000 million pesos (about £128 million) to 183,000 million (about £44 million). Within hours of the announcement, Nairo was in the Presidential Palace, obtaining assurances that the cuts would be revised.

All this, in a season when he was targeting two Grand Tour wins.

The 2017 Giro d'Italia was a race of two time trials: 39.8 kilometres through rugged Umbria on stage ten, and 29.3 slightly downhill kilometres from the Monza motor racing circuit into central Milan on the last day – the better part of 70 kilometres made to measure for the Dutchman Tom Dumoulin, not yet the world time trial champion but already the bronze and silver medallist, and twice the Dutch national champion.

At the Vuelta a España in 2015, Dumoulin had outclimbed Chris Froome to win at the Cumbre del Sol, and led the race outright until illness and Fabio Aru overcame him on the final mountain stage.

'We knew Dumoulin would be a contender after what he had done at the 2015 Vuelta,' Nairo recalled later, 'but he was much stronger than we all expected. The idea was that I would go to the Giro, then step up for the Tour, so I wasn't really at 100 per cent.'

Underestimating Dumoulin was to make Nairo's Giro d'Italia an ordeal.

The stage before the first of the time trials, with 6.6 kilometres to go to the finish line on Blockhaus, in the Majella massif in Abruzzo – the name simply means 'log cabin' – Nairo raised the pace. Only Vincenzo Nibali and Thibaut Pinot could stay with him. Dumoulin was part of a chasing group of three, a minute behind them. With 4.3 kilometres to go, after a series of exploratory accelerations, Nairo darted away alone to the stage win, and the race lead.

But Dumoulin's high-speed chase meant he conceded only 24 seconds – and the first of the time trials took place in head- and crosswinds that presented less of a challenge to a man of Dumoulin's mass and power than to a light physique like Nairo's. The Dutchman took the stage win. Nairo, continually buffeted by the wind, conceded 2 minutes 53 seconds and the Maglia Rosa.

Dumoulin came out leading the Giro by 2 minutes 23 seconds.

For the first time ever in a Grand Tour, Colombia took most of its joy from the sprint stages. Fernando Gaviria, already victorious in stages three and five, added wins in stages twelve and thirteen too.

Stage fourteen, culminating with a 12-kilometre climb up to the Sanctuary at Oropa, gave Nairo the chance to take back time. He attacked with four kilometres to go, speeding across to the Russian climber Ilnur Zakarin. They floated ten seconds ahead of Dumoulin. As his immense power began to devour their advantage, Nairo set off alone. But Dumoulin's relentless chase brought him up to Nairo with 1.5 kilometres still to ride. Once there, he sprinted straight past to win the stage.

Nairo, just fourth, conceded 14 more seconds, plus the stage winner's 10-second bonus. Suddenly, the tables turned decisively against him.

At 222 kilometres, stage sixteen was the longest mountain stage of the race. At the foot of the final climb, the Umbrailpass or Giogo di Santa Maria, with 33 kilometres left, Dumoulin stopped beneath a traffic sign, tore off the pink jersey and squatted in a nearby field. Whatever the public perception of cycling's unwritten codes, it was late in the stage for his rivals to suspend hostilities. Even so, Nairo instructed Winner Anacona to relax the pace and for twenty minutes the group containing Dumoulin's closest rivals neither waited nor attacked.

Then, with 26 kilometres remaining, Nibali lost patience. Soon he, Nairo, Zakarin and Pozzovivo had formed a single group, with Dumoulin less than a minute behind.

With 20 kilometres to go, and under a kilometre to the strategic final descent, Nibali attacked again. This time, only Nairo could respond. Third in the stage behind Nibali and Landa, he pulled back 2 minutes and 6 seconds on Dumoulin. He now lay just 31 seconds behind his rival.

Sixty kilometres into stage nineteen, on the long descent

from the village of Sappada, Nairo's teammate José Joaquím Rojas called his team car: Dumoulin was in the rear part of the peloton. Arrieta sent the rest of the Movistar team to sprint at the front. Dumoulin was on the wrong side of the split, but he had the good fortune to be with Mollema, Kruijswijk and Adam Yates, seventh, eighth and ninth overall. Forty kilometres of gruelling racing followed as their combined teammates, then the contenders themselves, closed the gap with 100 kilometres left in the stage.

On the early slopes of the final climb, 15.4 kilometres up to the ski resort of Piancavallo in the Dolomites, the race leader was hanging on to the back of the group of favourites. With 3.4 kilometres to go and Dumoulin 33 seconds behind, Nairo was the virtual Maglia Rosa. He crossed the finish line a handful of seconds behind Pinot, a handful ahead of Nibali. Then, the wait. Dumoulin crossed the line 1 minute, 9 seconds later. Nairo now led by 38 seconds. After 85 hours of racing, and despite everything that had happened, Nairo, Dumoulin, Nibali and Pinot lay within 53 seconds of each other.

For the final 80 kilometres of stage 20, Dumoulin yo-yoed at the back of the dwindling group of favourites. Pinot, Zakarin, Nibali, and Pozzovivo preceded Nairo to the line. Dumoulin came in at the back of a trailing group, but he had conceded no more than 15 seconds.

With only the 29.3km time trial from the Monza circuit to Milan left to ride, Nairo led Nibali by 39 seconds, Pinot by 43 and Dumoulin by 53. But the race route, and the slight descent, provided the perfect scenario for Dumoulin.

The Dutchman came through the first split, after 8.8 kilometres, in 10 minutes and a second. Nairo, hindered by a knee injury and constantly changing position, passed the same point 31 seconds down. He was still 75 seconds from the finish line when Dumoulin, watching the screens in the finish line area, raised his arms in triumph. Nairo finished three seconds inside

Pinot's time, but by then the Giro was lost. Dumoulin had beaten him by 31 seconds.

1	Tom Dumoulin	90:34:54
2	Nairo Quintana	at 31s
3	Vincenzo Nibali	at 40s
4	Thibaut Pinot	at 1m17s

At the 2017 Tour de France, he was never in contention. Only ninth at La Planche des Belles Filles on stage five, he was unable to follow the leaders on the Mont du Chat in stage nine, and on stage twelve, from Pau to Peyragudes, he could do no better than twelfth, conceding 2 minutes 4 seconds to the stage winner Romain Bardet, and 1 minute 42 seconds to Froome.

That day, his father Luis commented to Canal Caracol in Colombia that Nairo should not have ridden the Giro d'Italia when the Tour de France represented the greater goal. Movistar, he said, were burning his son out.

On stage thirteen, stranded in eighth place, over four minutes from the race lead, Nairo tried for a stage win, only to be outsprinted by Warren Barguil at Foix.

There would be no recovery and no stage win. Nairo finished the 2017 Tour de France twelfth, a quarter of an hour behind Froome, and eclipsed by his compatriot Rigoberto Urán, the stage winner at Chambéry, the runner-up at Peyragudes, Serre-Chevalier and in the final classification. Fourteenth and forty-second in the 2015 Giro and Tour, and then seventh in the 2016 Giro d'Italia, it was a brilliant comeback for a rider many had considered finished as a Grand Tour rider.

Now it was Nairo's turn to be written off. On the second rest day, an interview appeared on the website of the Spanish national daily *El País*. Under the title 'Eusebio Unzué: "Nairo started getting old very young"', the owner of the Movistar team responded to Nairo's father's comments: 'Nairo was already brilliant at

23. Now, other riders of the same generation, born in the 90s – Bardet, Landa, Aru, Dumoulin – are coming to maturity.'

Perhaps intending his comments as much for Mikel Landa, and the team's Spanish sponsors, as for Nairo, Unzué continued, '[Nairo's] level is still high, but he has made no progress. Before [this Tour] we were entitled to think that he wasn't getting any better, but he wasn't getting any worse either. I would say that this Tour has rather broken that line. There has been a decline. He started getting old very young.'

Landa's imminent arrival at Movistar was an open secret. Unzué needed the best Spanish rider on his team, and Telefónica, the team's Spanish sponsor, was making a special disbursement to secure the services of Spain's most talented stage racer after Alberto Contador's retirement. Indeed, at the time of the interview he lay six positions higher than Nairo in the general classification.

The message seemed to be that Nairo was so strong, so consistent, that he could be ridden hard year after year, piling win on win. But any dip in form, and he was on his own. There seemed to be no recognition that, riding against Froome and Team Sky, with its colossal budget, armies of sports scientists and tiers of top climbers drilled to neutralise him, Nairo had never had his own train of climbers allowing him to conserve energy until the higher slopes.

Nairo's results didn't sound like those of an old man. It was, after all, his fourth consecutive Grand Tour, having finished the previous three third, first and second. Before that run had started, he had won the 2016 editions of Catalunya and Romandie and taken podium places in San Luis, the Itzulia and the Route du Sud. Instead of resting between the 2016 Vuelta and the 2017 Giro, he had celebrated wins in the Volta a la Comunitat Valenciana and Tirreno–Adriatico, and second place in the Vuelta a Asturias.

The schedule would have been debilitating even for a rider

subjected to rigorous physiological monitoring. In the spring before Chris Froome started his record-breaking sequence of four Grand Tours between 2017 and 2018, for instance, and between each of the three-week races, he did not win a race. But, even after Nairo's physical problems at the 2016 Tour, his team had arranged no blanket screening, no great banks of tests to find the causes and set him back on track.

Indeed, Movistar's obsession with winning team titles meant that when his riders had finished their tasks as domestiques, instead of resting up to give their all for Nairo the coming day, they were often riding hard for team classification points. Its preoccupation with the world team rankings – cycling's booby prize for failure to win the Tour de France, which Movistar had achieved in 2013, 2014 and 2015 – meant that Nairo had never been free to focus solely on the Tour.

The conflicts concealed in the team's financial structure complicated Nairo's position. Telefónica was said to be cooling on its cycling sponsorship. The enthusiasm, and the larger part of the budget, came from Movistar's South American operation. This would seem to empower Nairo in the team. On the other hand, some day the Movistar contract would end and the team owner, Eusebio Unzué, would be looking for a new sponsor in Spain, not Latin America. Between the money and the team fell a shadow.

But for Nairo, Colombia's cyclists and cycling more generally, with its sponsorship-based finance model, there was a deeper question: how useful were dark-skinned, indigenous descendants with peasant farming origins really going to be for giant companies hawking holidays, mobile phone contracts and satellite TV accounts to European and North American consumers?

The season had ended with more Colombian success. At the 2017 Vuelta a España, Miguel Ángel López won two stages in brilliant fashion, outclimbing Froome, Nibali and Bardet to the Calar Alto Observatory, then on the Sierra Nevada attacking with six kilometres to go, dropping Contador, riding past the Briton Adam Yates and winning by 36 seconds. He finished the Vuelta eighth overall.

In November, no one was surprised when Nairo accepted the Attorney General's invitation to become the official Advocate for the Defence of Athletes' Rights.

'It is really just a symbolic role,' he told me. 'There is no concrete agreement yet. But the idea is that there would be a conduit allowing sportsmen and women to report corruption in Colombian sport. And there is always corruption.'

Yet, despite the institutional weakness of Colombian cycling, the long production line of brilliant young riders showed no signs of abating. In the final races of the season, Rigoberto Urán was third again in the Giro dell'Emilia, then, five days later, he succeeded López as Milano–Torino champion, with Nairo fourth and, in seventh place, another brilliant young Colombian prospect named Daniel Felipe Martínez Poveda.

19

The Yellow Man

The Pinzaima River has its source in Sutapá and its end in the Magdalena River, near the town of Honda. In summer, or during the run of sunny days they call summer here, where there are no seasons, the water is transparent, and beneath its churning surface you can make out the bowl gouged from the river bed by the pounding torrent in the lee of the bald rock from which children throw themselves as their families picnic on the bank.

But Cundinamarca's rainfall is abundant, and the day I visited Daniel Martínez, at the foot of a four-kilometre dirt track that loses, or gains, 600 metres in altitude, the Pinzaima was swollen and opaque with sediment. Between the house and the centre of Vergara, a village in north-west Cundinamarca, the gradient averages 15 per cent. The sullen Pinzaima is a little way down the track, below the house. Beneath the river, a seam of emeralds is said to lie, of inestimable worth but impossible to extract.

Daniel Martínez appears with a machete and invites me into the sugarcane crop that surrounds the house, and a peasant farming world to which he is a punctilious and articulate guide. 'It is too hot for coffee here,' he says. 'Sugarcane produces one harvest per month,' and immediately we are deep in the culture of *panela*, the traditional energy source for Colombia's cyclists: when they first went to Europe en masse, their European rivals took pieces of *panela* and sent them for chemical analysis, wondering if it perhaps contained the secret of their success.

Making the panela is a twenty-four-hour job, once a month.

'We cut the cane, load it onto a mule and carry it up to the *trapiche*' – the complex of presses and heated vats where *panela* is made – 'for the milling, which we call the *molienda*.'

The cut cane is fed into a mill, or *molino*, a mechanical crusher that in some parts is driven by a water wheel. The cane juice, or *guarapo*, is poured into a tank or cauldron called a *paila*. The fibre left over from the crushing, called the *bagazo*, is burned with wood beneath the *paila*, and the *guarapo* thickens as it boils. The foam that forms on the surface, called *cachaza*, is scooped off and used as cattle or pig feed.

Each tank or *paila* is smaller than the next. As the honey reduces, it is poured into the next, slightly smaller tank and the first one receives the next batch. The stiff, mud-thick liquid in the final *paila* is ladled into a mould to harden, forming a *libra* or pound of *panela*. Forty one-pound bricks of *panela* make a crate. It is sold on Saturdays. The price changes every week.

Cut the *panela* into cubes or sticks, dissolve it in boiling water, and you have *aguapanela* – a surefire cure for headaches, colds, and weak legs on a mountain stage.

A patio surrounds the house, and Dani's father, Guillermo, and his uncle, Manuel, are painting the balustrade. We go inside, and Dani's mother, Isabel, brings us *guarapo* in a *totuma* – a cup made of the skin of a fruit called the *totumo* or *güira* – and a meal of fried *mojarra*, a freshwater fish, and a plate of rice, potato, tomato and slices of fried plantain.

Every moment is an exhilarating, joyful education.

'We are sowing maize on the mountain opposite,' Dani continues. 'To clear the hillside, you hack down the undergrowth, then leave it to dry and burn it. In the ashes you often find stones carved with pre-Colombian patterns.

'I think that people who say, "Those poor peasant farmers,"

have never been in the countryside, because when you are in the countryside, you don't suffer. No one dies of hunger.'

And, when I think about it, we have done nothing but eat, drink and speak about food since I arrived.

But, in the next breath, Dani's father Guillermo tells me, 'Four or five months ago, they were paying 350,000 pesos for five crates of *panela*. This week they are paying 180,000 pesos. It's very cheap. Too cheap for the producers.'

'I often talk to Nairo,' Dani resumes. 'He asked me, "Where do your parents come from?"

'I said, "I'm from the countryside too. I had to wield a machete as a child." You are strong mentally because you come from below. Not having many resources is an advantage, because it brings out your mettle. It gives you one or two points on the others. You are brought up on hard knocks. If you want something, you have to put your back into it. It gives you character.'

But, for all his love of the countryside, Daniel Martínez was born in Bogotá and spent much of his childhood there. His elder brother, Yeison, was born in Vergara in 1992. At the time, the family lived on a finca left to Guillermo by his father. When Yeison was three years old, Guillermo and Isabel took him to Bogotá and moved into the neighbourhood of Roma with two of Guillermo's siblings. In Roma, Guillermo rode from candy store to candy store on an iron tricycle equipped with a huge box, delivering confectionery. Isabel worked in a kitchen making meat pasties known as *empanadas*, then took up selling food to pupils and teachers from a stall outside the gates of a school.

'We didn't work for anyone,' Guillermo tells me. 'We were entirely independent, so when the kids had time off school, we came to Vergara. We spent mid-November to mid-January here every year.

'When we first went to Bogotá, there was no violence. There were guerrillas, but they didn't cause trouble. All they were interested in was getting money out of the people who had some. They didn't bother people like us.'

Daniel's uncle, Manuel Mora Vega, explains, 'The guerrillas kept to the other bank.' He indicates the distant hillside where both of Daniel's parents grew up. 'They killed people on the other side of the river. There was a young man who was stealing yuca and plantain. Someone complained to the FARC and they executed him.

'Isabel fell pregnant with Daniel, and the growing family moved out of their shared accommodation and found a place in nearby Bosa, where Daniel was born in April 1996. Then, when President Pastrana came to power [in 1998], the violence flared. There were guerrillas everywhere.'

Isabel remembers, 'When Yeison was six' – making this, too, 1998 – 'we had a party that ended up going all night. The following day, I was told the house had been surrounded by guerrillas, who for reasons known only to themselves had decided not to intervene. It sent a chill though me.'

Manuel continues, 'A lot of people fled. They were afraid of their children being taken.'

Daniel's parents were among them. They took their three children, Yeison, Daniel, four years his junior, and Laura, another year younger, back to the capital, and stayed there.

'For three years we stayed away from Vergara,' Isabel tells me. 'We were afraid they would take Yeison, so we stayed in the capital. We only came back when Uribe was elected for the second time.'

That was in 2006. It was interpreted as a kind of guarantee that the progress Colombia had made was permanent. It was then that his parents bought the finca beside the Pinzaima.

One day, when Dani was ten, he went down to the river to play: 'The river was laden with mud and dead animals, and I fell ill. As a child, I was obese. But the fever was heavy, and I lost ten kilograms. I have never been fat again.'

During family holidays at Vergara, the only television was at his grandmother's, in the hills opposite the finca. 'The Tour came on at eight in the morning,' Dani told me. 'I took my bike, went out to train, then at about nine I sat down to watch the Tour de France, even the flat stages. This was when I was eleven or twelve. And when I was watching, I said, "One of these days, if God wills it, I'll be there in the Tour de France." I looked at the Englishmen, the Frenchmen, all tall and skinny. And the bikes.'

He started cycling three years later: 'I was good at football, and I was going to join a football academy, but, one day, the friend who was going to give me a lift didn't turn up. I was so frustrated, I decided to take up cycling instead. My first bike had belonged to my brother. It was heavy, with no brakes. He was holding a raffle to raise the money for another bike, so he gave me his old one. It was far too big for me. He was finishing fifteenth or twentieth in races on that bike. I started racing aged fifteen' – meaning in 2011 or 2012 – 'I did the same events that my brother had ridden, and won them.'

The family lived in Bosa, south-west Bogotá, where Daniel went to school, but they were just two blocks away from Soacha, which lies outside the capital and had more to offer in terms of coaching. Daniel began to attend the Soacha Institute for Recreation and Sport, which had produced the cyclist Walter Pedraza and the 2013 junior world three-cushion billiards champion, José Juan García.

Daniel's progress was instant. National time-trial champion in 2011, he repeated his success in 2012, and then, between 5 and 8 December, in the heat of the Caribbean coast, he won the Vuelta del Futuro riding for the Cundinamarca team: 'Most of my teammates abandoned.'

In July 2013 he became junior Pan-American time trial champion, and added the junior national road race title two weeks later. In August, at the Junior Track World Championships in Glasgow, a mechanical problem took him out of his qualifying heat in the scratch race.

In September, he joined the Colombian junior team in Italy to prepare for the UCI Road World Championships in Florence. Six days before the road race for junior men, he rode the Memorial Gino Calderini at Livorno, against many of the riders he would meet in Florence. He attacked on the first major climb, with more than 40 kilometres still to ride. He was then joined by his teammate Juan Felipe Osorio, and they rode together until Osorio crashed on a descent. Dani won the race alone.

In Florence a week later, he joined an early fifteen-man breakaway group that gained 5 minutes 5 seconds on the peloton. He and the Italian rider Seid Lizde were the last survivors of the group: Dani dropped the Italian on the last passage of Via Salviati.

'No one wanted to work, so I decided to go alone.'

The French rider Franck Bonnamour crossed to Martínez and the two of them started the final circuit with a lead of 14 seconds over the group of favourites.

Bonnamour dropped Martínez – 'I had nothing left,' Dani remembers – at the very moment Mathieu Van Der Poel attacked out of the peloton. He joined, then dropped Bonnamour, and held a small lead over the final five kilometres. Dani finished fifteenth in a group of twenty riders all given the same time, three seconds behind the winner.

'I crossed the line punching myself in the chest out of frustration,' Dani told me. 'I felt good enough to have won the world championships: the problem was, I didn't know how to race in Europe. I was used to riding in Colombia where, if you get into the breakaway, you have a good chance of winning. In Europe it is the opposite. If I'd ridden with more intelligence, I could at least have won a medal.'

Those European experiences whetted Daniel's appetite for more: 'I felt my time in Europe was a first step, and I wanted to go back for longer.'

Unknown to Martínez, Alejandro González Tablas, road

coach at the UCI World Cycling Centre in Switzerland, had been monitoring his results. In July 2014 Daniel flew to Switzerland. 'From the beginning, he was a diamond,' the coach remembers. 'In the laboratory, and in field tests, he was exceptional. He had some experience already, he could read a race quickly, which comes from track racing, although physically he was still very young. But even with that junior physique, he rode like an elite rider. He didn't speak English, but he integrated quite well into the group.'

The juniors raced most weekends in the Rhône-Alpes region of France. On 27 July 2014 the World Cycling Centre's junior team went to the Tour de la Vallée de Trambouze: Daniel came second in the morning time trial and fourth in the afternoon road race, finishing second overall and the best of the World Cycling Centre riders. The following week, he was second to Guillaume Barillot, a French rider six years his senior, in the Grand Prix du Cru Fleurie in the Rhône.

'These are Under-23 races,' Alejandro González Tablas explains, 'which in France means a mix of category ones, twos, threes and juniors, all riding together. They are mostly about 120 kilometres long – pure junior races are usually about 90 – and they are good prep for the World Championships.'

At the Grand Prix de Chardonnay on 7 August, Daniel was only seventh after missing the break, but on 10 August, at the end of a flat circuit race, he won the Grand Prix de Chamoux-sur-Gelon.

González Tablas recalls, 'Then we went to the Tour de Tarantaise, a stage race with a mix of elite, Under-23 and junior riders held in a valley near Grenoble. It was the event's first year, and they made it very demanding. Daniel won the first stage and took the race lead. He lost it in the second stage, through lack of experience – a junior's mistake – but he showed what he was capable of by winning it back again in the last stage.'

'They were training me for the World Championships in Ponferrada, but I fell ill a week before the championships,' Daniel explains. 'It was eventually diagnosed at the end of the year as mononucleosis [glandular fever].'

In 2015, aged eighteen, he joined Team Colombia and moved into a house in Brescia with Cayetano Sarmiento, Darwin Pantoja and Darwin Atapuma, by now riding for BMC. Tyrannical with the older riders, team director Claudio Corti was indulgent with Dani, whose €36,000 wage guaranteed a bank loan for his mother to buy a parcel of land. Then he paid for the house too: 'In Italy, my first thought was to invest my money well and get my family out of rented accommodation and into our own house.'

Riding now for Team Colombia and barely nineteen, he won the mountains jersey at June's Route du Sud and the best young rider category at the Tour of Utah in August. He told me, 'When I joined Team Colombia my managers were Alex and Johnny Carera. Corti came to me directly, and I told him to negotiate with them. When rumours began to go round that the team was ending, I called the Careras, but they told me Corti had assured them that all was well. I said, "If the team closes and I don't have a ride, I'll find another agent."'

When the team closed at the end of the year, all the riders faced a scramble for contracts: 'I called [Nairo Quintana's agent] Giuseppe Acquadro. It was already the end of October, but he spoke to Wilier-Southeast. It was that or nothing. I said I didn't care how much they were paying. I just wanted to keep riding.'

Acquadro put Daniel in touch with the former rider Michele Bartoli, who became his coach. For Wilier-Southeast, Daniel targeted best young rider titles: he was third in the category at Coppi and Bartali Week in March and second at the Giro del Trentino – in both races the title was won by Egan Bernal. He also rode his first Grand Tour, the 2016 Giro d'Italia, where he was the youngest rider, the race starting eleven days after his twentieth birthday.

By October 2017, still only twenty-one, he was achieving top tens in major races: ninth in the Three Valleys of Varese, with

Pinot, Nibali and Aru in plain sight ahead of him; seventh in Milano–Torino, with Nairo and Wout Poels finishing just before him; third on the Selçuk stage at the Tour of Turkey, behind WorldTour riders Diego Ulissi and Jesper Hansen, and fourth overall.

For all his success in Italy and elsewhere, Daniel's heart was set on France: 'I watched the Giro d'Italia and, yes, I liked it, but the Tour de France was where I fixed my sights. I've never been obsessed by any other race the way I am by the Tour de France. I want to win the yellow jersey. When I started riding, my dream was to win it. I guess it always will be.'

Wondering where the roots of his obsession lay, I mentioned that, in Muysca culture and its aftermath, yellow was everywhere. The Muysca were the '*hijos del maíz*' ('the children of sweetcorn'). Man was made of yellow earth. Their rituals were full of brightly coloured ceremonial garb: only the *psihipqua*, or Muysca chieftain, could wear golden jewels, agave bonnets and painted blankets.

While we were talking, Dani's uncle Manuel, who had been painting outside, came in, sat beside us – and began to speak.

'A long time ago – I must have been seven or eight years old, and I'm fifty-seven now, so about forty-nine years ago – there was a huge surge in the Pinzaima, and the neighbours who live lower down, by the river, climbed to higher ground. They were sitting shivering on the hillside when they saw a little girl floating down the churning water in a basket. She was tiny and yellow, surrounded by five chicks. 'They shouted, "Hey, *niña*, get out of there. It's dangerous."

'The little girl spun her basket around in the water and turned to look at them, and said, "Don't worry. This is nothing. When my daddy comes down, then it's going to be dangerous."

'She floated down through the rapids lower down, and away. The little girl left with the litter of chicks that she was carrying. And nothing more [was said]. And the river was hurling huge rocks down and *guadua* trunks.'

I ask Manuel, 'What colour was she wearing?'

'Yellow: the girl, the little chicks and the basket.'

The hairs rose on my neck as a worldview I only knew through books came to life before me. It was the communal background understanding of the cyclists from the high-altitude plateau of Cundinamarca and Boyacá laid bare.

In the oral culture of the Andean highlands, the thin air is full of yellow spirits or numina: sprites known as *encantos de agua* (water incantations) or *tunjos* are thought to dwell in caves high in the mountains, moving along rivers and waterways, or through underground passages. The sun sent a messenger, Bochica, the master of weaving, who controlled the weather and walked the Muysca territories from Pasca in the south to Iza in the north, giving things their names and indicating the points in the landscape, generally caves and lakes high in the mountains, from which his power radiated – places of pilgrimage, ritual locations where the Muysca made their offerings and sacrifices. The word *tunjo* also describes figurines made of gold, wood or cotton which the Muysca either buried or cast into rivers and lakes, as a means of restoring, or prolonging, harmony among the delicate balance of forces in the cosmos. On immersion in water, the *tunjo* became a spirit which could surface in times of flooding and high water. When they did, they were recognisable for their yellow garb, hair or skin.

This ancient colour symbolism, the ritual pilgrimage to places high in the mountains, belonged to a language in which Colombia was fluent, long before its cyclists rode the Tour de France. It seemed to me that it was not in their genes but in their culture, in the tacit, never fully formulated map we all have of our being in the world – the inarticulate, unacknowledged, taken-for-granted body of knowledge with which, without our even noticing it, we all of us orientate ourselves – that we should look to understand cycling's special hold on the Colombian imagination, and solve the mystery of its unique cycling culture.

20

Migrants' Stories

Daniel Martínez rode his third Tour de l'Avenir in August 2017, with Iván Sosa, Cristian Muñoz and Wldy Sandoval – 'Wl-' is pronounced 'ull' as in 'full' – as part of a team led, for the second year, by Egan Bernal, who had earned his leadership at the Tour de Savoie Mont Blanc in June and the Sibiu Cycling Tour in July, in both cases by winning the race overall, two stages, and the points and young rider categories.

The team sprinter was Álvaro Hodeg. He told me, 'I did not have a lead-out train, but the person who helped me most was Egan himself. Most climbers position themselves badly in the peloton. Not Egan. And, of course, he commands respect.'

Hodeg finished second in stages two and three, and went into the last day for the sprinters, stage six, Montrichard to Saint-Amand-Montrond, 139.1 kilometres, resigned to winning nothing. Things only got worse: 'At the stage start, there was a traffic divider in the middle of the road. I managed to crash into it on my own and scraped up my back.'

The stage finish came after a climb, and there was a roundabout with 400 metres to go. Three riders attacked: 'I said to Egan, "Hit it hard so no one else can attack." I started my sprint a long way out and came past the three attackers. I saw a wheel come alongside mine and crossed the finish line not knowing who had won. Then the journalists came running after me. I was overjoyed.

'I'm telling you, if Bernal wasn't a climber, he'd be a great lead-out man.'

On stage seven – Saint-Gervais Mont-Blanc to Hauteluce-Les Saisies, 118.4 kilometres – Bernal planned to let a small escape group go.

'I was really motivated to help Egan, so I said, "I'll take care of the first 60 kilometers." When Egan was happy with the constituents of the breakaway, I let it go.

'When we started climbing, Egan told me, "Alvarito, ride the first kilometre on the limit." When I had finished, the team was at the front. I crossed the finish line 24 minutes after Egan, and saw him on the podium with the yellow jersey. He called me over to the podium and hugged me. It was fantastic.'

Bernal won the following day too, sealing Colombia's fourth Tour de l'Avenir win since 2010. On 27 August, the day of the final stage, Team Sky announced that they had signed him up.

Paolo Alberati told me, 'I tried to insist on him staying one more year with Gianni Savio and ride the Giro d'Italia as leader. But he wanted to go to Sky. I said, "You will, but you'll go after winning two stages of the Giro as a twenty-year-old, earning four times what they are offering now."'

But Egan dispensed with Alberati, took on a new agent in Giuseppe Acquadro and the move went ahead.

Alberati told me, 'Egan has character, intelligence and a strong will. I didn't always have an easy relationship with him. I thought I needed to help him grow, but he was already fully grown. When he came to stay with me for the first time, my wife said, "He's eighteen, but he thinks like a forty-eight-year-old."

'But we patched things up,' he finishes, 'and we have a wonderful friendship.'

However, Álvaro Hodeg had beaten Egan Bernal to a World-Tour contract. Hodeg had joined Quick-Step Floors as a *stagiaire* or trainee rider on 1 August 2017. Of Arab and Scottish ancestry, Álvaro José Hodeg Chagüi was a rare rider from the sweltering town of Montería, 18 metres above sea level on the Sinú River, 400 kilometres due north of Medellín and just 50 kilometres from the Caribbean Coast. His story takes us into the melancholic store of migrant tales whose broken shards constitute a fascinating corner of the kaleidoscope that is modern Colombia. Through him, cycling began to colonise new parts of the national geography, and a new demographic.

Ⅲ

Between 1815 and 1930 more than 50 million migrants crossed the Atlantic to start new lives. The United States of America opened its arms to 32 million of them. Latin America welcomed more than 13 million. Argentina, which took half the Latin American intake, doubled its population between 1869 and 1895, did so again between 1895 and 1914, and again between 1914 and 1947. Brazil, in turn, took in 4.4 million immigrants, while Cuba, Chile, Uruguay and Mexico all received figures in the hundreds of thousands.

Colombia felt no more than a ripple of these vast migratory waves. Its lack of development and repeated civil wars after independence in 1819 discouraged mass migration. It welcomed handfuls of incomers from Spain, Germany, Italy and France, while racist immigration laws largely discouraged arrivals from China and the Arab world.

In the town of Cereté, 50 kilometres from the Caribbean Sea in the department of Córdoba, Álvaro Hodeg's great-uncle, Abraham Saker Chagüi, switching easily between Spanish and English, told me how the Chagüis came to Colombia.

'We were Melkites: Damascene Christians who used the Byzantine Rite.'

On 6 July 1860, frenzied Muslim bands had entered the Christian quarter in Damascus and cut 20,000 throats:

'The background was economic, as in all wars, but religion was laid over it. A Muslim belonging to the elite, an Algerian named Abd-El-Kader, took thousands of Christians into his palace and saved them. They included my father's family, the Saker, and my mother's family, the Chagüi.'

He takes a picture from the wall: 'This is the Damascus massacre by a Dutch painter named Jean-Baptiste Huysmans. Look at the city in the background, burned. This is Abd-El-Kader. And this woman is a Melkite Christian handing over her baby to be saved.'

After the massacre, Abraham Saker explains, a large part of Syria's Christian community left: 'They went to Beirut and took the Marseille boat. Most wanted to go to the United States, but, since Damascus had a lot of sandstorms, many of them were rejected because of conjunctivitis, so they went wherever the tide took them.'

After a lifetime of wandering, the tide eventually carried Abraham's grandfather Salomón Chagüi to Cartagena. He arrived alone in about 1910 and founded a general store and a trading company whose boats distributed their wares along Colombia's rivers. When the business was stable, Salomón Chagüi summoned the rest of his family to join him.

'My grandfather lived close to the ocean, in a village called San Bernardo del Viento. His wife, my grandmother, was travelling from Syria with her eldest daughter, her husband and their three sons when the June sou'westerlies began to blow. The storm overturned the boat and they all drowned. My grandfather was left a widower.'

He started a new family, and in 1925 he took his five Colombia-born sons back to Beirut to be educated at the Jesuit University.

'In 1929, after the Wall Street crash, the company went bankrupt,' Abraham told me. 'They returned to Colombia and Salomón's son, Elía, opened a store in Cereté and began to send palm nut butter to his brother Julio Chagüi in Barranquilla. And they started to prosper again.'

Colombia's Arabs – Syrians, Lebanese, Palestinians, all referred to as Turks by the locals – were busy importers and dynamic salesmen. The first to sell door-to-door, the first to offer credit, they changed their adopted nation's culture even before they became active in politics: the first woman mayor in Colombia, appointed at Ocaña in 1962, was María Susana Awad, whose Lebanese father sold fabrics and groceries, and exported coffee, cinchona bark and tagua nuts to Europe. The President of Colombia from 1978 to 1982, Julio César Turbay, was the son of a Lebanese businessman and a peasant woman from Cundinamarca, and unrelated to Gabriel Turbay Abunader, Foreign Minister and Ambassador to the United States in the 1930s and 1940s, another son of the Lebanese community.

Scotland's impact on Colombia has been less marked. An unsuccessful attempt in 1698 and 1699 to settle 4,000 Scots at Darien on the Panama Isthmus is said to have bankrupted Scotland, leaving it with little choice but to agree to the 1707 Acts of Union.

Fifty-four Scottish volunteers fought for Colombian independence from Spain between 1810 and 1830, and, in October 1825, a group of families from the Scottish Highlands emigrated from Cromarty to La Guajira in Gran Colombia. Finding the land there unproductive, they quickly left for Venezuela, Panama and Canada.

For the rest of the nineteenth century, Scottish migration to Colombia appears to have been close to non-existent: a few individuals slipping the moorings of the home country and disappearing into the landscape.

In Cereté, Álvaro Hodeg's great-aunt Puri Hodge explained that a Scotsman called Hodge – Christian name unknown – had reached Cartagena in the 1880s with three children: Enrique, Lorenzo and Elisa. Hodge's wife, the children's mother, had died in unexplained circumstances, perhaps during the voyage.

Once there, Hodge, Name Unknown, appears to have navigated the River Sinú, selling products from Cartagena and purchasing cattle in the Sinú that he later sold, at a profit, when he returned.

His eldest, Lorenzo, had another Lorenzo in 1929, who grew tall and ruddy and piloted a launch out of Cartagena, along the Sinú but also seabound to Panama. He had children with many women then settled on a large ranch in Montería, where he employed indigenous labour. In the family's various branches, Hodge was garbled into Hodges, even Hodeg.

The fourth of Lorenzo's five children was another Álvaro. He opened a shop in Montería, selling everything a ranch owner might need. Álvaro, the great-grandson of Hodge, Christian name unknown, married Salomón Chagüi's great-granddaughter Elsa who, on 16 September 1996, gave him their first son, Álvaro José Hodeg Chagüi.

Not knowing Hodge, Name Unknown's year or port of embarkation, it might have taken months or years to search the records in Cartagena. Scotland's statutory registers of births held no record of a Lorenzo, Enrique or Elisa Hodge, and I could find no Lawrence, Henry and Elizabeth in any single cluster. The General Register Office for England was just as unhelpful.

Even if I had found them, I doubted the records would have addressed the key question. After all, most Scottish migrants went to Australia and New Zealand. For those of them prepared to adopt Spanish, Argentina was a popular destination. There were even Scottish Hodges in the British Leeward Islands. So why Colombia? Was he running away from something?

Bright eyed, emotional, disarmingly open – 'I cry easily!' he says. 'I'm nervous enough as it is . . .' – Álvaro Hodeg is a joy to speak to. Every race is an adventure, every incident material for a yarn full of passion and colour.

On 8 July 2013 he was just an overweight schoolboy with an unbeatable sprint. It was the night before his Pan-American Games debut at Aguascalientes, 500 kilometres north-west of Mexico City, and he slept badly: 'I'm always nervous before races. I'm a bit better now, but that night I lay there all night thinking.'

At the time, he had only been riding on the track three weeks. He had only been riding at all a few months. 'I was hyperactive when I was very small,' he says. 'At school I played football, basketball and tennis. I was national table tennis champion, national volleyball champion, school sportsman of the year three times. I was good at everything. I told my mother, "I want to earn my living from sport." I didn't know if it would be tennis, football, ping pong, or whatever, but I loved sport.'

Cycling is not part of Montería culture. Its few competitive cyclists train at four in the morning because at nine the humidity is suffocating. When Álvaro Hodeg was small, cycling was a social activity on Sundays, nothing more. But his father Lorenzo's godson, a man named Salín Ghisays Martínez, was one of Montería's few keen cyclists. Sometime in 2012 – perhaps early in the year – Salín invited Álvaro to race: 'I finished third. They started telling me, "You're good." So I carried on, and within two months I was winning races. I said to my mother, "I like this!"'

Soon, he had no rivals in Montería.

Salín introduced Álvaro to a recreational rider from Medellín named Roivan Gomez Muñoz. Roivan remembers, 'I saw him ride two or three times, and the kid had great condition as a sprinter. I said, "He looks good, but if he's going to get anywhere he needs to go to Medellín."'

Álvaro took the message to heart, but his father tried to convince him to finish school in Montería. His mother, Elsa, promised him, 'I will look for a college for you, although it is not very likely they will accept a pupil just for year eleven, especially one they don't know. If they'll have you, then perhaps it is God's will.'

The first two schools turned him down. The third, the school attached to the Universidad Pontificia Bolivariana, accepted him.

Roivan Gomez offered him accommodation in the neighbourhood of Belén, near the Aeropark where the cyclists meet, and Álvaro Hodeg joined dozens, perhaps hundreds, of out-of-town kids, often from tiny villages, given temporary accommodation by other cyclists while they tried to make it in the sport.

When the other cyclists were out training in the morning, Álvaro was at school, meaning he mostly trained alone. To relieve the boredom, Roivan took him to the velodrome and introduced him to Benjamín Laverde, Mincho, who, in turn, introduced him to the track: 'Mincho welcomed me in and included me in his training sessions. I grew very attached to him because the Paisas are very regionalistic, and I'm from the coast.'

But Mincho could also be a hard taskmaster: 'On about my third day, it started raining. Mincho told me, "It's OK, you can sprint. Nothing's going to happen." I touched the blue line on the camber' – the stayer's line – 'and went down heavily. Mincho just stood their laughing. Inside, I cursed him.

'Another time, he sent me out to ride the kilometre. I was just starting, and the kilo is very hard, and there were a lot of people watching. I said, "Mincho, don't make me do this in front of everyone."

'"Just go and do it. Go, go."'

On the second lap, with aching legs, Álvaro stopped: '"No, Mincho, I'm not doing this."

'"Then get out and come back when you want to work," and he threw me out of the velodrome!'

Yet Álvaro's progress was as fast as his sprint: 'Two weeks later' – this would have been late June 2013 (Roivan says, 'He can't have been to the track more than five times') – 'I was doing some flying laps in the velodrome with Mincho, when the national coach Jhon Jaime González came in. He said, "Álvaro, do me the fastest lap you can." I didn't know what line to take or anything, but, from the look on his face, I must have set a good time.

'He said, "Álvaro, the Pan-American Championships are in two weeks' time in Mexico. Do you want to go?"

'I said, "The Pan-Americans? I'm in!"'

Ten days before the trip, he flew home to Montería, with Roivan and Rigoberto Urán, who had just finished second in the Giro d'Italia. Rigoberto was making a guest appearance at the annual Sea and Volcano Festival in the village of Arboletes, famous for its beaches and its mud volcano. The festival included a public cycling event. Rigoberto started it but did not finish. Álvaro won, but by the time he got back to the Martín Emilio Rodríguez Velodrome in Medellín, he had missed three days of track work and could no longer keep up.

The team sprint sees three riders race in single file, the lead rider dropping out after each lap until only one remains. Álvaro's companions John Castillo, from Barranquilla, and Juan David Gutiérrez, from Bogotá, were riding away from him, which brought him, if not to tears, at least to the point of asking to be excused from the Games: 'I said, "What happens if they drop me when we are in Mexico? I'll have to ride three laps on my own."'

The national track coach, Jhon Jaime González, just told him, 'Alvarito, you'll be fine.'

In round one the following morning, the starting pistol went off twice: 'Jhon Jaime told me, "False start. One more and you're disqualified."

'I thought, "What do I do now? If I go early, we're out. If I don't, I'm dropped."

'We started again. On the first curve, the other two began to ride away from me. I thought about giving up. But then I heard a voice, like an angel saying, "Come on, Álvarito. Now's the time."

'With half a lap to go, we led by almost half the velodrome.'

The following day, the team won the final against Mexico.

Next came individual sprint qualifying, where riders build up slowly, take a flying start then sprint all-out for 200 metres. Álvaro's time of 10.28 seconds, a new junior national record, put him in the final, although sprint finals are, until the final lap, not sprints at all: they are tactical duels, with several extremely slow laps when the rivals test each other's bike handling before the fast finish. Álvaro Hodeg had never ridden one before: 'I was up against a small Ecuadorean sprinter. Jhon Jaime said, "You'll beat him, easy."

'We set off watching each other. I was big, carrying a lot of weight, and he started riding his bars into mine and heading me off to force me into a track stand. I was new to it all, and I couldn't do anything like that. I started shouting, "Judge, judge!" They disqualified me. When I left the track, effing and blinding, Jhon Jaime and everyone were rolling about in laughter.'

That evening, Jhon Jaime visited him in his room: 'He said, "Alvarito, are you ready for tomorrow?"

'"What's on tomorrow?"

'"You're going to ride the kilometre."'

In qualifying he was trackside, warming up on the rollers, sneezing with nerves: 'I told Jhon Jaime, "My stomach hurts. Make someone else ride."

'"You'll be fine."'

The next day, in qualifying, his bike got caught in the starting gate: 'I wrenched it out, but on the first lap I was really slow. Jhon Jaime was shouting, "Good, good. Come on!"

'When I'd finished, he said, "Best time, *güevon*!"

'As I was leaving the track, Jhon Jaime said, "Careful when you put your foot down. It's easy to fall off." As I put my foot down, I fell off. In the end, two riders went faster than me, but at least I won the bronze medal. It is still probably the hardest I've ever ridden.'

After Mexico, Roivan introduced Álvaro to Carlos Mario Jaramillo, or 'Millo', the coach of the Claro-Coldeportes team. Before the end of 2013, aged seventeen, he was on the fringes of the team: 'They didn't pay me; they simply took me to races. At the velodrome I worked with Mincho: nothing specific, no heart-rate monitor or power meter, but learning everything I could.'

Mincho tells me, 'We did lots of work behind the motorbike, lots of leg speed, nothing too hard, nothing that could burn out the engine.'

Roivan says, 'Mincho was the most important person to him, as he was to so many riders before him: Laverde, Ardila, Rigoberto and many more. Mincho trained them, explained everything to them, became a substitute father to them.'

Their work together paid off: at the 2014 junior national track championships, Álvaro Hodeg won four gold medals. At the Pan-American Games, his improved bike handling allowed him to take a bronze medal in the individual sprint, and he finished eighth in the Pan-American road race.

Late in September 2015, Millo called from Richmond, Virginia, the venue for the UCI Road World Championships. It was three o'clock in the afternoon: '"Fernando Gaviria did not travel. You fly tomorrow morning."

'I went out straight away on my bike, trained for five hours, arrived home at ten at night and went to the airport first thing.'

The ground staff found him in the departure lounge, fast asleep: 'The lady from Avianca [the Colombian national airline] said, "Name, please?"

'"Me? Álvaro."

'"Come on! Your plane is leaving."

'They were my first World Championships, and with two laps to go I was in the main group, which was getting smaller. I really felt good. Just as we entered the cobblestones, I had a puncture. It took a minute to replace the wheel, and by then the race had gone. I'm not saying I was going to win, but I cried all the way to the paddock!'.

Before November's Vuelta del Porvenir, he prepared like a professional: 'I went with Roivan in the car, and we trained along the stages. Several climbs I rode repeatedly. I noted down the kilometres, the gradients and at night I studied my notes.'

By now, Claro-Coldeportes were sponsoring him as an individual, but, for the Vuelta del Porvenir, he had no team. Mincho assembled a group of support riders and they set off for the race: 'I began to target the intermediate sprints. I didn't take part in the first one – I didn't really know what I was doing – but I won the second one.'

In the end, Álvaro tied on points with his closest rival but won more intermediate sprints and took the competition. 'In Colombia,' he says, 'the sprints are very different from the sprints in Europe, because here the level is not so high, so everyone tries: the climbers, anyone who can get to the front. So there are crashes and chaos.'

One of Colombia's toughest races for sprinters is the Vuelta al Valle. Álvaro rode as a first year Under-23 rider in March 2015 for Coldeportes-Claro. His teammates included Fernando Gaviria and the future Katusha rider Jonathan Restrepo: 'In one of the stages, there was a climb, then a steep descent towards the finish line. I still did not have much ability. I was on Fernando Gaviria's wheel. He dodged a traffic separator. I rode straight into it.'

Behind him, his teammates Jonathan Restrepo and Germán Chavez hit the floor: 'I'd brought the whole team down. And *Pácora*' – Restrepo – 'was groaning. His knee was bad.'

Álvaro spent all night in a hospital waiting room: 'The doctor told me not to start the next day's stage. I did, but I abandoned after a kilometre. Every time I took a deep breath, it was painful. For weeks, if I coughed or sat up in bed, it was very uncomfortable. But I had not broken anything.'

In May 2017 Álvaro was due to fly to Italy for the Under-23 Giro d'Italia but fell ill. As he had before the 2013 Pan-American Championships, he begged his sports director, Carlos Mario Jaramillo, not to take him.

'You're just overtrained,' Millo told him. 'Don't ride any more until we leave.'

'I do tend to train a lot,' he told me.

In Italy, he did a preparation race. He told his coach, 'I'm taking it easy today,' then attacked when the flag went down.

'There were five of us. We gained two minutes. I felt good and forced the pace, until Millo said, "You're going too deep." They caught me on the last climb.'

At the Giro, Álvaro faced strong sprinters in Fabio Jakobsen and Bram Welten. Fifth in stage one, after finding himself boxed in, he crashed in stage two and soft-pedalled to the finish line, grazed all over. On stage five, he took the blue shirt as leader of the points competition. That afternoon he rode the 14-kilometre time trial wearing a blue skinsuit.

'I had been on the attack all morning and I was tired,' he tells me.

But, by now, he had signed his WorldTour contract, and Quick-Step had sent him a time trial bike to use in Italy.

'When the mechanic unpacked it, I saw Tom Boonen written on the frame. "Ha! I'm on Tom Boonen's bike."

'Millo said, "Alvarito, take the time trial easy. Just don't miss the cut."

'I did not warm up much, but when I rolled out, I felt good. The first climb was four kilometres long. I caught my minute man on its slopes. As I crossed the brow of the hill, I saw my two-minute man. I passed him on the way down. Then I caught my three-minute man. On the flat before the finish, I nearly caught the rider ahead of him.

'Millo said, "Best time!"

'I spent half an hour in the hot seat before my time was beaten.'

Álvaro Hodeg became a full-time professional in 2018. At the Handzame Classic in Belgium on 16 March, he was piloted towards the sprint by a well-drilled lead-out train, and took his first win in the professional ranks.

Three days later, in the first stage of the Volta a Catalunya, Álvaro took the win several lengths ahead of Bora-Hansgrohe teammates Sam Bennett and Jay McCarthy.

Five wins in his first year as a professional established him among the very best of the new generation of sprinters. If Álvaro Hodeg's progress – and that of another lowland sprinter, Nelson Soto, from the Caribbean port of Barranquilla – promoted cycling beyond its mountainous heartlands, the announcement of a race that would bring many of the world's top riders to Colombia caused national euphoria.

21

Order of Succession

Days before the Colombian Cycling Federation elections in January 2017, Jorge Ovidio González had announced an international cycling event to take place in February 2018. It was a decisive coup for his campaign, although the creation of the future *Oro y Paz* lay in the work of a small event organiser called the Fundación Sentimiento Cafetero, run by Alejandro Carrisoza, a Medellín native living in the coffee town of Armenia.

In 2011 Carrizosa had put on a five-day stage race in the departments of Risaralda and Quindío called the Clásica Internacional del Café-Coldeportes. The 80 million peso budget was to be paid in equal parts by Coldeportes and the Colombian Cycling Federation, but the federation never paid its share. At considerable personal cost, Carrizosa paid the prize money and other debts.

But he persisted. The agricultural crisis had led many coffee farms to diversify into tourism, and they needed international promotion. And, as Carrizosa told me, 'Our cyclists were flourishing; our cycling was not.'

Carrizosa met Rich Hincapie, brother of the former professional cyclist George and a partner in Medalist Sports, the US event organiser responsible for the Tour of Utah, the Colorado Classic and the USA Pro Challenge. Together they began to plan the Tour del Café. Carrizosa told me, 'We developed the project in 2012 and 2013, and sent the documentation to the federation in mid-2013. The first Tour del Café should have taken place in February 2014. But they told me, "All cycling sponsors have to work through the federation. All events have to be organised by the federation. The federation will not endorse your project."'

In most countries, cycling federations limit themselves to organising the annual national championships. They entrust other events to private companies, as recommended by the UCI. The Colombian Federation departs from the norm in organising the Vuelta del Porvenir, Vuelta al Futuro and Vuelta de la Juventud, as well as the country's premier domestic event, the Vuelta a Colombia. Carrizosa threatened the Federation's monopoly.

In September 2015 Carrizosa travelled to the UCI Road World Championships in Richmond, Virginia, organised by Medalist Sports. There, he was told by the UCI that, if the National Federation would not help, the UCI could intervene directly: 'I came back to Medellín and resumed talks with the sponsors. Everyone was motivated. The Department of Quindío proposed a meeting with the Cycling Federación, the government, the UCI, the sponsors and me. The Cycling Federación president refused on the abstruse grounds that only he was authorised to issue an invitaion to the UCI.'

Echoes of the federation's aggression can be heard in a UCI email to the Colombian Cycling Federation dated 18 April 2016:

We are very surprised that you speak of 'piracy', given that the UCI Regulations are unambiguous: national federations are responsible and hold all rights in the drafting of their national calendar but, as regards international events, the UCI is the sole authority . . . However, as Article 1.2.06 of the UCI Regulations clearly explains, if a national federation refuses to complete the process of registering an event in the UCI international calendar, the organizer has the right to register his race directly with the UCI. There is therefore no piracy – at least, not by the organizer or the UCI.

News of the Colombian Cycling Federation's intransigence reached the press in September 2016. After the January 2017 elections, Carrizosa tried again. He recalls a tense meeting attended by the Secretary for Commerce and Tourism of the Department of Quindío, Carrizosa's company, now called The Cycling Company SAS.

'The chairman of our company told him, among other things, "The model you propose channels all financial resources through the federation. We cannot do that because we do not handle money ourselves, we manage it through a fiduciary, and you are not a bank."'

Two months later, President González rejected the proposal. That 18 April 2016 email from the UCI also noted:

We are very happy to know that one of the sponsors of the national Federation intends to organize a category 2.1 event. As I understand, the organizer will be the Federation itself. If you have the capacity to do so, then fine.

The event was eventually held as the 2018 Oro y Paz. It was not even a decent cut-and-paste of Carrizosa's original project. The riders essentially spent five days going up and down a single 315-kilometre stretch of Highway 25 between the coffee-producing towns of Santander de Quilichao and Manizales, with various U-turns. Hardly an international showcase for the 'New Colombia'.

The race's main goal seemed to be to shore up political power among the cycling federation. As an exercise in marketing Colombia internationally, the race was a missed opportunity. Beyond the bare race results, there were no press releases at all.

Although huge crowds turned out, few outside observers learned much about the country.

Poor radio signals meant chaotic television coverage. Even Rigoberto Urán, never normally a grumbler, complained that incorrect information about the advantage of various attacks had affected the result. Even so, on stage five in the pretty village of Salento, set among the 60-metre palm trees of the Cocora Valley, Nairo, Egan, Rigo and Sergio Luís, pressed in on both sides by jubilant fans a hundred metres from the finish line, sprinted side by side. The image quickly became an icon.

The race was decided on the final day, when Dayer Quintana won the stage and Egan Bernal took overall victory by eight seconds. The win launched Bernal's professional career perfectly, and led to an immediate pay rise. Six weeks later, at the end of stage four of the Volta a Catalunya, he finished second to Alejandro Valverde in the sprint at La Molina and moved into second place overall. There he would have stayed had the Movistar rider José Joaquín Rojas, riding just ahead of him, not slipped on a patch of oil six kilometres from the finish. With no time to react, Bernal suffered collarbone and shoulder-blade fractures. Incredibly, thirty-two days after the accident, in April's Tour de Romandie, he won the mountain time trial ahead of Primož Roglič, Richie Porte and Steven Kruijswijk, three of the world's best climbers. The win led to yet another pay increase, as did two stage wins and overall victory in May's Tour of California.

It felt like the passing of the baton, even if Rigoberto Urán, 31, and Nairo, 28, still had plenty of racing in them. As Bernal grew in stature, Miguel Ángel López, three years his senior, duelled at the Giro d'Italia with Richard Carapaz, who became the first Ecuadorean to take a Grand Tour stage win at Montevergine di Mercogliano, 65 kilometres inland from Naples.

After stage fourteen, López stood sixth overall, with Carapaz seventh. After stage fifteen, they lay fifth and sixth. After stage nineteen, they were fourth and fifth. Stage twenty saw Carapaz move up into fourth place and López step up onto the podium, in the distinguished company of Froome and Dumoulin.

At June's Tour de Suisse, Nairo showed that he was still a formidable competitor by attacking alone 28 kilometres from the end of a stage ending at Arosa, holding off Jakob Fuglsang and Richie Porte, working together, and winning the stage by 22 seconds.

But the chaos that reigned in his team quickly put paid to his Tour ambitions. Movistar went into the Tour with three declared leaders in Nairo, Landa and Alejandro Valverde. The impossibility of protecting them all was proven four kilometres from the end of stage one, when Nairo careered into a traffic island and broke both wheels. With no teammate to hand, he lost a minute and 15 seconds to contenders such as Dumoulin, Roglič and Geraint Thomas. The stage winner that day, Fernando Gaviria, took the yellow, green and white jerseys.

Then, in stage three's team time trial over a technical course with 80kph descents and gusting wind, Movistar could do no better than tenth. Even so, Nairo went into stage eleven, a short mountain stage over two Hors Catégorie giants before La Rosière, near the Italian border, confident. Valverde attacked early. Dumoulin bridged across to him, then disposed of him on the last climb. Inside the final five kilometres, Thomas darted across to Dumoulin, Dan Martin attacked behind him with Froome on his wheel, leaving Nairo, in the company of Bardet, Nibali and Roglič, unable to follow. Nairo's hopes of winning the 2018 Tour dissolved there and then.

Stage seventeen was a 65-kilometre mountain sprint over two colossal climbs before the final 16-kilometre ascent on the Col du Portet. At the foot of the final climb, he attacked, chased by Dan Martin. Without ever gaining 30 seconds on the Irishman, Nairo redeemed his Tour with a stage win, gaining 47 seconds on the race leader and moving into fifth place. At dinner, there was no team celebration of his success.

The following day, an arm went out at the back of the peloton, sending Nairo into the verge. His injuries were still being treated at midnight. The following day, he sat up on the final climb. He would finish the Tour only tenth, 14 minutes 18 seconds behind the winner, Geraint Thomas.

The previous year's runner-up, Rigoberto Urán, fared even worse, falling twice on the Paris–Roubaix-inspired ninth stage and losing a minute and a half. The first mountain stages quietly removed him from the list of contenders, and he abandoned on stage twelve. Behind Nairo and Rigoberto, the younger Colombians vied for their place in the order of succession. Urán's teammate Daniel Martínez, the Tour's third-youngest participant, had been there for him at every incident. Freed from his domestic duties, he joined the breakaways in stages fourteen and fifteen.

Egan Bernal, the youngest rider in the race, overcame crashes in stages one and nine to offer his leaders precious help in the mountains. On Alpe d'Huez at the end of stage twelve, he closed down an attack by Nairo and positioned Thomas for his stage win. In stages seventeen and nineteen, he paced an ailing Froome through the Pyrenees.

On 4 August, six days after the Tour had finished, Egan started the Clásica San Sebastián. With fewer than 20 kilometres remaining, a fall ahead of him brought him crashing down. Despite a brain bleed, he underwent surgery that evening to repair his upper lip and reduce a nasal fracture. A series of dental interventions was needed to replace and repair the missing and fractured teeth.

On 5 October, during Egan's sixty-three-day lay-off, Team Sky showed their faith in him by announcing that Egan had signed a five-year contract with the team. Team manager Sir David Brailsford agreed: 'A five-year deal in cycling is exceptional, but Egan is an exceptional talent ... we have even greater ambitions to keep on improving, and Egan will be at the very heart of that.'

At Il Lombardia on 13 October, Bernal showed he had lost

none of his nerve by chasing down the leading group of Nibali, Pinot and Roglič in a vertiginous descent from the Sormano. His vitality ebbed on the penultimate climb, and, inside the final 15 kilometres he was caught by the chasing group. Urán finished the race fourth, with Bernal fading to twelfth.

At the Vuelta a España, López managed to overshadow Quintana and Urán. True, Nairo lay third overall, ten seconds ahead of López and just 33 seconds behind the race leader Simon Yates, after fifteen stages. They were fourth and sixth after the following day's time trial but still well placed to bid for podium places, if not victory overall.

However, 2.9 kilometres from the stage eighteen finish line on the Balcón de Bizkaia climb, as Nairo began to struggle, his teammate Alejandro Valverde forced the pace at the front. López stayed with the race leader Yates, while Nairo, without ever losing sight of the leading group, rode alone to the finish line, conceding 54 seconds to Yates and 52 to Miguel Ángel López. He dropped to sixth overall, eventually slipping to eighth, one place behind Urán.

On the Colada de la Gallina climb in Andorra, Miguel Ángel López moved into third place overall, and stayed there for the rest of the race. He had only taken three victories all year, but, with podium finishes in the Giro d'Italia and the Vuelta a España, it was the best season of his career. He finished it with another second place, in the Milano Torino. Inside the final 1.5 kilometres, he and the young French rider David Gaudu tangled and went down. By the time Miguel Ángel had leapt to his feet and remounted, Thibaut Pinot had gone. López could only follow him in for second place.

◈

At August's Vuelta a Burgos, a compatriot even younger than Egan Bernal had challenged Miguel Ángel López's hegemony. Four kilometres from the finish line on Picón Blanco, López launched what looked like a winning attack. Under the *flamme rouge*, he led the chasing group of six by 21 seconds. With 800 metres to go, a figure hurtled out of the following pack. With 300 metres to go, Iván Ramiro Sosa, 20 years, 9 months and 7 days old, caught López, who accelerated and moved into his slipstream. On the final, right-hand bend, López took the inside line. Position alone gave him the win, with Sosa beside him.

On the final stage, on the traditional climb up to Lagunas de Neila, Sosa tracked López. Five hundred metres from the finish line, he attacked, gaining 19 seconds. They gave him the stage win and victory overall. Another Colombian career was underway.

22

Constant Gardeners

From the corner of your eye, *Espeletia grandiflora* – colloquially, *frailejón*, 'the big friar' – resembles a human figure at prayer. It even sounds like one, its voice the busy burble of the peat underfoot. Ecologically the most sympathetic of plants, it captures moisture in its hairy leaves, and releases it through its roots. The high-altitude grassland where the *frailejón* grows is called the *páramo*. Considered an evolutionary hotspot, it is also a vast repository of fresh water: the peat is said to be able to retain up to twenty-six times its weight in water.

From its sap, the Muysca holy men prepared a sacred resin in which they washed the prospective *psihipqua*. Then, they dusted him with powdered gold. In the last moments of the night, they joined him on a raft heavy with jewels and burning incense. As they rowed out into the crucible lake at Guatavita, dawn's early glow glistened green on the water's surface. The villagers at the water's edge saw off the darkness with a wailing of reed instruments and jangling of bells. Day broke, and a plane of golden light sliced through the penumbra, revealing the *psihipqua* to his people. Six years spent hidden from them and the sun in a sacred cave, abstaining from salt, chilli pepper and sexual relations, had prepared him for this moment.

An incantation went up, and offerings were cast into the lake: gold like pieces of sun, emeralds that echoed the water's hue, figurines in stone, wood and cotton. The new *psihipqua* stepped to the edge of the raft and, to a collective gasp, he plunged into the deep.

There can scarcely have been a more dramatic sight in all human history.

The Spanish called him *El Dorado*, the golden one. Not that European eyes ever saw him: Sebastián de Belalcázar, who died in 1551, heard of the ceremony during his subjugation of Quito. A generation later, Don Juan, *cacique* of Guatavita, described it to his friend, the chronicler Juan Rodríguez Freile. Over the centuries to come, El Dorado bedded down into the stock of global fantasies.

But then, in 1856, at one of the lagunas at Siecha, east of Bogotá, a remarkable discovery proved the stories of the ritual of El Dorado true: a tiny golden model, twenty centimetres by ten, of a raft bearing ten human figures. Acquired by the German Consul in Bogotá, it was sold to the Altes Museum in Berlin and sent by sea. But the ship caught fire in Bremen harbour, and the priceless sacred object, fulfilling its ancient destiny, disappeared beneath the waves. After all, the Muysca cosmos was one of opposing principles: night/day, sun/moon, right/wrong, man/woman, earth/water. When equilibrium was lost – at times of drought, flood or conflict – sacred golden figurines, ritually cast by expert craftsmen, were buried in the earth, deposited in caves, or tossed into lakes or rivers to restore the harmony of the spirit world.

To the metal-working cultures of the pre-Colombian Andes, gold was a medium for speaking to the gods. To the European conquerors, it meant earthly wealth and power. So, in the 1580s, the Spanish blasted a cleft in the holy lake's perimeter to lower the water level and get access to the sunken gold. In 1898 a Briton named Hartley Knowles went further, draining the lake down to four feet of mud, although he only had time to pilfer a few artefacts before the silt set like concrete in the sun.

Then, in 1969, a peasant farmer named Cruz María Dimaté came across a pile of ceramic and metal fragments in a cave near the village of Pasca, 90 kilometres south of Bogotá. Sorting through the pieces, he found himself holding perhaps the most sought-after artefact in the Americas: a second golden Muysca raft. Acquired by the Bank of the Republic, it quickly became the centrepiece of Bogotá's extraordinary Gold Museum.

The find was made within living memory. In Pasca, more than anywhere, it seemed to me, the *campesinos* must still tell the old stories. But, of the old Muysca legends, Iván Ramiro Sosa Cuervo told me, 'I don't know them. It is another world now.'

Colombia had moved on.

On 15 July 1537, when the Conquistador Juan de Céspedes is said to have both conquered and founded the village – although, I wondered, how could it be both? – Pasca was a hamlet set between two rivers whose clear waters washed over a bed of polished white stones as enormous as prehistoric eggs.

A Muysca word meaning 'the father's enclosure', Pasca looks up at the mountains of Sumapaz, which contain the world's largest *páramo* ecosystem. In 1990 Colombia was ranked as the country with the fourth greatest water wealth in the world, although environmental mismanagement since then has seen it plummet to twenty-fourth.

In the 1960s Sumapaz was one of eight rebel-controlled areas dubbed 'Independent Republics' by the right – peasant communities that rejected the state and denied the Colombian armed forces entry. The FARC were founded in 1964 by survivors of military assaults on these rebel strongholds.

Iván's parents, Jorge Antonio Sosa and Thelma Johana Cuervo, both have their origins in Boyacá: the Sosas were from Turmequé, the Cuervos from Ramiriquí, 35 kilometres away, although Antonio and Thelma were born in Fusagasugá, Antonio, one of seven siblings, Thelma one of four. But they decided against a large family.

'There isn't much money in the countryside,' Antonio told me, 'so to educate your children properly, you can't have too many of them.'

They moved to Finca El Caucho, a parcel of land north-east of the village on a vereda known as Gúchipas, in 1995. Iván was born in nearby Fusagasugá on 31 October 1997. They named him after Iván Ramiro Parra, who, in October 1996 had won his second Vuelta de la Juventud and was said to be so good that he would supersede even his eldest brother Fabio's achievements.

At the time of my visit, Iván Ramiro Sosa Cuervo was still living in the family's house built on the finca by his father. Wealth must only have been weeks away from transforming his life, and that of his family. He had recently refused Trek-Segafredo's offer of €250,000 a year and signed for Team Sky for a similar figure or more. It rewarded his parents for seeing beyond a life of peasant toil for their children. They were sorting pea pods into 50 kilo sacks when I arrived.

'We've always grown the same things here: peas, beans, chilli peppers, potatoes, tamarillo and blackberries,' Antonio told me.

He had grown up on a coffee plantation, but vegetable prices were no more reliable and, in any case, he nurtured other dreams for his son: 'I liked cycling and, since the day we bought him his first bike, I wanted him to be a cyclist. The radio journalists said, "If you are good, you can do well. If you are average, it's hard," and I thought, "That is like any job."'

The qualities needed, he said, were the same as those needed by peasant farmers: 'Perseverance, constancy, as in anything else. I used to say to him, if you have a dream, you have to start at the bottom and lay solid foundations.'

Twelve years on from her son's first win, his mother places the trophy on the table. The best riders in the eight- to eleven-year-olds category of the 2006 Pasca Mountain Bike Cup, round eight, were Iván and his cousin Jhojan García Sosa, both eleven – Jhojan's mother, Beatriz, is Antonio's sister. They were so equally matched in the final uphill sprint along the main street, and so proud and unyielding, that each nearly undid the other and himself when, twenty metres from the finish in the square, they collided and fell. It was Iván who rose more quickly and crossed the line first.

Jhoján's family had no car but had always travelled – mother, father and two children – together on a motorbike. When Jhojan was eight and growing too big for the saddle, his uncle Joaquín, the youngest of the Sosa siblings and a PE teacher in Fusagasugá, bought him a bike, and he began to ride the eight kilometres to his grandmother's behind the motorbike.

Joaquín began to take Iván, Jhojan, their cousins Arley and Andrés, and Iván's half-brother, Diego, on weekend rides in the surrounding mountains. Iván and Jhojan, eight years old and the youngest of the group, were the only ones who stuck with it. When Diego was diagnosed with cancer and died soon afterwards, Iván and Jhojan were deeply affected. Their 2006 Pasca Mountain Bike Cup duel came a year later.

From the age of twelve, Iván took the school bus home from Fusagasugá, his cousin Jhojan's – and Lucho Herrera's – home town. He spent his afternoons picking and packing seven or eight fifteen-pound punnets of blackberries. Iván and Jhojan joined the Gigra Cycling Club in Fusagasugá. They trained and raced like brothers, although Jhojan was the more constant of the two, and he was selected for the 2013 Vuelta del Futuro. He finished 54th, 31 places behind Egan Bernal, and one place behind Esteban Chaves' brother Brayan. The following year, he was fourth in the first three stages, and first in the fourth. It earned him victory overall, and an invitation from Luis Fernando Saldarriaga to join him in Medellín. There, Jhojan finished 300 metres short of Nairo Quintana's time for the climb up Las

Palmas, and Saldarriaga offered him a contract with his team, 4-72.

Iván too flourished at the cycling club, despite his regular school's lack of enthusiasm. His mother told me, 'I went to the Instituto Triángulo in Fusagasugá, who said they would send him to the Interschool Games, and Iván changed schools.'

In 2015 he prepared for his school certificate while riding for a team sponsored by the teacher's cooperative society, Canapro.

In August 2015 he took a solo win by 1 minute 15 seconds in stage three of the four-day Clásica Ciudad de Soacha, from Fusagsugá to Soacha, over two passes, San Miguel and the Alto de Romeral. It brought him overall victory in the race. In the last week of November, he went to the Tour del Porvenir. After finishing eighth in the stage-two time trial, won by Julián Cardona, he threw away 39 seconds in the final kilometre of stage three, Sutamarchán–Chiquinquirá–Barbosa–Arcabuco, due to a hunger knock. The following day, on El Crucero, the climb above Sogamoso, he won the stage, 27 seconds ahead of Sergio Andrés Higuita. In stage five, a circuit around Tunja, he finished fourth.

Just after the Tour del Porvenir, he had passed his school certificate with a mark good enough to earn a 50 per cent grant to go to the San José University in Bogotá. He went to Italy instead: Andrea Bianco had seen Iván win on El Crucero and invited him to Bogotá for testing. Blanco spoke to Paolo Alberati, who found him a place with Winner Anacona's old team, Maltinti-Lampadari.

'People said life was hard in Europe, but my coach at Canapro, Fabio Chíngate, told me I should go and try for a year.'

His mother Thelma recalls, 'He spent eight months in Europe. He travelled out on 14 February and came back on 14 October.'

Living in San Miniato, between Pisa and Florence, he adjusted quickly. At the Coppa del Grano in March at San Giovanni Valdarno, he came tenth. At the Trofeo San Leolino in April, he finished second. On 5 June he was eighth in the Trofeo Figros; on 19 June second in the Trofeo Citta' di Malmantile; and on the 25th he won the Schio-Ossario del Pasubio.

Sosa and Bernal then rode the 2016 Tour de l'Avenir together. Bernal led the Colombia team and finished fourth. 'It wasn't the result we wanted,' Sosa reflects, 'but I think I was still adjusting to life in Europe.'

Even so, his race results prompted Paolo Alberati to approach Gianni Savio at Androni Giocattoli-Sidermec. However, on 10 June, soon after the Trofeo Figros, Sosa had taken an oxygen uptake test, returning figures of 84.4 ml/min/kg: a high result, but not in Bernal's range.

Iván told me, 'To begin with, Gianni was not very encouraging. He put a lot of trust in the test result. But oxygen uptake after five hours in the mountains is rather different from during a twenty-minute lab test, and in the end he offered me a contract.'

Iván's first race as a professional cyclist was the 2017 Tour of Táchira State in Venezuela. He won the best young rider competition there. Of his remaining forty-two race days, twenty-seven were spent riding with Egan Bernal. They became close friends.

It was only when Bernal had moved on that Sosa came into his own. In Folgaria, on day one of the Tour of the Alps in April 2018, he darted away from a group containing Thibaut Pinot, Christopher Froome, Fabio Aru and Miguel Angel López to take third place. The following day, after climbing the Alpe di Pampeago with Pinot, Froome, López and Domenico Pozzovivo, he finished third again and took the race lead.

The following day, Sosa watched Froome and López attack before the crest of the Passo Palade: 'I let them go, because I knew I was going to catch them, until the bike slid away from me on a curve.'

He rolled across the finish line having lost four minutes and the leader's jersey, but his performance in the first two stages had been as impressive as Egan Bernal's the year before.

The results began to pile up. At the start of June, he won a stage and the general classification at the Tour of Bihor-Bellotto in Romania, then, at the end of the month, began a remarkable sequence of three consecutive stage-race wins. At the Adriatica Ionica Race, he won stage three on the Passo Giau, high in the Dolomites, and the race overall, 41 seconds ahead of the Italian climber Giulio Ciccone. At the Sibiu Cycling Tour in Romania, he triumphed in stage two at Balea Lac, with a time for the final ascent 1 minute 38 seconds faster than Bernal's mark the previous year.

But it was victory in his next race, the Vuelta a Burgos, not a WorldTour race but a key preparation event for the Vuelta a España, featuring four WorldTour teams and a Vuelta contender in Miguel Ángel López, that brought him international admiration.

'And I only went to Burgos to find my rhythm for the Tour de l'Avenir.'

By the time of the 2018 Tour de l'Avenir, Iván's contract negotations for 2019 were the topic of public speculation. In April, soon after the Tour of the Alps, he had taken physiological tests at the Mapei Centre in Castellanza, north-west of Milan. The Trek-Segafredo team had reportedly paid Gianni Savio €120,000 as early as June to activate Iván Sosa's contract-release clause, perhaps trying to make the signing a fait accompli in advance of the 1 August contract window.

After Sosa's successful Vuelta a Burgos, Trek-Segafredo manager Luca Guercilena agreed to increase his future yearly wage to €250,000. On 24 August Trek-Segafredo sent a twenty-five-page contract to Sosa and his agents, followed, days later, by a full Spanish translation. But Sosa did not sign.

At the Tour de l'Avenir, riding for the Colombian national team, Sosa won the first mountain stage. The following day, he was second in a stage he says he should have won.

'I felt a stomach problem coming on. The following day, I was very ill, and all the contract speculation affected my mind.'

Overall, he could finish only sixth.

The day after the Tour de l'Avenir finished, on 27 August, it was announced that Sosa would be riding for Trek-Segafredo in 2019. The deal had been brokered by Alberati, Fondriest and their lawyer Marco Angelini. According to the website cyclingnews.com, Alberati called Sosa on Monday 3 September to discuss preparations for the Under-23 road race at the World Championships. Over the days that followed, Sosa received a call from Bernal's agent, Giuseppe Acquadro.

'He said, "I want to talk to you in person." I said, "Come over." He said, "I would like to work with you," and so on. He wanted to know if I had signed anything. I showed him the contract with Alberati, and he told me the contract was not valid because it was for four years, and the UCI only recognises two-year contracts. I told him I had not signed anything with Trek-Segafredo.

'Alberati said that I had given my word and that was what counted. Giuseppe told me, "If you haven't signed anything, you haven't signed anything."

'He said, "Suppose that you hadn't won Burgos, and the team had said, 'We're going to offer you this: take it or leave it,' how much would your word be worth then? Suppose I told you that next time I come, I'll bring you a contract with Team Sky?"'

Iván told me, 'I think every cyclist in the world would like to go there.'

Before Acquadro returned, Iván's father Antonio took a phone call from Alberati: 'The Italians called us to put pressure on us, so that we would tell him to sign with Trek. But he already had his heart set on Sky, and we didn't want him to miss the opportunity. Every sportsman dreams of joining the best team in the world.'

Sosa says he received a visit from Alberati, Fondriest and Angelini: 'They said I had to sign the contract. Otherwise Trek were going to sue me. They gave me half an hour to sign.'

He resisted: 'I said, "If your problem is with me, why do you want to involve my parents?"'

'I was an innocent,' he told me. 'I don't know anything about law or anything like that. Giuseppe advised me, and I spoke to Egan, who wanted me at Sky. He told me that Giuseppe was genuine.'

The contract was signed in time for Iván to attend Team Sky's camp in the first week of November 2018. It meant that Colombia had nineteen WorldTour riders distributed among eight of the eighteen WorldTour teams, and another twenty-five in the Professional-Continental ranks, the second tier of global cycling. Six of the WorldTour riders were twenty-two or younger. The abundance of talent was causing a feeding frenzy among riders' agents, but none of the wealth generated was being reinvested in Colombian cycling. At its highest level, the national sport was becoming an advertisement for the country's inability to manage its own resources. This was in stark contrast with the near-miracles being worked at cycling's grass roots by some remarkable local projects.

23

Chiaroscuro

The Vueltas a Colombia of the 1960s rolled over poor, potholed roads, so the contenders needed solid support vehicles. Colombia's top rider, Martín Emilio 'Cochise' Rodríguez, had a friend in construction who drove an indestructible 1955 Ford pick-up, so Cochise asked him along. So it was that Luis Fernando Saldarriaga's grandfather, Jesús María Saldarriaga, came to drive in the champion's wake during many of his greatest triumphs.

The oldest of Jesús María's ten children, Fernando – Luís Fernando's father – was a promising cyclist. His chance came at the 1968 RCN Clásico, but he started stage one ill, did not start stage two at all and went into construction like his father.

In January 2017 I stayed with Fernando Saldarriaga and his wife Amparo, as Esteban Chaves had done during his time with Bike House-Trek – as Nairo Quintana and Sergio Luís Henao had done, too, in their Colombia Es Pasión years. From their home in Barrio Santa Fé, close to the Olaya Herrera airport in northern Medellín, Fernando and Amparo have built a remarkable sporting project – a homespun, humanitarian recycling machine that takes in devastated lives and turns out well-balanced, self-respecting athletes, some of them world-class. Seeing the strictness of their nurturing, the sternness of the support they give the boys and girls of Club Nueva Generación, makes it easier to understand the moral rigour of their only son. When their young riders send

Fernando text messages, they have to use correct Spanish. If there are orthographical mistakes, Fernando does not reply. One morning during my stay, a young rider arrived after an all-night bus journey. Fernando sent him straight to bed to recover, then, later in the day, cast frequent glances over the boy's shoulder as, in his best handwriting, he copied his teammates' contact details into an exercise book.

Fernando whispered to me, 'It's the only time he writes.'

One morning, at the Aeropark near Medellín's Olaya Herrera airport, I watched as Henry Daniel Restrepo, fourteen years old, showed off his Peter Sagan-style one-handed wheelie to sixteen-year-old Carlos Daniel Echeverri. Henry Daniel had come to Medellín in 2014 from Tarazá, Antioquia, the country's third largest gold-producing town, 220 kilometres north of Medellín and close to the drug traffickers' routes north to the Caribbean and the natural ports of the Gulf of Morrosquillo.

The FARC had first entered Tarazá in 1983. By 2000 a paramilitary force known as the Bloque Mineros or 'Miners' Division' had displaced them and built an empire of arms, drugs and illegal gold. Paramilitary rule meant fear and summary justice, but also, occasionally, welcome reforms. To win over Tarazá's 42,000 inhabitants, the Bloque Mineros had provided road paving, zinc roofing and community kitchens. They had remodelled the asylum, funded clinics with sophisticated equipment, helped a hundred families through its *Tarazá Sin Hambre* ('Tarazá Without Hunger') programme, arranged tubal ligation for 270 women and a sex-change operation for a village member of the LGBTQ community.

But the demobilisation of the Bloque Mineros in January 2006 opened a vacuum, and President Uribe's offensive on illicit crops coincided with a leap in international gold prices, leading to an influx of coca workers and investors into the semi-clandestine economy of river gold mining. An alliance of former paramilitaries called the Urabeños – the country's most powerful criminal organisation – soon filled the gap.

Henry Daniel had been a member of Ciclotara, the Tarazá cycling school, but the violence brought by the Urabeños prompted the family to move to Medellín, where he joined Club Nueva Generación. In 2016 he won all the races he entered.

In 2017 Carlos Daniel Echeverri had become national sprint gold medallist on the track, succeeding another Club Nueva Generación member, Santiago Betancur, who had come to Medellín from the town of Caucasia, 60 kilometres from Tarazá and with many of the same problems. Santiago's mother had been a nurse at Caucasia hospital, where a doorman was murdered by one of the armed factions as a warning to hospital workers not to treat the wounded from their enemies.

When one of the grenades that exploded daily in the street left Santiago temporarily deaf, the family fled for Medellín.

His mother commented, 'In Medellín you wear your hospital uniform in the street for safety. In Caucasia you took it off before you left the clinic. It was my home village. I thought I'd spend my whole life there. But the gunmen imposed a curfew and banned family celebrations. If they suspected you of sympathising with their enemies, they entered your house and gunned you down.'

In Medellín, Santiago enrolled in Club Nueva Generation and met Juan Dario Davíd, sixteen, another boy who, like him, was not technically displaced. His parents had sent him to stay with an uncle in Buenos Aires, Medellín – a neighbourhood built by Pablo Escobar – to grow up free from the insecurity in his home town, Cañasgordas, western Antioquia.

I spoke to José Manuel Marín too, a promising young rider from a farm near the artificial lake at Guatapé. He had been found, three weeks old, suckling at the breast of his still-warm mother, murdered with her husband in the conflict. Warm and welcoming, José Manuel told me that one day he would like to invite me to the farm where he was brought up.

Through Fernando and Amparo, all of these young riders knew Nairo Quintana and trained alongside Sergio Andrés

Higuita, Wilmar Paredes and Kevin Cano, all Club Nueva Generación graduates who moved on to Colombia Es Pasión's final manifestation, Manzana Postobón. They knew that the distance between Club Nueva Generación and cycling at its highest level was not unbridgeable.

Another young rider, Juan Pablo Ortega, fourteen, held the record for the Baby Ciclismo, a 400-metre time trial organised in Medellín each January, with riders from all over Colombia. A month after he won the 2016 edition, his mother died of cancer. Sergio Higuita quietly told Fernando Saldarriaga to persevere with Juan Pablo: he would cover Juan Pablo's expenses. More than just a family, the club is a life-support system. Perhaps one day it will produce the Nairo Quintana or Egan Bernal of the future. Perhaps it already has: at the end of 2018, Sergio Higuita, from the deprived neighbourhood of Comuna Castilla – famous for another Higuita, René, the long-haired, scorpion-kicking goalkeeper of the 1990s – signed a contract with the WorldTour team EF Education First. In September 2019 he capped a brilliant season with a mountain stage win at the Vuelta a España, and fourteenth overall, at his first attempt.

Yet, like one of those opposing pairs dear to the Muysca, the silver cloud of Club Nueva Generación had a dark lining. On 5 April 2019 Wilmar Paredes was provisionally suspended by the UCI after an out-of-competition test on 27 February detected traces of EPO. On 20 May 2019, the UCI announced that, in a test taken seven months before, another Manzana Postobón rider, Juan José Amador, had returned an adverse analytical finding – the precursor to a positive doping test – for boldenone, an anabolic steroid.

Luisa Ríos had known Paredes all his life. She told me, 'I felt it was partly our responsibility too. It's too easy to blame the riders. It is the fault of all of us, as directors.'

Luís Fernando Saldarriaga said, 'I was asked my opinion, and I said we should close the team down. We can't tolerate unethical behaviour. We have damaged our sponsor, we have sinned, and we have to pay the price.'

On 24 May the Corporación Pedaleamos por Colombia – the management entity for the various manifestations of Colombia Es Pasión, 4-72 Colombia, and now Manzana Postobón – issued a statement that read, in part, 'Due to the regrettable facts published in the past weeks, in which athletes belonging to the professional cycling team have been implicated, we have taken the decision not to continue with the squad, and henceforth the team will no longer participate in the national and international race calendar.'

The problems had been a long time brewing. On 1 September 2018 Juan Pablo Villegas, once the soul of the team, resigned. In January 2019 he had spoken to Luisa Ríos, telling her 'I don't think the team will be around for long. In these conditions, they're going to have a positive.'

It was Villegas's second retirement. Brought up labouring in the coffee-growing department of Caldas, he was working full-time by the time he was eleven, rising at 4.30 a.m., walking to the fields and carrying 70kg loads of coffee and plantains. Honest, tough, he told me, 'Colombia Es Pasión didn't teach me new values. They were my values.'

In February 2015, in a frank interview with the Colombian writer Klaus Bellón, published on Bellón's bilingual website Alps & Andes, Villegas said:

The talent at Colombia Es Pasion was amazing, with Nairo, Esteban Chaves, Pantano. There was internal testing and a strong ethical component with the focus on clean sport, as well as a team of guys who we can now see are capable of winning the biggest races against the best riders in the world. Yet in Colombia our best rider could lose 20 minutes in a stage and

finish thirtieth in GC [general classification, the overall time]
. . . we were taunted and laughed at.

Then we'd go abroad to race and win . . .

In February 2015 the Colombian soft drinks giant Postobón had moved in to save the 4-72 team, and Vélez, Saldarriaga and Ríos had invited Villegas back to the team now known as Manzana Postobón, despite death threats made to him on social media. Far from offering protection, a senior Colombian Cycling Federation official threatened Villegas with a ban unless he issued a retraction. Gustavo Duncan, a journalist with the national daily *El Tiempo*, published a report about the Villegas scandal. Visibility in one of the country's leading newspapers allowed him to race safely at the 2015 Vuelta al Caribe and Vuelta a Cundinamarca. Still, it was decided that he would not ride in the Clásico RCN or Vuelta a Colombia. It was too dangerous.

Ignacio Vélez too had been receiving death threats for his anti-doping stance. His family had long pleaded with him to get out of cycling, but he had refused to be intimidated. He finally walked away in 2015, out of not fear but frustration. He told me, 'I was tired of the incompetence, the lack of vision, and the shady deals over doping between the cycling federation and Coldeportes.'

He had left the Corporación Pedaleamos por Colombia in 2015, to be replaced by a Medellín industrialist named Alejandro Restrepo.

Saldarriaga's principled approach to cycling was diluted by the arrival of other sports directors, and Juan Pablo Villegas was attacked for his anti-doping stance. He considered resigning, but when his wife became pregnant, with no job waiting for him, he had to stay.

'The last three years in the team were torture. If I had a chance of winning, I was sent to collect water. If I went down to the hotel bar for a coffee or chocolate to relieve the boredom of being in my room all day, it was like I'd committed a crime. Only the thought of feeding my son made me carry on.'

Manzana Postobón became a conventional team, its management team motivated more by victories than by any kind of moral mission. In November 2017 Ríos left the team. With her no longer at the helm, Colsanitas downgraded their involvement. The team's internal testing became sporadic.

In August 2018 the team went to China for the Tour of Qinghai Lake. The riders finished first, second, fifth and eighth, but their achievement was marred by a row over the distribution of the prize money. Two days after arriving home from China, the Manzana Postobón rider Juan José Amador was drug tested, and the spiral of events that led to the team's downfall began.

On 15 April 2019 another scandal broke when Jarlinson Pantano's positive test became public knowledge. At the end of July, *El Tiempo* newspaper reported that US federal agents and European investigators sought to interview Dr Alberto Beltrán in connection with the spate of doping scandals. The newpaper found that Beltrán had been arrested in a Bogotá gym in June 2016, and extradition proceedings to Spain initiated soon afterwards, only for the Colombia Prosecutor's Office to cancel the arrest warrant four months later and order his release, on the grounds that doping was not a crime in Colombia.

Beltrán, the report continued, had returned to work, with no charges filed against him.

Yet, despite these foundations of sand – this background of corruption and mismanagement, to which the outside world could plead blissful ignorance – Colombia's international cyclists went from strength to strength.

Egan Bernal won the 2019 Paris–Nice in March, with Nairo Quintana second. Dani Martínez had taken a brilliant victory on the Col de Turini in stage seven. Miguel Ángel López, second that day, went on to win the Volta a Catalunya, with Bernal third and Quintana fourth. Egan had then returned to Colombia, to prepare for a Giro d'Italia he was fated not to start.

On Saturday 4 May, descending from the Port d'Envalira, a mountain pass in Andorra, he had crashed. That left Miguel Ángel López carrying Colombia's ambitions, until a series of mechanical problems ended his hopes of victory. He finished as the best young rider, as he had in 2018, but only seventh in the final classification.

The Giro started badly for his old rival Richard Carapaz too. With eight kilometres left in stage three, the Ecuadorean had a mechanical problem and took a teammate's bike. He ended the stage 78th, having lost 46 crucial seconds. The following day at Frascati, he started his Giro again. With 600 metres to go on 6 per cent slopes, he attacked. The Australian sprinter Caleb Ewan tied up on the gradients and Carapaz took the stage win.

Ten days later, with 16 kilometres to go up to the finish line beside Lake Serrù, his teammate Mikel Landa attacked the group of favourites, followed by a TV camera bike. Behind him, unseen, Carapaz made his own, even more impressive incursion, recording the fastest time for the ascent. Landa and Carapaz finished the stage third and fourth, and slotted into sixth and eighth overall.

That evening, a Canyon bikes rep was talking to Carapaz's mechanic Tomás Amezaga. As Richard walked past, he said to Tomás, 'Tell him to start preparing a pink bike for me, because we're going to be wearing pink.' It was said lightheartedly, but it showed the ambition in his mindset.

The following day, with 28 kilometres to go and three to the top of the Colle San Carlo, Carapaz accelerated hard. At the top, he led by 30 seconds. On the 16.6-kilometre descent, he lost 5 seconds, before powering up the final, 8.3-kilometre ramp, gaining time with every turn of the pedals. He finished the stage 1 minute 54 seconds before his closest rivals, added a 10-second bonus for the stage win, and took the Maglia Rosa by 7 seconds.

During the rest-day press conferences, the race favourites Vincenzo Nibali and Primož Roglič conceded that it had been a mistake to let the Ecuadorean go. Carapaz punished them for their insolence by adding handfuls of seconds to his overall lead on each of the next three stages. He received his pink bike on stage eighteen, his twenty-sixth birthday, 30 May, then went into the final time trial with a lead of 1:54 over Nibali, 2:53 over his teammate Landa, and 3:16 over Roglič.

He told me, 'I had no reason to take any risks.'

After playing it safe on a technical course, he won the Giro by 1 minute 5 seconds, with Nibali second and Roglič third. The first Ecuadorean to win a three-week Tour, Richard is certainly also the first Grand Tour champion to be simultaneously indigenous (through his father) and Afro-American (through his mother). It was a triumph for diversity, inclusion, and the fellowship of humankind.

It was in 2008, when he was fifteen, that Juan Carlos Rosero had visited his school at El Playón de San Francisco, on the line between the border provinces of Carchi and Sucumbíos, and invited the pupils to join his newly constituted cycling club. Rosero had been Ecuador's most successful cyclist: the winner of three Vueltas a Ecuador, in 1992 he had worn the leader's jersey from start to finish, become the only ever foreign winner of the hard-fought Vuelta a Boyacá, and finished fifth in the Vuelta a Colombia, even taking the race lead for a day, replacing Lucho Herrera. He briefly rode for the Pepsi Cola-Alba-Fanini team in Italy, where he was listed as Colombian. As Richard remembers it, almost every child in the school, all sixty of them, signed up.

Carapaz showed immediate talent. Twice the national junior champion on the road, he won bronze medals in the individual pursuit and madison. In 2010 Rosero called Oliverio Cárdenas in Colombia. With no berth left in his own team, Cárdenas recommended him to the Bogotá team Canapro, for whom Richard won a stage and finished fourth in the 2010 Vuelta del Porvenir. A year later, he won the 2011 edition – the first non-Colombian to do so.

On the morning of 23 January 2013, he went out for a pre-season jog in the mountains with his teammates and Rosero.

> We dropped him on the climbs and he caught us on the descents, until he began to feel ill and decided to turn back. I called him later to see if he could pick us up. At first he said no. Then he called back and said, 'I'm on my way.' He picked us up, dropped us off, then, three hours later, the phone rang. I thought there had been some sort of mix up. Or it was a bad joke. I ran to the emergency room. They sent me to the morgue where I found his family weeping. It was my first experience of death.

Travelling to races all over northern Ecuador and Colombia, Richard and Juan Carlos Rosero became close: he describes Rosero as 'my first coach, my brother, my second father'. Yet, Richard says, there are no pictures of them together.

'We shared so many moments together that it never occurred to either of us to stop and take a photograph.'

Richard Carapaz was born on 29 May 1993 in El Carmelo, on the Carchi side of the line where the Ecuadorean provinces of Carchi and Sucumbíos meet, on land that had been Colombian until 1916, when the current land border was demarcated.

'Most of my relations have been farmers all their lives, like my father, until he switched to driving a truck,' Richard recalls. 'For fifteen years he transported coffee from the Ecuadorean Amazon, through the border controls with Colombia, to the coffee warehouses in Ipiales.'

Even so, the family continued to grow crops and keep cattle, and Richard had to play his part. When he was fifteen, he was left in charge of the family finca with only his grandfather to help.

'My mother had been diagnosed with breast cancer, and my

parents had to go away to the hospital. We had eight or nine cows, so I had to milk them very early, then go to school and study, then prepare a meal and go out to train.'

His mother, thankfully, recovered from her illness.

He lived with his family six kilometres from El Playón de San Francisco near the Guandera Ecological Reserve, a forested area. He took the school bus, or used an old bike he had recovered from a batch of junk he picked up in his truck.

'The reserve was only semi-explored,' he told me. 'The sort of terrain the guerrillas liked to hide in. It is still a protected area today. You were always hearing about FARC attacks, car bombs, and so on, the other side of the border. They closed the crossings from time to time, but you got used to it: they always opened again. I remember particularly the attack which killed Raúl Reyes: it had a huge impact on the border population.'

Raúl Reyes was a member of the FARC's ruling Secretariat and one of the commanders of its Southern Bloc, in the Colombian Amazon. He operated out of a FARC camp in Sucumbíos province, Ecuador, less than two kilometres from the border. Since the start of 2007 the Colombian armed forces had launched at least four operations against him: each time he had slipped through their hands. On the night of 29 February 2008, intel reports suggested that Reyes would be re-entering Colombia to meet a known drugs trafficker. Super Tucano light attack aircraft were already in the air when news came through that Reyes had not crossed the border: he was at the camp in Ecuador.

The Colombian Defence Minister and future President, Juan Manuel Santos, could see no other path but to continue the operation.

At 12:02 a.m. on Saturday 1 March 2008, high-precision missiles then Colombian Special Forces hit the camp. Reyes' body was recovered, together with computers and hard drives. President Rafael Correa of Ecuador recalled his ambassador and deployed the Ecuadorean army along the border.

For those whose livelihoods depended on cross-border trade, the episode created serious hardship. But Richard Carapaz was already looking beyond the Colombian border at a career in the wider arena of global sport.

卌

Rosero had fixed as Richard's 2013 goal May's Pan-American under-23 road race in Zacatecas, Mexico. 'He said, "It will open the door to Colombia, and then Europe."'

Richard finished 1 minute 52 seconds ahead of the runner-up. A month later, an 18-year-old among elite riders, he was riding the four-day Tour des Pays de Savoie for the national team. He finished fourth, fifth and second in the first three stages, and ninth overall.

Then, while training the following year, disaster struck him, in the form of a car whose driver was using a mobile phone. Two operations were needed to repair the sciatic nerve in his right leg. After six months unable to ride, he resumed training and crossed the border to join the Medellín-based Strongman-Campagnolo team. In April 2015 he won the third stage of the Vuelta de la Juventud and pulled on the leader's jersey. The following day, he reinforced his lead by winning atop the 22.3-kilometre climb to Concordia. Three days after that, he became the first non-Colombian rider to win the Vuelta de la Juventud. In Tulcán, the capital of Carchi province, he was received as a hero. The parade through the city streets took five hours.

It was the start of a meteoric ascent. He started 2016 riding for Strongman-Campagnolo Wilier. In March he went to Spain to ride for the Navarre-based amateur team Lizarte. In an eight-week period between March and May 2016, he took four wins, four second places, and a third. By August he had signed for Movistar to become the first ever Ecuadorean on a WorldTour team. Over the next two years, two more of his compatriots would join him: Jhonatan Narváez went to Quick-Step Floors in

2018 before moving to Team Sky in 2019; and Jonathan 'Jhonny' Caicedo, the winner of the 2018 Vuelta a Colombia, joined EF Education First in 2019. Both riders had been coached by Juan Carlos Rosero. Caicedo, a month older than Richard Carapaz, from Santa Martha de Cuba, about forty kilometres from El Carmelo, had been his teammate as a junior.

With Colombia well established in WorldTour geography, Ecuador was global cycling's new frontier.

In May, after rehab in Andorra, Egan Bernal and his coach Xabier Artetxe had headed back to Zipaquirá.

'We had worked very hard for the Giro d'Italia,' Artetxe told me, 'and then we had to refocus on the Tour. It was a conundrum. If you keep working hard, you won't make it to the Tour, but if you relax, you won't either. Luckily, we got it right.'

They returned to Europe mid-June for the Tour of Switzerland. By then, on the morning of the stage-four time trial at the Critérium du Dauphiné in France, Chris Froome had suffered a terrible crash – the second of the conspiracy of accidents that surrounded Bernal that summer.

On stage four of the Swiss Tour, in the third of the fateful crashes, Egan's teammate Geraint Thomas, the reigning Tour de France champion, fell and abandoned. The following day, Egan took the race lead. He ended the week with a stage win and victory overall.

'We knew he wasn't 100 per cent in Switzerland,' Artetxe pointed out. 'Winning wasn't the objective.'

In Brussels for the Grand Départ, Egan did not have the emaciated look of a rider in absolute peak form. Artetxe told me, 'He was in good shape, and the first task was not to lose the Tour in the team time trial' – on stage two – 'and at La Planche des Belles Filles' – the mountain finish on day six.

'Of course,' Egan's coach continued, 'you have good days and bad ones.' Egan's bad day was in the individual time trial at Pau on stage thirteen. He finished the stage 22nd, after conceding 1 minute 36 seconds to Julian Alaphilippe, 1 minute 22 seconds to Geraint Thomas, and between 50 seconds and a minute to likely contenders like Rigoberto Urán, Steven Kruijswijk and Thibaut Pinot.

'He lost 45 seconds more than we expected,' Artetxe told me. 'After the stage, he doubted himself, and wondered if his form was tailing off. With all the data I had, I thought not.

'I told him, "It was just a bad day. You lost one and a half minutes to the winner, but you are still in contention, and all the mountains are still ahead of you."'

Xabier Artetxe feels that Egan's frustration may paradoxically have allowed him to cast caution to the wind: 'If everything had been going well, he would have been under enormous pressure. Having a bad day allowed him to reset his thinking, and say, "OK, let's try and win this damn Tour."'

The contrast between Artetxe's constant, detailed monitoring and Movistar's haphazard approach was absolute. In spring 2019 the Tour of the Basque Country and the Ardennes classics were suddenly removed from Nairo's calendar, and the Critérium du Dauphiné added. Nairo was told that the full Tour team would ride the Dauphiné, and then go to pre-Tour training camp to reconnoitre mountains and prepare the team time trial. Come June, only three of Nairo's Tour teammates went to the Dauphiné and the training camp was cancelled. Nairo was sent to prepare in Andorra: the journey cost him a day of training. And there were no team time trial drills. Sure enough, on stage two Movistar lost 1 minute 5 seconds to the winners Jumbo-Visma, and 45 seconds to Team Ineos (as Team Sky were now known).

The individual time trial was followed by a short, punishing stage that finished atop the western side of the Col du Tourmalet. The stage was won brilliantly by the French rider Thibaut Pinot. Egan was fifth, conceding 8 seconds. Nairo, who had fallen three days earlier, lost contact with the leaders low down on the Tourmalet and crossed the finish line 17th, 3 minutes 24 seconds after Pinot, and out of contention for the Tour win.

After the stage, Egan told me, 'When Pinot attacked, I was looking at my computer, and my power figures were going crazy, so I came off the gas and let him go.'

It sounded as though he was riding to a programme intended to bring him to peak form for stages eighteen, nineteen and twenty in the Alps.

Xabier Artetxe says things were more complicated: 'It wasn't all measured. Egan knew what his level was that day. And it is true that his best performances were in the third week, when he was less tired than the rest.'

On the first of the crucial Alpine stages, Nairo Quintana joined the early breakaway then attacked alone, 6.8 kilometres from the top of the Galibier. He won the stage at Valloire by 1 minute 35 seconds and he leapfrogged five places into seventh overall, despite his own team pulling behind. Back in the peloton, Egan attacked a little over three kilometres from the summit of the Galibier. He caught a small group of survivors from the early breakaway, and finished the stage 32 seconds ahead of the yellow jersey group. This moved him up to second overall.

Thirty-six kilometres into stage nineteen, Thibaut Pinot, who had torn one of the quadriceps in his left thigh in a crash on stage seventeen to Gap – the fourth of the providential accidents that affected the race's outcome – abandoned the Tour.

◈

As Egan rode away on the Col de l'Iseran, a continent away, the Alto de Las Margaritas, with its views over green, fertile hills and the artificial lake formed by the dam at Neusa, was quiet. Normally at this hour – it was still just nine in the morning – Las Margaritas was teeming with cyclists. Today, the riders had stayed at home to see the stage unfold. A gentle, 11-kilometre climb at an average gradient of 4.7 per cent, the Alto de Las Margaritas bears no comparison to the mighty Iseran, the highest paved mountain pass in the Alps, its gradients exceeding 10 per cent, first included in the Tour de France in 1938. Las Margaritas has never even featured in the Vuelta a Colombia, but it rises to 3,151 metres, or 10,340 feet, into the sky. As the sea-level natives around him began to suffer in the altitude of the Iseran, Egan approached the altitudes where he had spent most of his twenty-two years. As he extended his lead, and secured the yellow jersey, the reordering in the sporting realm seemed to resonate in nature itself. Black clouds opened over the valley ahead, shedding twenty million litres of ice on the valley below. The very mountains seemed to shake.

On 7 August, Gustavo Petro, the losing candidate in the June 2018 presidential elections, published a tweet that mentioned the new Tour de France winner.

'Egan Bernal lived in a neighbourhood that is part of the history of Zipaquirá: Bolívar 83, the M19 neighbourhood, the neighbourhood that, with my own hands, aged 21, I helped build and lead in the midst of the struggle with their entire community.

'From there I went to torture and jail.'

The tweet was greeted by a storm of replies taking Petro to task for claiming a part in Egan's Tour win. Typical was this:

'There you have it, gentlemen: we really owe the Tour de France win to Petro. They should stop paying so many tributes to Egan and concentrate on the important thing: how the M19 built the road to our first Tour win.'

A week later, during an interview for W Radio, the journalist Vicky Dávila asked Egan about Petro's tweet.

'I saw it and, truthfully, I didn't understand why people were so hard on him. I'd heard that he built the barrio. Sincerely, it didn't seem bad to me. It seemed normal. It didn't seem to me that he was appropriating the win.' In such a polarised society, it was a salutary call for calm and balance.

24

Tsantsøn Kauyi

On the final climb of the 2019 Tour Colombia – its name having been changed at the President's insistence from *Oro y Paz*, the former having largely cancelled out the latter in most of the country's history – squadrons of frantic 'me withs', their mobile phones in self-shooting mode, darted out to harry the riders, concerned not so much with holding infinity in the palm of their hand as propping up fragile egos through the urban economy of exhibitionism: 'Me with Nairo.' 'Me with Miguel Ángel.' 'Me with Egan.'

As Nairo described it after the stage, 'We were arriving at such speed, in such a state of concentration, that every movement, every detail, was in full definition. Then a spectator appeared from the roadside.'

López added, 'I didn't fully realise what was happening. I was forcing the pace when I felt a fan touch me – I think it was his mobile phone. I just carried on at my rhythm.'

One shortsighted smartphone user ran into another, then stumbled buttocks-first into Nairo and Iván Sosa, the flabby mediocrity of modern metropolitan solipsism colliding with the fragile excellence of the peasant cyclists.

Nairo made a parable of the incident: 'You fall, you are suddenly behind, and that special state is broken. You have to recover your rhythm and motivation, and carry on. It's not easy.

Then again, there are moments like that in every life. You get up and you carry on the struggle. It was our turn today.'

The promised nirvana of digital connectivity was probably undoing peasant cultures all around the world. Its numinous glow could hardly be further removed from the peasant farmer's daily struggle and the old, close-woven patterns of feeling, while the dull black ore containing tantalum, used in the capacitors on which smartphone technology depends, of which Colombia is thought to harbour 5 per cent of global reserves, is sold on the international black market, its profits bolstering the power of criminal bands.

I walked the final kilometre of the stage, on the climb of Las Palmas, looking down on Medellín. The logoed cycling products at the roadside – Scott, Specialized, Rapha, BMC, Go Rigo Go – betrayed the presence of Medellín's affluent classes, out in force to watch the sons of the disinherited peasantry do battle. I had seen a variant of the same scenario at the massive public subscription ride that Nairo Quintana had organised two months earlier, sauntering through the Boyacá countryside with two thousand participants, many on expensive, carbon-fibre machines. Between fields of spring onions where rural workers performed their daily, backbreaking labour, the leisure riders consumed the spectacle of peasant life as they rode past, some even stopping to take photographs. This stratification, this voyeurism may itself be a sign of development – and the distance Colombia has travelled.

Meanwhile, as Nairo closed in on the finish line, espresso bars and delicatessens offering soya and almond milk, vegan biscuits and organic chocolate – the tastes, allergies and technologies of global urban living – lined the final metres. If it proved anything at all, it was that identity was up for grabs in modern Colombia.

And yet, as Antonio Gramsci, a man of such intellectual powers that, when he was tried for conspiracy in Mussolini's Italy, the state prosecutor is said to have declared, 'This brain must be kept from functioning for twenty years,' once wrote:

> The personality is a bizarre fusion of ideas borrowed from the cave men, and state-of-the-art scientific thought; of the most provincial, backward-looking prejudices, mingled with futuristic philosophical intuitions . . . true awareness of who we are means 'Knowing thyself' as the outcome of the processes of history all the way down to the present, which have deposited in all of us an infinity of traces, without deigning to leave an inventory.

Nairo had never heard of Gramsci or his *Prison Notebooks*. His viewpoint came from his own life experience. Yet what he said came down to the same thing: 'Too little remains to resurrect what we once were,' he told me. 'Historical reconstruction for the purposes of tourism? Sure. But it ends there.'

His Muyscan past was both constitutive of his identity and unknowable.

Not everyone agreed. After all, Spanish crown records from the sixteenth century, indigenous councils from the nineteenth, and modern land registry entries, prove continuous residence of the same lands by the same Muysca communities right down to the present. Collective ownership of the reservation of Suba in north-west Bogotá was abolished in 1875 and its land reallocated to the resident Muysca families as private lots. Many families were dispossessed when Bogotá annexed the area in 1954. So, in 1990, their descendants began a class action to recover the lost estates. After the 1991 Constitution had undertaken to recognise and protect Colombia's ethnic diversity, the Ministry of the Interior recognised it and three other Muysca councils. Muysca was one of the 101 ethnic identity options listed in the 2005 census form.

After 2006, noting that the community in Suba had tripled its membership in a decade and that many new organisations were emerging, the state made no further formal recognitions.

Meanwhile, organisations were springing up that advanced the reawakening of the Muysca identity through the re-creation of language, the elaboration of new myths and rituals, the re-enchantment of the landscape. Even in an age of fluid identities and experimentation with the self, with social networks providing an audience – a world where people have a right to choose for themselves their own pattern of life, to decide in conscience what convictions to espouse, to determine the shape of their lives in a host of ways that their ancestors couldn't control – the so-called re-ethnicisation they proposed was anything but uncontroversial.

In the highlands of Cundinamarca and Boyacá, the concept *campesino* has always contained within it an indigenous hue. When I asked Egan Bernal's mother Flor Marina her thoughts on the indigenous component of her family identity, she told me, conflating indigenous with rural, 'They are part of our roots. I feel very proud of being what I am. That is, I come from the countryside. I love and respect and value the land.'

Asked the same, Rodrigo Anacona told me, 'On my mother's side, there is no one left. On my father's side, I have one uncle. I asked him once if we had indigenous blood, since we come from the countryside, and he said, "Of course. My father" – that is, my grandfather, Winner's great-grandfather – "was the leader of his indigenous community."'

Winner told me, 'My name, Anacona, comes from our indigenous ancestors, and I carry it with pride. I am also a Gómez, which is Colombian, or Spanish, on my mother's side, so I have both bloodlines in my veins.'

Darwin Atapuma is on record as saying, 'I have deeper indigenous roots than most, and I am happy to admit it. Atapuma is an Ecuadorean *cacique* name. It is in the Indigenous Registry, with all the community of the Pastos, and I am proud of being indigenous.'

Quintessentially Colombian but also off-centre with respect to official or mainstream society, this indigenous aspect potentially offers many of Colombia's cyclists a locus of the soul from which to distance themselves from some aspects of the mainstream – even if the riders I spoke to from more developed Antioquia, where cycling enjoys greater official support, made much less of their indigenous heritage. Sebastián Henao would only acknowledge, 'I have probably been grazed by an arrow or two.'

ᨒ

Not all Colombia's indigenous cyclists are from groups requiring cultural reconstruction. Nineteen-year-old Jimy Morales, a brilliant young rider belonging to the indigenous Misak people in south-west Colombia, and brought up on a reservation near Silvia, in the department of Cauca (*Kauca* means 'Mother of the Forests' in their language, Guambiano or Namtrik), told me proudly that the Misak were never conquered by the Spanish.

Jimy inherited the dream of cycling from his father, a former soldier, and an uncle. Bright, communicative, enthusiastic, he is keen to teach you a few words of his mother tongue and travels with his ceremonial dress in his bags. Of their colour scheme, he says, 'The pink threads represent the blood shed by our predecessors in the struggle against the Spanish conquest. So pink is an important colour for us.'

'Then you'll have to win the Giro d'Italia,' I tease.

'And yellow means purity, and all the wealth that the Spanish stole!'

'You'd better win the Tour de France too.'

'I like the sound of that!'

Much of the story told in this book relates to the triumph of normalisation: how cycling has helped Colombia become a much more ordinary, regular member of the global community than ever before. However, like Nairo and Darwin, Jimy believes that success as a professional cyclist may allow him to add to his community's resilience in the face of pressure from the majority urban culture: 'We Misak are very proud, and we want to show the world that the original inhabitants still exist. I think cycling gives us a way of protecting our identity.'

How appropriate that it should be the bicycle, that relic of the past reshaped in wind tunnels, made over in carbon fibre and reconceived as the most desirable of the desire's objects, that is the vehicle of this carrying over of the past into the future.

On the other hand, sport is tightly woven with nationalism, and media coverage of sporting events is only available in the national language. As well as several distinct varieties of Spanish and two Creoles spoken by Afro-descendants, sixty-three indigenous languages are spoken in Colombia, but many of these tongues are sadly at risk of extinction. In less robust indigenous cultures than the Misak, sport may also be influential in drawing young people away from their mother tongues. Even Jimy configures, with every pedal stroke, a Colombian national identity alongside his Misak indigenous self.

He says, 'My father was my first coach. He coaches me in Guambiano. I only began to acquire Spanish when I was at school. Now I want to learn English and other languages.'

The Guambiano expression for bicycle, he tells me, is *tsantsøn kauyi*, literally 'iron horse', and I suppose that *kauyi* derives from *caballo*, but when I quiz him about more technical terms, he says, 'You can invent ways of saying bike computer and power meter in Guambiano, but we just use the Spanish words.'

Jimy started racing in 2012, when he was twelve years old, during a Misak cultural week: 'My father and my uncle Felipe raced when they were younger, but they couldn't follow their dreams. So when I started they encouraged me and supported me.'

The following year he went to Medellín and ran into Fernando Saldarriaga and the Club Nueva Generación. He spent two years in the city, learning about cycling. In 2015 he went to Ramiriquí in Boyacá to race for Club Deportivo Ponimar-Ramiriquí, the team supported by the Mauricio Soler Foundation: '2016 was a good year for me. At the Clásica Esteban Chaves, I was second and third in different stages. At the Clásica Nacional Ciudad de Aguazul, I won the last stage and finished fourth in the GC. And at the Vuelta del Futuro, I was fourth in the time trial and moved into fifth overall, but I fell and dropped out of contention.

'I made contact with the Jarlinson Pantano Foundation through friends in Cali, and in early 2017 I took part in a competition they held at the velodrome. I told Jarlinson's wife Jessenia about my situation. I had no team, and I wanted to join the foundation. Everyone else was from Valle del Cauca, but they made an exception for me.' Through the foundation, Jimy made contact with Club Ciclista Sant Boi in San Baudilio de Llobregat, Catalunya, and travelled to Europe to continue his development.

☰

Colombians manage to be deeply attached to their origins, despite a remarkable lack of nationalist sentiment. Their response to one of the most important issues facing the nation, the massive influx of economic migrants from Venezuela since 2017, has been conspicuously free of xenophobic outrage. In the absence of nationalistic urges, the role its cyclists perform in unifying and focusing national pride is key: their renown extends to the national boundaries and beyond. Karina Vélez of Movistar Colombia, who managed Nairo's press relations at the 2018 Tour de France, told me of the crowds who gathered around the team bus.

'You form an idea of what most people are about from their garb and posture: social class, prosperity, whether they live abroad or have come as tourists,' she said. 'But there were other figures at the Tour who were difficult to place. Their stance, clothes and other things – tattoos and so on – that set them apart.'

She went over to talk to them: '[They were] demobilised guerrillas. One said that the thing he most wanted to see in life was

Nairo racing at the Tour de France. He had spent his demobilisation payment on the trip.'

Juan Manuel Santos used to quip – although it was also true – that he was elected by the right in 2010 and by the left in 2014. In 2018, the right replaced him with Iván Duque, at forty-two years and six days old on the day of his investiture, Colombia's youngest leader in seventy years – and an opponent of Santos's peace deal.

Of Duque's inaugural speech, the losing electoral candidate, Gustavo Petro – many years before, the founder of the Zipaquirá barrio of Bolívar 83 – noted, 'Peace got one mention, inequality, none at all': this, in the second most unequal country in Latin America, and the seventh in the world, according to World Bank figures.

This is why the Colombian peasantry is prepared to pursue a strategy as high-risk as professional cycling to bridge the gap themselves – and why, even in the absence of good management, Colombian cycling continues to produce so many champion peasant-cyclists.

Ask Colombians today where their nation is heading, and many will tell you they are not sure. The car bomb detonated by the ELN in Bogotá on 17 January 2019 was a sign that the peace had not yet been won. On 29 August two former FARC peace negotiators, Iván Márquez and Jesús Santrich, announced that they were recommencing revolutionary armed struggle – in the company of Ricardo de Jesús Agudelo, alias 'El Paisa', the man who ordered Guillermo Gaviria Correa's execution north of Urrao in 2003.

Whatever the politics of Colombian peace, the cultures and identities that have flourished since the turn of the millennium – of which cycling, inspired by the nation's WorldTour idols, is an integral part – are surely too deeply rooted to allow Colombia ever to go back. Even so, the illegal armed groups did perform one vital function: by frightening off the loggers and farmers, they helped preserve Colombia's 5.5 million square kilometres of rainforest. In their absence, the forests are being razed. Not even peace is unequivocal.

◈

During a recent visit to Colombia, a friend beheld the beautiful, rugged, high-altitude landscape around Nairo's childhood home and thought of Geraint Thomas.

'Just look at it,' he said. 'It explains everything. It makes you wonder how someone who comes from South Wales can even compete.'

It was a simple enough observation, and a generous one, but it contained a fundamental misunderstanding. It is not that altitude was the only thing Nairo, Egan, Miguel Ángel, Iván, and the Ecuadorean, Richard Carapaz, had going for them. They had good families too, great sporting genes, a wholesome rural diet of fresh food, and a surrounding, everyday culture that understood and supported its cyclists. What they lacked was everything else: life-chances, freedom from financial worry, some insulation from the struggle for survival, the chance to live what the post-industrial world likes to call childhood.

In sporting terms, they grew up with none of that integration of the service sector, industry, the universities and the state – or any semblance of that rough match between family buying power, and the sporting goods on offer in the market place – that defines the post-industrial world. There was no supportive state; no up-to-date equipment or cutting-edge sports science – the expert coaching, nutritional expertise, specialist technology, analytical software or recovery advice; no opportunity to travel, be stimulated and gain experience that, from an early age, shape the future careers of riders in the developed world. In the face of a collapsing rural economy and diminishing opportunity, the peasant-cyclists of Colombia and Ecuador pursued their own life-projects by dint of unbelievable mental resilience, determination, personal organisation and astonishing hard work.

For a few, elite-level sport pays off. For the majority, it is not even an option. It is sink or swim – and most, of course, sink. The few who ever reach the Grand Tours are the cycling equivalents of statistical error. Their successes are triumphs for values like diversity and inclusion, and unfashionable ideas like the fellowship of humankind. They are victories for the underdogs we should always support. They also allow cycling's tiny corner of globalised sport to look just a little more like the majority of the 220 countries to whom it is broadcast.

True, their successes can still be cast in terms of Third World muscle working for First World brains and wages. There should be more team directors, coaches and sports scientists from the wider world, more exchanges, more technology and experience transfer, more support for clean sport and honest organisation, more elite-level events outside the rich world. In terms of human potential, the triumphs described in this book are the conclusion of one set of stories, and the beginnings of another.

That will depend on whether sport as we know it can find an environmentally sustainable way to carry on. After all, Colombia's first Tour de France win took place in a summer of extremes – perhaps the first of many, as climate change deepens in its intensity. On this threshold of our own devising, the climate emergency, deforestation and mass extinction are joined by a global eradication of memory. On the green slopes below Iguaque, where five hundred years of history seem to have passed in the blink of an eye, I asked Isabel Monroy, *Mamá Chavita*, how much of the old ways survived. She told me, 'My mother is in her nineties. Her generation remember many things, although they will be gone soon.'

Richard Carapaz said, 'My grandfather tells me things, but he didn't pass them on to my father's generation. The culture has gone now.'

In a few short years, their world will be lost.

Acknowledgements

This book is the product of generous assistance from a wide number of global sports stars who already had enormous demands on their time, including from the media, before my own humble entreaties. Most of the people interviewed for this book are mentioned in the text, and it is unnecessary to repeat their names here. I would especially like to thank Darwin Atapuma, Daniel Martínez, Jarlinson Pantano, Álvaro Hodeg, and their families, for their kind hospitality in Túquerres, Vergara, Cali and Montería.

Above all, despite an impossible number of journalistic enquiries from other quarters, and the infinite number of good causes and commitments to which he gives his time, Nairo Quintana took my work to heart and found space to give me a number of extended interviews, and introduced me to his wonderful mother, Doña Eloísa, whose other sons Alfredo and Dayer were also unfailingly helpful.

Luís Fernando Saldarriaga's contribution both to Colombian cycling and to this work is immeasurable. He, Gustavo Duncan and Ignacio Vélez – three of the four *enemigos del ciclismo* (I can proudly claim to be the fourth) – are longstanding friends, and they should consider many of these pages their own. So too should my wonderful guides and accomplices Luisa Fernanda Ríos, Libardo Leyton, and the exceptional, the irreplaceable Karina Vélez.

However, in addition to long interviews, the following kindly made themselves available over periods of days and weeks for supplementary fact-checking via telephone and text: Rafael Acevedo, Giuseppe Acquadro, Paolo Alberati, Alex Atapuma, Jairo Chaves, Jorge Flores Guzmán, Diana Herrera, Benjamín Laverde, Pablo Mazuera, Carlos Julián Quintero and Óscar de J. Vargas.

Special thanks to Juan Pablo Villegas and Richard Carapaz, two sources of sporting and human inspiration.

My generous journalistic colleague and admired craftsman Carlos Arribas shared several of the visits, and interviews, that were integral to this book.

Readers of early drafts included Dr Matthew Brown, the journalist Gustavo Duncan, my father, John Rendell, and the writer and campaigner Andrew Simms: their comments improved its content and clarity.

Other cherished friends whose advice and support were of great value to me include Ned Boulting, Steve Docherty, Eder Garcés, Osvaldo Hernández, Gary Imlach, Jørgen Leth, Ana Marín, Edgar Medellín, Ricardo Montezuma, Diego Morales, Alfredo Muñoz, Hugo Muñoz, Roberto Nitti, Consuelo Onofre, Jean-François Quenet, Lisandro Rengifo, Alfredo Saldarriaga, Pascale Schyns, Mauricio Silva, James Venner, Carolyn Viccari and the staff of VSquared TV and Aurora Media Worldwide UK Ltd.

The genealogist David Dobson, and Joaquín González, very kindly responded to my enquiries with personal communications.

Paul Murphy's close reading led to great improvements in the final manuscript, while Alan Samson and Lucinda McNeile at Orion Books provided solid and consistent support. I also thank John English for his careful line edit and Steve Marking for his beautiful cover design. My literary agent, Laetitia Rutherford, has been an unstoppable whirlwind of energy, driving me on throughout.

The sensation of cultural distance I have always found

Acknowledgements

intoxicating, perhaps, in part, perhaps because of the invigorating challenge, and ultimate reinforcement, it offers to the conviction that, in their infinite differences, human beings are all equal. There is also the self-centred pleasure of looking back at oneself from a great distance and discovering the unexpected – and the simple fun of speaking another language, which converts simple, almost invisible exchanges like everyday small talk into entertaining acts of cross-cultural play. Colombia has also enlarged my consciousness with a new repertoire of literature, music, fruit and vegetables, a new perspective on history, my culture of birth, and Europe, as seen by Colombians, Afro-Colombians and on the indigenous people of Colombia.

For all these things, and for many, life-enriching friendships, I am grateful.

Above all, thanks to my wife, I-Lin Chen, for putting up with my absences, physical and mental, during the composition of this book.

All errors, omissions and oversights are the responsibility of the author alone.

Sources

Books are also made of other books, and, among the many I have consulted, I have particularly depended on the following:

On recent Colombian political history, the memoirs of Presidents Uribe and Santos, *No hay causa perdida* and *La batalla por la paz*; Julio Sánchez Cristo's excellent *El País que se hizo posible*, and León Valencia's *Los Retos del Postconflicto* (with Ariel Ávila).

On recent social history, the essays in *Entre Dos Paces: Colombia y Antioquia 1991–2016*, edited by Jorge Giraldo Ramírez and Leonardo García Jaramillo; those in *Colombia 1930–1960: Mirando hacia dentro*, and *1960/2010: La búsqueda de la democracia*, part of the *América Latina en la Historia Contemporánea* series published by the Fundación Mapfre, and two books by Gustavo Duncan, *Los Señores de la Guerra*, and *Democracia Feroz: ¿Por qué la sociedad en Colombia no es capaz de controlar a su clase política?*

On the peace process, Francisco Barbosa's *Justicia transicional o impunidad?*

On emeralds, Petrit Baquero's *La nueva guerra verde. ¿Quiénes son los nuevos patrones de las esmeraldas en Colombia y por qué se siguen matando?*

On Urrao and Vereda Pabón, Mary Roldán's brilliant *Blood and Fire: La Violencia in Antioquia, Colombia, 1946–1953*.

On the Muysca at the time of the Spanish conquest and subsequently, J. Michael Francis's *Invading Colombia: Spanish Accounts of the Gonzalo Jimenez de Quesada Expedition of Conquest*; J. H.

Elliott's astonishing *Empires of the Atlantic World. Britain and Spain in America 1492–1830*; the wonderful and provocative work by researchers at the Universidad Nacional de Colombia, including the essays in *Muysca: memoria y presencia*, edited by María Emilia Montes Rodríguez and Constanza Moya Pardo; François Correa Rubio's monumental *El Sol del poder* on Muysca symbolism and politics; Jorge Augusto Gamboa's equally imposing *El cacicazgo muisca en los años posteriores a la Conquista: del psihipqua al cacique colonial*; the work on contemporary Muysca movements published by Universidad de San Tomás, especially the essays in *Territorios y Memorias Culturales Muiscas*, edited by Pablo Felipe Gómez Montañez and Fredy Leonardo Reyes Albarracín, and, of course, the classic *Peasant Society in the Colombian Andes: A sociological study of Saucío* by Orlando Fals-Borda.

On peasant culture generally, and the current crisis of Colombian agriculture in particular, the essays in Teodor Shanin's classic collection *Peasants and Peasant Societies* (Penguin Modern Sociology Readings); the more recent *Peasant Poverty and Persistence in the Twenty-First Century*, edited by Julio Boltvinik and Susan Archer Mann, and the hardhitting newspaper reports in *El Tiempo* by Aurelio Suárez Montoya collected in *¡El tal paro agrario . . . sí existió! Crisis y movilizaciones campesinas 2013–2014*.

On Colombian flora and fauna, Edward O. Wilson and José M. Gómez Durán's *Kingdom of Ants. José Celestino Mutis and the Dawn of Natural History in the New World*, a beautiful introduction to Colombia's flora and fauna, and to the singular Celestino Mutis.

Finally, on the international anti-doping system, Larry D. Bowers' 'The International Antidoping System and Why It Works' in the periodical *Clinical Chemistry*.

Index

Index

Index

Index

Index